BEAUTIFUL BUTTONS

BEAUTIFUL BUTTONS

a memoir of survival and triumph

CATHRINE ANN

BPS
books
Toronto and New York
www.bpsbooks.com

Published in 2011 by
BPS Books
Toronto and New York
www.bpsbooks.com
A division of Bastian Publishing Services Ltd.

ISBN 978-1-926645-62-9

First published in hardcover in 2010 by Key Porter Books, Toronto, Canada.

Cataloguing-in-Publication Data available from Library and Archives Canada.

Cover: Alison Carr
Text design and typesetting: Alison Carr
Cover and author photos: Alison Carr

Some names and details have been changed to protect the privacy of individuals.

Somebody once said you never know what's enough
until you know what's more than enough.
—Billie Holliday

Come to the edge.
We might fall.
Come to the edge.
It's too high!
Come to the edge!
And they came,
and he pushed,
and they flew.
—Christopher Logue

Nothing in this world can take the place of persistence.
Talent will not; nothing is more common than unsuccessful
people with talent. Genius will not; unrewarded genius is
almost a proverb. Education will not; the world is full of
educated derelicts. Persistence and determination alone
are omnipotent. The slogan "press on" has solved and
always will solve the problems of the human race.
—Calvin Coolidge

I fell. I got up. I fell again. I got up again.
Even when I fell on my face, I was still falling forward.
—Cathrine Ann

For Marc
For Michael

Contents

Acknowledgements   xi
Preface   xiii
Introduction   1

ONE   In the beginning ...   9
TWO   The house that got away   31
THREE   Trust   53
FOUR   Hello, God? It's me. No, Cathrine ... *Cathrine*   60
FIVE   Death and pets   73
SIX   Mommy's perfect angel   80
SEVEN   School daze   89
EIGHT   Food   98
NINE   Trust ... again   102
TEN   Self-esteem issues   113
ELEVEN   The "budding" entrepreneur   118
TWELVE   Eddie   124
THIRTEEN   The joys of motherhood   135
FOURTEEN   Now what?   148
FIFTEEN   Out of the frying pan ...   154
SIXTEEN   My hero   159
SEVENTEEN   You can always depend on family   163

EIGHTEEN   Learning from my mistakes?   170

NINETEEN   I fly into the cuckoo's nest   176

TWENTY   My ball and chain   185

TWENTY-ONE   Livin' the high life   192

TWENTY-TWO   Looking in the mirror ... and who do I see?   210

TWENTY-THREE   The jackpot   222

TWENTY-FOUR   Picking up the pieces   240

TWENTY-FIVE   Dad and med school   256

TWENTY-SIX   The mob   266

TWENTY-SEVEN   A second chance   285

TWENTY-EIGHT   Struggles, heartbreak and the
                whole damn thing   297

TWENTY-NINE   Looking back without regrets.
                Well, maybe a few ...   306

Acknowledgements

I HAVE A FEW PEOPLE to thank for helping me write this book. Some may know how much they helped me get to this point, and others may not.

First, I would like to thank everyone who never meant a bloody thing to me or to whom I never meant anything. Without you, I wouldn't be the person I am.

Second, I would like to thank everyone who did mean something to me, either now, or in my past, whom I am not acknowledging individually on this page. Without you, I wouldn't be the person I am.

I would like to thank my husband, Marc. A yin to my yang. How does he put up with me? He is one in a gazillion! Marc never judged me. He accepted me the way I was and he believed that I could become a better person. He knew exactly what to do and say, and maybe more importantly, what to not say, to help me get to a better place in my life with him by my side. I wouldn't be where I am without my best friend, Marc.

To Dr. Jennifer Rodrigues: when I met you a few years ago, I was ready to pack it all in. Your help was instrumental in my staying just a little bit longer with my memories and pain and guilt and everything else that represented the dark and nasty that I felt was part of me, so I could make sense of my crazy life and be able to cope. You helped me immensely and I sincerely thank you for not feeling sorry for me, just as you promised me you wouldn't in our very first meeting!

Thank you Farah Perelmuter, CEO, Co-founder of Speakers' Spotlight. You believed in me the first time you heard me speak publicly years ago, in all my rawness and inexperience as a speaker—and you still signed me up! You were right, though—my story continues to resonate with people everywhere. It was you who also introduced me to my amazing literary agent, Hilary McMahon at Westwood Creative Artists, whom I also thank for giving me the chance I needed as a first-time author.

And thank you, Jonathan Schmidt, at Key Porter, for your help with the first publication of this book. You were very brave to tackle this one!

Preface

WHAT YOU ARE ABOUT TO READ is the story of my life—thus far, anyway. But there are at least a few lifetimes in it already, so I don't think you'll wonder why I didn't wait a few more years first. Plus, sometimes I think that life is way too long anyway. Or, at least it felt that way for me at times. I guess that's because nothing really ever was easy for me. But it doesn't matter if you see life as too short or too long or just right. What I think you will agree with is that life is like a grindstone: either you get polished up or you get ground down to smithereens.

My story is not so neat and straightforward and organized. Of course while it was happening to me, I didn't realize how messed up it really was. But the older I got, the more I found myself thinking about the past. I wanted to review everything so I could do some much needed healing and hopefully find myself. And then I realized that I didn't have to find myself at all. Instead, I had to create myself. But I did have to heal. I kept making the same mistakes over and over, expecting a different or better outcome. Isn't that one of the definitions of insanity?

I first attempted to write this book over five years ago. I scribbled a few chapters and then I ran. It was too much. But I realized I couldn't run away from myself, so I forced myself to feel the pain and deal with it; otherwise I couldn't have gone on in my life. I thought it would be good therapy for me to face my past. Instead, it threw me into a state of deep, dark depression that would take a professional therapist years to help me unravel. And then, it was still difficult for me to write. It's amazing what a little—strike that—*a lot* of therapy and determination will get a person in life. And it isn't a question of what I became. It's a question of who I am becoming in spite of it all. The point is, we all have it in us to be the person we want to be. We just have to want it bad enough.

So I went into therapy and I'm still here, still curious about who I will ultimately become. Who knew that at fifty-four I would still wonder about that?

I am not the kind of person who wants to blame the past for what I am. The past defined me. Yes, I made lots of mistakes. Some I knew were outright wrong and for one reason or another I just didn't care. Other times, I didn't really know until after the fact and somehow I did care. Sure, there are lots of people I let down. And there were a lot of people that let me down. For a long time I let myself down.

My toughest years in life were from the time I was born until fifty. Hell, it's still tough! As a result, I wasn't always the nicest person. In fact, the trouble with me was, I could sometimes be a real bitch. And then other times I was a real doormat. But when you have only yourself to rely on, or to care about, you forget about how your actions and words affect other people. A lot of times, I was frustrated. Sometimes I was misunderstood. Other times, I really didn't care what anyone thought of me because I figured I was simply trying to even the score. I'm not happy about that. It's just a fact.

Welcome to my story!

Introduction

IF I HAD PLANNED THINGS better, I would have prepared the kind of acceptance speech that all the people who had just finished their meal expected to hear. But I hadn't. Basically, I'm a fly-by-the-seat-of-your-pants type of person but with a driven, Type A personality, if that makes sense. On top of that, I tend to talk first and think second. Sometimes I think I've got a brain like a Ferrari and a mouth like the brakes on a Model T Ford, if you get the picture. Or, if you're into dogs more than cars, like I am, my brain is a greyhound and my mouth is a bulldog. I think I'd better stop with the analogies now.

Besides, I hadn't written a speech because that would have meant assuming I had won and might have jinxed things. I'm pretty superstitious so I do believe in luck, but over the years I've learned the harder I work, the luckier I get.

I really wanted to win this award. I meandered up to the stage before the event started and took a peek at the Oscar-like statues. I was oh-so-tempted to touch but I didn't dare—that might have jinxed things too. I was now sitting at a formally decorated table of ten people, including me, in a formally decorated room of about a thousand more people, all of whom were strangers except for my husband, Marc. There I was, trying to stay positive about my chance of winning, looking around and smiling like I was as confident as anybody could be, but that was just on the outside. Inside, I was still the insecure little kid who was the last one chosen for teams at school or the one who never had anyone show up for her birthday parties. But that was all in the past. Things had been getting better for me since I met Marc and started our company, Consumer Connection, in 1998. Still, I was nervous as hell, and when they announced me as the winner of the 2006 YWCA Entrepreneur/ Innovator of the Year Award, my first reaction was shock.

I wasn't going to show it, of course. I sat there, grinning just as I had before my name was announced, while all the people in the banquet room began looking around to see who this person was, this winner of such a prestigious award. I might still be sitting there if Marc hadn't called my name, snapping me back to reality. I turned to see him applauding as madly as anyone else, with tears streaming down his cheeks, and that's when I got up and started weaving my way between the tables while the guests applauded more loudly now that they could see who the winner was.

My heart was racing. I kept smiling and now my tears started flowing. I hated the idea of tears in front of strangers, so I started to think of other things to distract myself, as this was a pretty easy thing to do—distracting myself, that is—as I manoeuvred among the guests. Like, what the hell was I wearing anyway?

Why do I always put something on and then later wish I were wearing something different? Or you know how you think you look really good and someone takes your picture and then you look at the picture later on and think, "What the hell was I thinking?!" Well, I figured that was going to happen given what I was wearing: a sexy—practically see-through—chiffon blouse that needless to say failed the test for "appropriate business attire." I had never been good at rules. I'm still not.

Oh, no, will I have to smile in the picture? I didn't smile in pictures any more because my teeth had somehow gone from perfect white Chiclets to uneven yellow stone chips.

Was my hair all right, thin as it was?

Lordy, why did I wear these high heels? They're a bitch to walk in. But at least those are something that I know looks great.

And why did I eat all that dessert?! I feel stuffed! Do I want to get fat again?!

I had a lot of thoughts because it was a long walk. As I approached the stage, where the presenter stood behind the Plexiglas lectern holding my award, my internal conversation with myself switched gears. Now instead of berating myself about my clothes and eating habits in the voice that sounds like some annoying little sister living inside my brain, I started kicking my butt over not preparing a speech. The best I could do, I decided, was to say the first thing that entered my mind as long as it didn't have any swear words in it. And I couldn't even guarantee that.

The presenter, a nice man in a designer suit with a purple flower in his lapel, handed me my award with his left hand and stuck out his right hand, inviting me to shake it. He had a big grin on his face and was beaming. I didn't think he could have looked happier or prouder if his own daughter herself had won.

I didn't immediately shake his hand. I said, "First things first!" Then I took the award and examined it quickly, saying to him, "Holy Hannah, this is like an Oscar!" He laughed as I gave him a hug. He then waved his hand, letting me know that I now needed to pose for the photographers. I then walked to the lectern, took a big breath, exhaled and faced the crowd. They could see me, but I couldn't see them. I was blinded by the spotlights and the cameras flashing, over and over to the point that I felt like a movie star. Actually, *not* seeing the crowd proved an advantage. I had been told the audience included a few Order of Canada members, some university and college presidents and a lot of pink-shirt executives and their partners. For a moment they were all invisible to me, which made me feel a bit more relaxed.

That's when I began to talk.

"Thanks for this amazing award," I said, which quieted the audience down and ended the applause. Then I added in a strong, clear, friendly voice, thinking of the banquet meal I had just consumed and the beautiful hotel room that I would be spending the night in: "Boy, this sure beats being homeless and eating out of garbage cans."

The camera flashes ended and my eyes began adjusting to the spotlights, so I could make out some blurry ghost-like shoulders rising and falling and heads tilting toward one another and whispers of "What did she just say?" floating back to me.

The annoying little-sister voice began nattering inside my head again. Why can't I just say "Thank you" and get the hell off the stage? What are they going to think of me now? What if some of my clients are out there and decide they'd rather not do business with a woman who admits to eating out of garbage cans?

People with their bellies full of a roast beef dinner and not-bad wine, sitting under luxury hotel chandeliers and wearing tailored suits and designer gowns, don't like to hear about other people eating out of garbage cans or sharing a jail cell with rats or selling their bodies to feed themselves and their children. I was prepared to talk about all these things, but I began to wonder if this was really the best time or place.

Standing there, holding my award and smiling out at the audience, I was watching a movie of the past nine years of my life being projected on the inside of my head in fast-forward mode. As the movie ran I realized that I was right where I belonged. I belonged here in front of these people, and I deserved the award I held in my hands. I had been living with pain and embarrassment and secrets and lies for most of my life. I had just revealed one of those secrets. I might as well reveal at least a few more. And I did.

That's when the words poured out of me, not because I had written them down or even thought about them in detail beforehand, but because I had been living with the thoughts and the memories and the pain for so many years. This is what I said:

I can hardly believe that I am here today, let alone accepting this amazing award. I know what it's like to eat from the garbage. I know what it's like to be homeless. I know what it's like to grow up unloved and un-wanted. I know what it's like to be locked up in jail and to associate with criminals and to feel as though life holds nothing in its big hands that is worthwhile for you. I am not my past. I am what I am today and what I will be tomorrow. I am a successful entrepreneur who has made millions of dollars because I found the courage, strength and determination to change. My message to you is this: Believe.

Hands started clapping, people rose to their feet and I stood there thinking, I bet they believe they've heard it all.

In truth, they hadn't heard a thing when it came to the nitty-gritty of my life.

Someone in the audience approached me later and suggested I become an inspirational speaker. Over the years since, I've provided details of my life during those speeches and in radio, TV and magazine interviews. Some of my stories have shocked people and even scandalized them, but I don't regret revealing details of my past. Fact of the matter is, my story helps more people than I could ever have imagined.

If everyone else like me knew that they could be accepted regardless of their background and whatever they did in the past, as long as they were committed to doing better in the future, as long as they redeemed themselves in some manner, it doesn't matter where they came from or how they dressed or what their title was at work. That's what I wanted—want—to tell the world.

My story isn't important because I managed to become a successful businesswoman. It is important as a lesson to *other* people that they can do it as well. It took me ten years to become an overnight success. It might take less time for other people to do it. Or more time. It didn't matter. They needed to believe it was possible, because when you start believing in yourself others begin believing in you too.

The people who are inspired by my story are the ones I am most interested in reaching. In the past—when people have heard me tell my story—they appreciated what I went through because they faced similar challenges in their lives and many had given up hope of finding happiness, success and contentment. Most, but not all, were women who were victims of various kinds of abuse: sexual, physical, emotional, economic—take your pick.

A man who approached me after I spoke at an event in Toronto particularly moved me. A lineup of women had gathered to speak to me, and among the crowd towered one man. At least six feet tall with grey hair, he was very well dressed in a suit and colourful tie. When it was his turn to speak to me, he reached down and I reached up and we hugged each other. He stood back a bit, but he was still very close. He told me that he worked as a CEO for a large communications company and it was his company that was actually one of the sponsors for the event. Then he lowered his head and his eyes searched the floor, as though he was looking for something he'd dropped. I saw a few tears run down his cheek and plop to the floor. When he looked up to meet my eyes, he said that he'd been sexually abused as a child and he had kept it a secret for more than forty years. Not even his wife of twenty years knew of his harsh past. But hearing my story there that day did something to him. He wasn't sure what it was but he had to thank me. He also said that he promised himself to get some help for the demons still haunting him, the demons he'd tried to forget about and push out of his mind but never could.

Hearing about the abuse I suffered as a child and as an adult let people like him know they were not alone. More important, it confirmed that they should never give up on their dreams, or healing, or changing whatever it was in their lives they need to change in order to feel and do better.

Nothing is as emotionally powerful, as mind-blowing, as receiving a letter from someone who thanks you for saving their life. I have received those letters. And the hidden message, the one that's behind this book, is the fact that in many ways I save their lives by saving my own first.

Through it all, things for me never got great one day and stayed that way. It was always two steps forward and one step back: a little trot and I'd fall down, get back up, take more baby steps, and on and on. Even when I fell on my face, I was still moving forward.

So here's the whole sad, sordid and sometimes funny tale. It even has a happy ending. Too bad it took so damn long to arrive.

What I remember: My father is sitting on the floor in front of the black-and-white television. Awkwardly, he fiddles and fusses with the aerial and attached coat hanger, trying to bring the picture into focus. He is drunk, of course. Like he could bring anything into focus.

I sit on the couch about five feet away from him. His friend—his eyes never off my father—moves his hand gently up my pyjama leg. He smiles, glancing at me for a second. I can smell his breath. His fingers play lightly between my legs.

Why doesn't Daddy do something? I wonder.

I keep my eyes on the TV. On my father. I sense the man's hands. It feels good.

I am five years old.

CHAPTER ONE

In the beginning ...

OF ALL THE MYSTERIES I have encountered in my life, none is more difficult to understand than why my mother and father ever married or why they ever stayed together after they did.

They didn't do it because they enjoyed each other's company, that's for sure.

"We had sex before we were married," my mother confessed years later. "We got married. It's what people did."

From what I knew, it probably was the first—and except for having me—probably the last time she had sex with my father. She, on the other hand, would accuse my father of having sex with basically anything that moved, including—as I would discover—men.

MARY HELEN EOTOFF—nicknamed "Sister Marie" by her family because of "saintly" behaviour as a child and claims made later as an adult that she never lied—had thick, almost-black shoulder-length hair that she usually wore in a ponytail or soft curls styled by a multitude of bobby pins or soft squishy pink curlers. What I remember is mostly her hair in curlers. Sometimes she would leave her hair in curlers for days on end.

"Why don't you take your curlers out now that your hair is dry?" I would ask.

"Mind your own business," she'd snap and take a long drag on her cigarette.

I often wished I had known my mother as a child or as a young girl. She must have been a lot different.

She was from a large Ukrainian family, with four sisters and two brothers. I would see and hear her laugh when she was with her sisters, but rarely at home when my father and I were the only ones around. She had a permanent scowl on her face, and that alone scared me.

By the time I arrived, in the middle of the 1950s, in Toronto, her life must have turned so sour that she had just given up. She resented her husband and her marriage, and resented me as well. Her job became trying to manage my dad's addictions, and I felt that I was an inconvenience.

She had a habit when she thought no one was watching her of slowly scratching her head and appearing to go somewhere else mentally. She just gazed off into space and scratched. "Always expect the worst," she would tell me. "That way you'll never be disappointed."

Her beautiful dark hair turned grey early. Every time she noticed a new grey hair, she would carefully isolate it and then wrap it around her pointy finger and give it a quick tug and wince. "For every one grey you pull out," she said, "ten grow in its place." I never understood the point of pulling them out and told her so. She would just shrug.

Life was a battle she could not win.

It used to bother me that she didn't take better care of her appearance, even if we were dirt poor. I remember thinking that her unshaven legs looked like the coarse hair you might see on spider legs, and the hairs used to poke through her beige stockings—hopefully only noticeable to me.

"Mom, why don't you shave your legs?"

"Why? What difference does it make? Who sees me?" she answered.

She lost her teeth when she was pregnant with me when she was twenty-eight. "Babies take everything good out of you when you're pregnant. That's why I lost all my teeth."

I used to have nightmares of my birth and my mother's happy

face, and then all of a sudden her eyes would go crazy as one by one all her teeth fell out of her head and onto the floor. It only made me feel even more guilty because I knew I was responsible for helping her look worse than she should have.

She kept her false teeth in a glass jar in the kitchen, and it embarrassed me that often she didn't bother wearing them at all. It made her look as old as my grandmother. I guess I was bothered a lot, for a kid, by people's physical appearances when they didn't try to always look their best. I guess I was embarrassed for myself too. It's probably why to this day it means a lot to me to have nice things and to look good. I like seeing other people have nice things and look good too.

I remember a picture of my mother when she was pregnant. She was skinny.

"Mom, didn't you eat when you were pregnant with me?"

"Who the hell had anything to eat? I was ninety-eight pounds when I got married and I've been starving ever since." She would always get angry, remembering the past, but she just couldn't let go of it.

On the rare occasions she was feeling nostalgic, she would tell me stories about "the nice German boy"—the one that got away. "I should have married him instead. Not that whoremaster of a bastard I married." Apparently she had been "too stupid" to date him because he was too nice. Well, they say the apple doesn't fall far from the tree. There were a lot of things that I didn't like about my mother, but I still ended up doing some of the very same things that I swore I would never do myself when I got older. My mother, my self.

Anyway, that isn't the first time I have heard that from various women in my life. Later on, my mother would have something negative to say about all her sisters' husbands and boyfriends; she'd give advice to everyone without them asking for it about how they needed to dump the bastards (and they all were, in my opinion as well), but she never took her own advice. She would visibly light right up like a Christmas tree when she compared this nice German boy to my father. She would go off into her own little world, sitting on the couch, eyes searching the ceiling left and right, telling me about his height and weight and eye colour and how he dressed so nicely and what a gentleman he was and on and on, as though trying to grab those feelings of long ago with every blink. That was another reason I wondered why she stayed with my dad. But maybe she figured there was only one other great guy out there and she'd missed her opportunity, so she would settle. Who knows?

Anyway, she never missed an opportunity to remind me that I was the product of the biggest mistake she ever made in her life. "Son of a bitch, I must have been dumb or something to marry the bastard just because I slept with him! And my stupid father loved him because *he* was just as rotten as your father! He was a cheap drunken rotten bastard too and I hated him!"

She complained about everything she didn't have or had lost because of my father and about the things she knew she would never have.

Since we never had any money, she made most of her own dresses in a sleeveless cotton style she wore year round. I always wanted her to wear something prettier, more modern, but she never did. The clothes she made always looked the same. She would say that she needed a new summer dress, so she would buy some flowery material and sew a sleeveless design with front darts on the bodice. It always fell below her knees. Then she would say that she needed a fall dress, and she would pick out some orangey-coloured material and sew the exact same pattern as the summer one—but she would wear a sweater over it. They were never pretty dresses either. They just did the job, that's all. Her sewing machine was a big old wooden dinosaur that she got from her mother. It had a huge metal foot pedal that she would have to pump in order to move the needle and sew. When that machine broke down, she got a new basic model on layaway at Eaton's and it took her about two years to pay for it.

I used to wish that she would dress to impress other mothers. I wanted to be proud of her, to know that other mothers were look-ing at her and envying her life instead of knowing that they felt sorry for her. I used to wonder why she couldn't she take more of an interest in her appearance. If not for herself than for us. Me. All she ever told me was that she had never had anything and never would so why hide it from people.

She never really talked about dating my father or their court-ship or what it was that attracted her to him except for the fact that her father liked him. Mostly by the time I heard what little there was to hear, it had been poisoned; the few memories were not happy ones.

When I used to ask about her dating my dad, she had only one story to tell me, about how when he went to visit her he always arrived with a bottle. My grandfather used to insist on answering the front door whenever my dad came calling. He would look to see if my dad had that familiar brown paper bag in his hand, which he always did, and he would then open his arms wide to hug my dad saying, "Oh, my sonny boy! Come right in, sonny boy!" Then, instead of going on a date with my mother, my dad would get drunk with my grandfather while my mother sat and watched.

Kind of like what I did most nights but now it was her and my father getting drunk. She also said that she didn't smoke or drink when they first met. Then she would shrug. "I figured if you can't beat them, you may as well join them."

She was nineteen when she married. My father was thirty. In their wedding photos, my mother isn't smiling. Not in a single one.

She once said she married just to escape her parents' house because she hated her father and she wanted to eat regular meals. Unfortunately, that didn't happen. Then I came along nine and a half years later. She said that her mother was a saint and she never understood why she stayed with her father. It was history repeating itself pure and simple, I thought. I started fearing my future well before it even happened.

"I don't know why my mother had seven goddamn kids with an asshole that couldn't take care of them all," she'd say. "My moth-er worked her ass off cleaning houses so that jerk could stay drunk. Thank God I only had one. I should have had none!"

MY PARENTS WERE an unlikely and even odd-looking pair. The first thing that anyone might notice seeing them for the very first time was that my mother stood an imposing and statuesque five foot nine, but my father was a good head shorter. He barely came up to her shoulder. It's no wonder she chose kitten heels or flats over high heels every time. Those types of shoes matched her dowdy dresses.

My mother claimed she never had enough food as a child. What made the memory so bitter for her was that my grandfather used to work at an abattoir in Toronto. Supposedly he got lots of meat free but he would always lock it away and never share.

"None of the kids could eat any meat! Well, none of us except Sophie, who was the baby of the family and always got special treatment, goddamn it!" she said.

"Why?" I would ask.

"Oh, how the hell do I know why? That's just what happened. We all ate potatoes every bloody night!" She oozed palpable anger and hatred.

There were lots of sad stories about her family when she was growing up too.

"All five of us girls slept on one double bed with us all lying horizontal," she'd tell me.

"Why?" I would ask.

"Why the hell do you always have to ask so many damn questions? So we could all fit! Why do you think?"

The two boys, my uncles, slept on one single bed together, she said. While she talked I would think more about those potatoes she ate every night, wondering how that was so bad. That was more than I ate growing up. I dreamed up all kinds of delicious ways to eat potatoes: boiled or baked or mashed or French fries or potato pancakes. Frankly, I couldn't understand why recollecting eating potatoes every night made her so angry. I couldn't imagine anything more luxurious than eating *every* night, no matter what it was. In any event, my mother had more to eat growing up than I did, but somehow she felt that she was harder done by as a kid than I was. Maybe she was just too caught up in her own pain to see mine.

MY FATHER, WALTER JOSEPH GWIZD, was born in Warsaw, Poland (Gwizd means whistle in Polish, he told me), sometime in the 1930s. When he was a boy, he and his stepmother and father came to Canada, along with his three half-brothers and two stepsisters. His mother, Cathrine, whom I'm named after, died when he was a baby. His friends referred to him as Whizman later on in life because he had a way of always getting what he wanted—a whiz of a character, I heard a friend of his say once.

He wore a moustache that got progressively greyer over the years but never thinned. Only a handful of times do I recall him shaving it off completely, and that was only because he made a rare, albeit fatal, mistaken right-hand move in front of the bathroom mirror.

"Shit! Son of a bitch!" I'd hear him yell to himself and I knew what had happened.

His hair was thick and dark and never receded, but like his moustache, it also became grey over time, but only in places where it made him look better. Women get old and men mature, I would think to myself when I compared my parents as they aged. He had clear skin and bright hazel eyes, just like mine. As a matter of fact, if you looked at a picture of only our eyes, you might think that they were of the same person.

I suppose he was what one would have called dapper. He was, for the most part, fastidious about his appearance. At least, that was the look he affected. What I do know is that he was considered quite handsome by women and must have had some charisma. He could be—when he wanted to be—quite the charmer.

He claimed he learned how to take care of himself while fighting overseas in the army. My mother said he was a goddamn liar: he was never overseas in the army. Whenever a car drove by and the engine backfired with a large bang, he used to jump three feet out of his seat. "Oh my God! Jesus! That was too much." He would complain about symptoms of shell shock.

"Shell shock, my ass," my mother said. "It's just his excuse to lap up the booze."

IMPROBABLY, CONSIDERING HIS FUSSINESS about his appearance, he kept about twenty pairs of reading glasses in a basket in the kitchen—all broken. None of the glasses ever had both stems, and a few had no nose rests. Mostly my father would find the glasses in dumpsters or garbage cans.

Nothing we had was ever bought new, and everything old was repaired or taped or patched way longer than might be acceptable by anyone else's standard. If it wasn't second- or third-hand—or, even better, free—we did without.

We usually had an old black-and-white TV that my dad had to regularly change tubes in to keep it working and a few older appliances such as a fridge and stove, but we never had a toaster until the early seventies. Only once did we have a washing machine, an ancient one, and that was only for about a year because it came with an apartment we were renting. When we did have a phone, it was regularly cut off for non-payment of the bill, as were the heating and hydro. Waking up every morning was like a crapshoot for me. The apartments we lived in would always be freezing cold and I'd have to guess whether the lights were turned off again or not. I couldn't rely on anything electrical being either available or working.

The only trade my father knew was lathing and plastering, which was good-paying work in the fifties and sixties. He was good enough, in fact, to launch his own lathing and plastering company, and to get contracts for some of the most important office buildings constructed in Toronto. He wasn't clever enough, however, to stop drinking even when he was working. If it contained alcohol and was within Dad's reach, he drank it. He tended to hire workers who enjoyed drinking as much as he did, which meant, I guess, that he didn't have to drink alone when he was working, even though that wouldn't have been a problem. There was always enough booze to go around, unlike food.

Other crews showed up on the construction site with thermoses of tea or coffee in their lunch pails; Dad and his buddies arrived with a bottle of whisky or cheap sherry. By the end of their shift they would be more plastered than the walls. How they managed to build flat, straight walls with so much alcohol in their systems is both a medical and architectural mystery. They'd slurp booze from dawn to dusk while nailing up the lathing and smearing on the plaster, and they would slide the empties between the walls and plaster them over. I like to picture all those shiny office towers in Toronto whose walls are covered in expensive wood panelling or pricey silk fabric, while inside and out of sight sit dozens of empty bottles reeking of cheap sherry and whisky.

My father's career as an employer ended just after I was born. One day, drunk as usual, he fell three stories off a scaffold and shattered his ankle so badly it had to be held together with screws and pins. The surgery not only left his leg an inch shorter than the other, but he could no longer flex his ankle either, so he walked with a noticeable limp the rest of his life. The pain he endured was one reason he could justify his "medicine": his daily bottle or two of whiskey. "You've got to hit the steel when it's hot!" he would say if he had money to buy two bottles instead of one.

The experience might have convinced some men that staggering around on a bunch of planks while working on a high ceiling was a habit worth dropping, but not my father. He drank as heavily as ever. He never wanted to take pills and would say, almost proudly, "I drink to deal with the pain of my ankle and by God it's better than being hopped up, like some people, on pills." He liked those two words, "hopped up." I would come home late some nights and he would say, "What are you hopped up on?" even though he was drunk as a skunk. A few times I caught him smoking pot right in the house. If booze wasn't around, then pot was. And when things got really desperate for him, anything containing alcohol would do very nicely instead.

I remember once in particular. He was acting weird and I asked what he was doing.

"I'm getting hopped up myself," he said, assuming I was high. He dropped his head back to look dreamily up at the ceiling. He offered me a "puff." I declined. "Takes the bloody pain away so I can walk just like everyone else!" he said. He showed me by walking around the room.

"Dad, you're *still* limping; you're just stoned."

"I'm not stoned, I'm hopped up! And if I can't feel it, it ain't happening!"

If my mother caught him smoking weed she would freak right out. He would just laugh and ignore her until she started slapping him upside the head and face, and sometimes he would laugh harder, which made her even more mad. Sometimes there would be no laughter and that's when the other side of him would appear: the dark side. I never knew when this side would come out. It could be when the moon shone bright or when the sun was shining, and it was up to me to carefully walk on eggshells around my dad until I sussed the situation out. And that is a crazy, stressed-out thing for any kid to have to learn how to do.

My father had three basic personalities. Which personality emerged at any one time depended on how drunk he was. The first was distant and cool: this meant he was sober. This was the personality I was least familiar with. The third was mean and nasty: he was drunk. But there was another personality that was an in-between stage after he'd had his first two or three drinks. It was like an edge had come off and he was actually a lot of fun to be around. He could feel, I guess, the first warmth of an alcohol haze creeping into his soul.

This was also when he'd open his arms and say, "Come here, my million dollars," and let me sit on his knee.

I would smile and enjoy the experience because I knew it would not last long: he would keep drinking and either he'd get mean or my mother would. Whenever she heard him call me his "million dollars" she'd say, "Yeah, yeah, million dollar shit," or "Million dollars, my ass."

I hated when she said that. I just thought, man, if I was worth a million dollars, then that must not be worth very much. I mean, it sounded like a lot, but when I looked around me and eventually became aware of how little we actually did have, well, a million didn't impress me much.

Like I said, my father was a pretty good-looking guy. His personality might have made him more attractive sometimes too. As I said, at times he could be very funny and engaging. He wasn't stupid, yet he did some of the stupidest things I can imagine any man doing. Some of the worst experiences of my life happened to me because of him. I guess deep down he had a good heart. But it was a long way down. I always thought he had a decent business sense too, which I think I may have inherited, but he screwed it up with bad friends and alcohol.

When he was in the mood, I would get some paper and pencils and we would play X's and O's with bets involved, and I would beat him over and over, winning all his pennies and nickels. Sometimes when he got up to go to the bathroom or the fridge, I would erase his moves if I thought that he was going to win and replace them with a losing mark. He would come back to the kitchen table and squint at the game and say, "What the—?" He always said that. You can fill in the rest of the sentence yourself. I'd just sit there pretending to not know "what the" anything and go on to win the game. He got distracted very easily and I took advantage of it whenever I could.

One night when I had won all his change, he broke into my mother's white pleather suitcase where she saved rare coins and bills that she claimed were worth a lot of money. He used those to bet with, but lost them all to me. When my mother came home and saw what I had won and how, she slapped him repeatedly while he laughed and laughed, saying "What the—?" over and over again. I didn't find it so funny because she used to take my winnings back. But he'd find it amusing sometimes to really piss my mother off. When I used to shout for her to stop hitting him, he'd say, "Now, Cathy, leave your mother alone." Crazy.

Over the years my dad broke into that suitcase time and time again until eventually almost all the rare and valuable items she had collected over twenty years—the upside-down dollars and upside-down coins and all the other freaks of the Canadian mint—were lost forever to the local liquor and tobacco stores around our neighborhoods, where he used them as regular cash when he needed cigarettes or booze. Whenever I saw him walking into their bedroom with a screwdriver in his hand when my mother wasn't home I would panic, knowing there was a potentially long and horrible night coming.

When my dad was feeling good about life and about me, he was my idea of a real father, somebody who cared about his daughter and was eccentric and childlike enough to be loveable. Like the day he suggested I become a circus performer. I would travel and make lots of money in a circus, he said. The thing is, I think he was dead serious. Most parents traditionally encourage their kid to become a lawyer or doctor or some other similar profession. My dad was absolutely sure I could make it in the circus. "You could be a tumbler and an acrobat!" he said, as though he had discovered some rare and great talent in me that I should not be wasting.

Just to prove it, he tried to teach me how to do flips and stand on my head, and between his drunken incompetence and my eagerness to please—my dad was teaching me something special!—I spent hours trying to do a headstand and cartwheel. But I was just too scared of getting hurt, so I made a few half-hearted attempts and then gave up on the circus.

He realized I wasn't any good. After that he suggested I become a lawyer.

IN GRADE 3 the kids in my class thought it would be fun to gather behind the school and throw rocks at me and call me ugly and skinny and make fun of the clothes I wore. At most of the schools, it was just the girls who teased me and started fights. But at this school, a few of the boys joined in. One time a boy threw a rock that hit me right in the forehead—I didn't see it coming, I just saw him laugh and point after it made contact. Blood gushed onto my face, burning my eyes. It tasted warm and salty. As I tried to blink the blood out of my eyes, I could hardly see where I was running, but I still ran. I ran and ran all the way home. When I got there, I washed the blood off my face and thought I would tell my dad so he could do something about these kids being so mean to me for no reason other than my being poor. I walked into the kitchen and told him what had just happened.

"I'll teach you karate! That way you can defend yourself."

"Do you know karate?"

He kicked his chair out of the way and dropped into a karate stance. He was drunk and wobbled unsteadily. He made his hands into blades and aimed two blows at me. The first hit me in the arm; it really hurt. But the next caught me in the neck and I passed out. I woke up to find him sitting at the kitchen table, drunkenly staring at me laughing his head off. I learned nothing about karate and the kids kept beating me up and throwing stones at me. But from the drunken recesses of his heart, he had at least tried to teach me something I might use.

I used to love hearing my dad describe the highest mountain peaks around the world. He recited them in descending order of their heights. He could figure out any mathematical equation in his head, and if you called out ten random numbers to him he would tell you their sum instantly. He was conversational in a number of foreign languages. One day he came home lugging an entire set of legal textbooks that he had found in the dump. It took him months to read them all, but every night he would have a different volume out on the kitchen table, and he'd drink and smoke and read.

"If you can't make it in the circus, maybe someday, you will be a lawyer instead. And you can use those books to learn how to get your old man out of jail, my million dollars!" Then he laughed.

I tried to read the books, but they were far too advanced for a child of eight. I knew if I had to read all those books to become a lawyer, well, that would never happen and my dad would just have to stay in jail!

Instead, I took to carrying those books under my arm, walking up and down the street by myself. I wanted people in the neighbourhood to see me with the big books and think that I was smart. That's when my mother started calling me a phony.

MY DAD LOVED JOHNNY CASH. So whenever his songs would pipe through the radio, my dad would turn the volume *way* up and sing along, continuing to sing and imitate his idol long after the song had ended. He would laugh and have a good old time doing this whenever the mood struck him. But my mother didn't like it.

She didn't like Johnny Cash or my dad being happy. Ever. One day he was seated on the floor drinking while trying to repair the TV set, and who should come on the radio but Johnny Cash. He got up off the floor to blast the volume, saying "Hello everybody, my name is Johnny Cash!" as though he were stepping on stage.

When my mother heard him laughing and the radio blasting, she flew into the room and turned the radio off—just like she always did.

"Yeah, yeah, goddamn Johnny Cash, eh? Figures. Another drunk just like you, you drunk bastard!" She stormed out of the room and my father instantly stopped singing and smiling.

And so did I.

Anyway, my dad was better at imitating Johnny Cash than he was at repairing the TV set or any other damn thing. He could take anything apart, but he was lousy at putting things back together. The fact that he tended to take them apart when he was drunk and tried to reassemble them when he was sober complicated things even more. Our houses always had piles of electric things taken apart that would stay that way until he brought home another similar item from the dump. And then the garbage parts would be put into a cupboard or somewhere else for potential future use, and the whole process would start all over again. He used to really look like he knew what he was doing when he was "repairing" something, but he never successfully fixed anything. As a matter of fact, he broke almost everything instead.

"That guy is goddamn useless!" my mother would say when she came across an item my dad was trying to repair. "Stay with a drunk and you'll have nothing new your entire life!"

MY MOTHER HAD A THING for Engelbert Humperdinck. When his songs came on the radio, it would be fine to turn the radio *way* up for him. "Oh, I just love that man. Ahhhh. Now *that's* a man," she would say. One time I said, "Mom, do you know his name is really Arnold George Dorsey?"

"Who gives a shit what his real name is."

I wondered why she didn't call him a phony too. Why was I one in her eyes and he wasn't?

DAD NEVER COMPLAINED about the broken reading glasses or decrepit furniture that was always picked up from the garbage or the appliances that he sometimes brought home from the dump because he liked to try to fix everything himself. So we never had anything new. Ever. And the dumpy furniture and everything else that was used and old always lived in houses or apartments that were just as old and dumpy.

Every now and again when he was drunk he would decide to repair the kitchen chairs. They were garbage when we first got them and never got any better. All three of the had a bland brown leaf pattern on the vinyl and were torn or ripped—from being old mostly but also from being hurled and kicked around in past fights. I'll never forget those chairs. They were practically rusted through where the nuts and bolts held the framework in place. Two chairs rocked when you sat in them, and you had to find a piece of cardboard or paper and fold it over a few times before stuffing it under one of the legs if you wanted to sit down without rocking endlessly.

The "repairs" never worked, of course. For the next few weeks, every time you sat in one of the kitchen chairs the edges of the tape would start peeling off and stick to your clothes. Eventually the tape would peel completely and when you stood up the whole length of tape rose and the chair would drag after you as you walked across the kitchen floor. Honestly, why I remember those chairs so vividly is the feeling of being stuck—I mean, deep-down stuck—stuck in my life, in that kitchen with these parents and being broke, poor, always fighting and always hungry and never having anything that was nice or—God forbid—new. It was like I knew I could never drag myself free.

His next favourite things to fix would be anything electronic, like the radio or TV. These repairs were about as successful as the chairs. I used to wonder if there really was anything he was good at, because to me it seemed that he continued losing his whole life.

My father was always trying to fix things. Stupid, meaningless things. He was no good at it. And the things that were in his control to fix? Those things he never bothered trying to fix. Maybe he had tried to once. I don't know. But by the time I turned up, it seemed like he just didn't care. Maybe he had given up by then.

My father was no saint, that's for sure. My mother surely had her reasons for resenting him. The thing is, I really felt sorry for my dad. He was like a bad dog that was always getting into trouble. He seemed more—I don't know—more helpless than anything else. What I do know is that as one gets older you tend to see your parents differently. Maybe that's why I feel like I do. I think that's why I developed such an attachment to animals. Animals are helpless too. They can't help being who they are. It always breaks my heart when people treat an animal cruelly and I get angry.

EVERY NEW YEAR'S EVE that I was with my parents growing up, my mother was very adamant that whatever and however you were on that night, at the stroke of midnight, was how you and your life would be for the whole next year. Worried that I could have such influence, I took that pretty seriously. So, every New Year's Eve, at the stroke of midnight, I used to be bathed and dressed as best as I could be, hair brushed, room clean, sitting on a chair or my bed as straight as I possibly could, smiling and thinking about how next year would be better for us all. However, listening to the fighting and arguing going on in the kitchen at the same time made it quite clear that the "rents" were the reason things would still no doubt remain the same. (I started calling my parents the "rents" because we rarely had the money to pay the rent, and "rent" formed part of the word "parents.")

Some parents have endearing names for each other, using them in front of their children or saving them for the bedroom. The name I usually heard my mother use to describe my father was "whoremaster." "He'll screw anything that walks," she said one time when no one was around, and then I'd hear her talk about my dad to a neighbour or someone and she would say, "Oh, Walter is very charismatic, that's for sure," and add, smiling, "Yes, everyone loves him— he's very good." And then she would walk by me and say under her breath, "Good for shit!" But by then, I knew this behaviour was part of the "what goes on in this house, stays in this house" crock that my mother and father hammered into my head as often as they could. I would think, Who the hell wants to know the type of crappola that goes on in our house anyway! I couldn't figure out why my parents were so paranoid about that, so I asked one time. "Because you goddamn tell everyone everything about you. You can't keep your mouth shut!" was the answer.

My dad's names for my mother were no better: "two bit whore" or simply "whore." "Cunt." "Bitch." This was what they were worried about me sharing with the outside world. But back then I would much rather tell people my version of my family. Sometimes when I was outside, I would talk to strangers. Okay, I always talked to strangers. If someone was waiting at the bus stop or streetcar stop near where we lived, I knew that they would be standing in one place and able to have a conversation. I would stand right beside them, waiting for them to say something. Usually they would say hello and ask me my name and then I would get right into it. "I'm waiting for my father to get off the bus," adding, "He's a doctor." And then I would get a reply something like, "Oh, my, isn't that nice."

"Yeah, and he's going to take my sister and me and my mother out to eat when he gets home." I would make up all kinds of stories but they usually included a sister, a family outing and food.

Both parents liked to drink, though from what I know of them it was my father who had the taste for it and my mother basically went along for the ride. When they both got drunk, that was bad news for me. And if they were both sober, that was sometimes worse news. Like on "Sober Sundays," when there was no money left to spend on booze and cigarettes. Two nasty personalities would emerge and I would wonder how I could find a few bucks for them to get them out of their misery. My mother used to collect bottles in the neighbourhood and cash them in. She did that for years. "I've got to collect goddamn bottles to pay for milk and tea!" she'd complain when she would walk in with a bag full of empties. But I knew that my dad would get that money too. She would hide things and he would find them. That's the game they played.

During my childhood my parents were bootleggers on and off. But they kept dipping into the merchandise themselves and that sort of defeated the purpose. My mom would still collect empties even if they did have this business going on the side. I guess in some ways she was sort of entrepreneurial herself.

Sober or drunk, they fought. It always started out half civil; they would actually begin speaking to each other about things that seemed to matter to them. I would be in my room or another part of the apartment, and I would hear them in the kitchen talking to each other in low murmurs, the same way I guessed that parents of other kids would discuss things. Some of the things they would say or do would be kind of cute or funny. And then it would always get ugly, booze or no booze: if there was booze, it was because they got drunk, and if there was no booze, because they couldn't get drunk.

I should have been pleased they were acting like real people who had something pleasant to say to each other. I wasn't. I hated it. It was as though they were teasing me, saying, "See, when we try, we can be the kind of parents a kid like you should have." It couldn't last, and never did. I knew the routine. I would be in a state of suspended animation, waiting for their voices to grow louder and angrier until they exploded into screams and shouts of rage. Soon I'd hear fists thumping the table followed by slaps and punches and broken glass and thrown furniture. I think it was worse when they weren't drunk, though. Especially because when they were sober, my mother would often cry after getting hit. When she was drinking, she just hit harder. I hated seeing my mother cry. I used to pray that God would help her because I couldn't.

Whenever I heard those murmurs from the kitchen, and the sound of booze being poured into a glass, I wanted to scream, *Hurry up and get plastered. Stop pretending you're nice people who give a damn about each other because it's just another lie. Hurry up and end this fake dance you're doing and start the fight because the sooner you start the sooner it will be over one way or another.*

WHEN I WAS EIGHT we moved to the second floor apartment above a restaurant a few doors down from the Cameron Hotel on Queen Street.

Down the block, my Auntie May lived in a two-bedroom apartment on the third floor above a shoe store. Auntie May was a widow who drank and smoked as much as my parents did, and so they were good friends. That was the pre-requisite to being friends with my parents wherever we lived. You had to smoke like a chimney and drink like a fish. Auntie May lived with her teenage son, Billy, who was rarely home when I was there. When he was home, he shut his bedroom door and didn't talk to me.

I don't know why everyone called my aunt's bedroom the Foxhole. I guess it was supposed to be some cutesy name for a plain, small, dark, windowless broom-closet sort of room that had been converted into a bedroom. There was barely space enough for a single person to stand up in, let alone a single bed with a small dresser that was pushed right up against the foot of the bed. The Foxhole's ceiling had a slope to it, so if you sat up suddenly from lying down in the bed, you would whack your head pretty good and have a goose egg on your noggin for a week. I don't know why the room was wallpapered either because it didn't make it look any better, but it was, with big flowers that were the size of watermelons. If you stared at an area of the wallpaper and you were too close, which you always were because the room was so small, you couldn't make out a pattern. It just looked like some purple psychedelic mess. But if you were standing at the doorway looking in, you could see that the wallpaper had a floral pattern to it. The wallpaper made the room look even smaller than it actually was.

I didn't like it. I tried to tell my mother that I didn't want to stay in the Foxhole, but she would tell me that I needed to "talk less and listen more." My Auntie May would tell me how wonderful a time I would have. My mother would say, acting all smiley, "I'll bring you a hot beef sandwich when I come back." Sure. I rarely got a hot beef sandwich and if I did, it was never hot.

Sleeping in the Foxhole was even worse than sleeping in the tub in our bathroom at home when my dad got really drunk. True, I had a pillow and a few blankets when sleeping in the Foxhole's bed compared to the tub, but at least I was at home in the tub. I just wished my parents would stay home with me and that they would be sober. Every time I asked my dad why he got drunk, he never gave me an answer except for the odd time that he told me it was because his ankle hurt him so much. As I got older, I didn't buy that story, but for a long time I did.

I always followed my parents to the hotel, so they started lecturing me before they left me alone in the Foxhole. "Cathy, you need to stay in the Foxhole all night, okay? You can't come to the hotel. You have to stay in the Foxhole. Don't you like it in the Foxhole? It's nice and safe and cozy. So be sure you stay here all night. If you need to go to the bathroom, go now, okay? Once we leave you here, you need to be sure you don't follow us." The only bathroom in the place was downstairs and real spooky and I was too afraid to go by myself. Maybe that is why I peed the bed.

Lots of times I would leave the Foxhole and wander the streets. I always eventually made my way to the Cameron Hotel, where my parents were drinking inside, and I would sit on the curb of the street and wait there for hours. Once in a while, especially when it started getting dark and cold outside, I would stand in front of the hotel's big front door and ask strangers to get my mom and dad for me. I would tell them what they looked like or get a peek at them as the door opened, and as a swoosh of hot air combined with the smell of booze enveloped me and blew my hair back for a quick second, I'd be able to tell the stranger where my parents were sitting. "Oh, oh, there they are, there they are, can you see the man with the white shirt right there!"

I had about five different people a night going into the Cameron to tell my parents to come out to talk to me and to come home. But they only sent me home instead. My dad was the one that usually came out of the hotel if at all, and he would give me some money to go to the store to buy some chips or some other crap item to eat and tell me to go home. It was as if my parents would die without the Cameron and booze, but I was just a pesky hungry kid who would still be alive as long as a few coins were tossed my way.

Eventually I would be too tired and go back to the "hole" and maybe fall asleep. Before I knew it, it seemed, I would get woken up abruptly by loud drunk voices sometimes arguing and sometimes laughing, and loud footsteps would come into the bedroom and my mother would announce, "Cathy! Time to get up and come home!" By this time I would be too tired to eat. Not that it mattered. They would have forgotten about my sandwich anyway.

My Auntie May, by the way, wasn't my real auntie, but I was told by my parents when they were drunk to call people they introduced me to Auntie or Uncle, so I did. But then when they sobered up and I would refer to someone as Auntie or Uncle, my mother would say, "They're not your uncle" or "They're not your auntie," and tell me to stop calling them that. When I would say something like, "Well, you just told me to call them that last night when they were at our house drinking with you and Daddy," she would say, "Stop giving me your crap. I don't know why parents make their kids call strangers 'Uncle' when they're not. That's so bloody stupid. Then kids get molested."

Yeah, it made just about that much sense to me too.

So, if my parents were drunk, everyone was Auntie or Uncle as the booze flowed. I learned to give descriptions of people if I had any questions or comments for my parents later. "Mommy, what was that woman's name that had red hair that was here last night?" I asked one time. "Oh, that's Patty." The following week when they were all drunk she would be Auntie Patty.

I DON'T REMEMBER my parents ever hugging or kissing me. They certainly never displayed any affection to one another. Not at home anyway.

The weird thing is, my mother used to kiss my cousins when we saw them. One time while I was out with my mother and my Auntie Nellie, my mother told a stranger that she was chatting with, "I'm out with my sister and my daughter shopping. We're all very close."

My Auntie Nellie swung on the stranger: "She's a goddamn liar. We're not close at all!" My mother gave her one of her infamous looks that meant, *Shut the fuck up or you're in trouble.* My Auntie Nellie just sniffed twice like she always did when she was uncomfortable or angry. Sniff, sniff and look away, shaking her head while she looked at me.

Like the cliché says, denial isn't a river in Egypt!

My mother never hugged me or ever seemed as happy as she appeared when she saw my cousins or people we barely knew. I would just smile and think, "How come you don't hug or kiss me?"

But I learned not to ask too many questions. It was just easier that way.

CHAPTER TWO

The house that got away

"GOD IS GOING to strike that drunkard down dead one day!"

My mother was of course referring to my father.

Of the many disappointments in her married life, she would tell me, nothing surpassed the loss of our house on Montrose Avenue. From the time I was about five right until I moved out of the house at around eighteen it was the flashpoint for their worst confrontations.

My mother would say or do something to upset my father. He would leap up from his chair. He would shove her and call her a stupid son of a bitch or miserable whore or something. And with her being taller than him, he had to shove upwards a bit in order to get her just below the shoulders.

Typically my mother would respond by slapping his face and sending his single-stemmed reading glasses flying. Before he could recover she would kick his surgically repaired ankle. Hard.

Dad would scream out loudly in pain and try to stand back up. He would get angrier and angrier and his face would get redder and redder. They would then both start hurling whatever was closest in reach at each other, like chairs or plates or glasses, while throwing blows left and right whenever they could get them in as well. Most of the things they threw at each other hit the walls, ceiling or windows; only the slaps and punches hit their mark. In every place we lived, the kitchen had chunks of wall and ceiling missing. I don't know why they only fought in the kitchen, but they did.

And I always watched from the kitchen entrances, terrified, screaming for them to stop.

Anyway, after this went on for a while, my mother would scream, "And who was the goddamn bastard that lost my house on Montrose Avenue to those Jewish bailiffs? Who didn't pay the goddamn mortgage and got drunk at the Wheatsheaf Tavern instead, eh? Who was it? It was you, you rotten bastard!"

No matter how vicious the fight had become at that point—no matter how drunk or incoherent—my father would suddenly grow quiet and sit back down at the kitchen table, pour himself three inches of whiskey and a thimble full of 7UP and fall into a stony, brooding contemplative silence.

Realizing he was lost to further abuse, my mother would walk away into another room, bitterly triumphant but still swearing under her breath.

SHORTLY AFTER I WAS BORN my parents moved into their first home.

They had been married about ten years. My dad had launched his own lathing and plastering company with a friend, and he was doing well enough to have saved the required deposit to buy a house. It was an attached two-storey brick home on Montrose Avenue, not far from downtown Toronto ("Do you know how much that house on Montrose would be worth today?" my mother reminded me year after year) with three bedrooms, a full basement and a fully fenced backyard. It wasn't in the most expensive part of the city by any means, but it was a pleasant neighbourhood, with lots of trees, parks and playgrounds.

To hear my mother tell it, the home on Montrose was as good as life would ever get. That house was the first thing she really owned. I think she enjoyed the status of being a home-owner. Apparently they even rented out a room for extra money. She washed our clothes by hand or foot in a tub (she still does to this day) and hung them on the clothesline to dry. She told me she used to love talking to neighbours and gossiping. It seemed as though she had exactly what she wanted in life in that house with my dad. I think having a house made her feel important, like a somebody. She had a house. She had a baby. She was married. She was a landlord.

The thing is, my mother was at heart a very conventional woman. She was a product of the times. So what if her husband was a drunk? She'd tell me that you must always stand by your man. "The man can do what he likes. A woman's place is to take care of him no matter what he does."

For a few months after they got the house, things were perfect. My father supposedly handed over his paycheque to my mother, who cashed it and then gave my dad spending money along with enough to cover the other bills, including the mortgage.

My father starting spending all his allowance at the bar. Then—short of cash—he started dipping into food money. Then the utility money and the mortgage money and before too long he was not coming home at all.

He would drink up his entire paycheque. Then he'd start selling whatever else there was at home that might be worth a few bucks, regardless of whether it was my mother's or his. She would be looking for an item one day and then realize that my dad must have done something and freak out at him. But the few smacks and the argument that would ensue on Wednesday would be a small price to pay for the drink he needed on Monday.

One cold fall evening she hears a loud knock on the front door. My father, as my mother tells it—is out "whoring around as usual." She is home with me. I am in my crib. Standing on the front stoop are two bailiffs.

"Jewish bailiffs," she says.

"How'd you know they were Jewish?" I asked once.

"Oh, because I'm telling you they were Jewish for God's sake. The Jews owned everything, don't you know that?!"

Anyway, the bailiffs explain to my mother that the mortgage hasn't been paid for months and they've arrived to evict us and take possession of the house. Now. Not tomorrow. Not next month, after she finds another place to live. Now.

My mother becomes frantic; I am crying in my crib. It's total chaos. Two movers show up.

"Sol, what's up?" asks one of the movers.

Sol tells the mover to throw everything that's in the house and not nailed down onto the street. This upsets the mover, who says, "Come on, Sol. There's a woman and baby here, I can't do that!"

The bailiff tells the mover if he doesn't do it, he doesn't get paid.

While the mover is mulling this over and watching my mother cry, Sol loses his patience. He picks up an upholstered fabric chair from the living room, heaves it past my mother, opens the front door, and throws the chair down the front steps where it rolls onto the sidewalk and ends up in the street. Then he wipes his hands together and says, "That's how you do it, Pete. Now hurry up, you're getting paid by the hour and we've already lost money on this deal."

My mother—tears streaking her face—is clinging to the second bailiff. "Please, please get your boss to stop. My husband will be home soon and we can sort this out, I promise. Please!" The bailiff puts up his hands, like "What can I do?" Meanwhile more and more of our belongings are being hauled onto the street. Neighbours have appeared at their doors and wandered onto the sidewalk to watch.

Finally it's over. Sol warns my mother that she had better be out of the house by midnight or she will be in even bigger trouble. "Let's get the hell out of here," he says and clumps down the steps.

Realizing she has been defeated, my mother puts on her coat, wraps me in a blanket, walks out of the house, and sits on the sidewalk curb and cries while the neighbours watch.

She sat with me on the curb for two hours, waiting for my father to come home.

My Auntie Sophie showed up eventually to take us to her house. My cousin Diane remembers my mother and me sitting on the curb crying.

My father—blind drunk—stumbled home in the wee hours of the morning, well after my mother and I were at my Auntie Sophie's house, to find the house empty and locked up and all the furniture on the street. He supposedly dragged the couch from the sidewalk back onto the lawn in front of the house and fell asleep on it as though nothing happened.

I THINK ABOUT my mother and her resolve.

"I should have left that fucking bastard after that!" she says.

How often I wished that she had.

Instead of leaving, she would make excuses for him. The bill collectors would come by demanding payment for this or that. She would tell them that, yes, her husband would be paying that bill in a day or two each time the same bill collector would call. The bills never got paid and it was easier to just move and start all over again. "At least he came to get us and got another place for us right away," my mother would sometimes say when I asked for more information about how the Montrose story ended.

I think my mom lost a part of herself the day she lost that house on Montrose Avenue. In a way, the best part of her might have been turned out in the same way the furniture had been turned out. She had been left vacant too. Not only did she start smoking and drinking, she also started gambling. Often when I came home from school or on the weekends, she would spend her time reading the racing pages in the newspaper. She would sit at the kitchen table, pen in hand, and circle all her winners. She did a bit better than my dad. Our mother-daughter table talk was her showing me all the triactors and quinellas she had either won or was going to win. She used to tell me all about the jockeys and how much they weighed and who owned and managed the horses—I mean, she knew it all. Now that I look back, I think a lot of the time when she was gone she was at the racetrack.

I used to wonder what the appeal of gambling was to my mother. It seemed stupidly reckless—especially given our circumstances. And maybe that was the point. When you have nothing, there's nothing to lose. Only there is, of course. There is always more to lose. My mother lost often.

"It's all fucking fixed!" she complained when she lost. But she never stopped. For my mother, hope did spring eternal. But it turned bitter. Each loss for her was a cruel reminder of how unfair the world had been to her. "See, I was going to pick number five but I bet on number seven at the last damn minute!"

MY DAD ONLY BEAT ME a couple of times that I can remember. But they were memorable enough.

Usually what he would do is make this real ugly face as he pounced out of the blue at something I said or did that he didn't like, and then he would stop, his nose exactly two inches away from my nose. To be honest, sometimes I think it would have been easier if he had just hit me. At least it would have been over. What I hated was the anxiety of not knowing if there was going to be something after the threat.

I remember one time turning my nose up at eating bread for dinner. My father went ballistic. "Eat the goddamn bread. Son of a bitch! Eat the goddamned bread! Huh! Huh!" He was crazy-eyed and in my face and biting down on his lower lip, threatening to whack me upside the head.

I hated bread—especially because it was never fresh. We always had to buy food that was old to save money. Tearing off all the green, mouldy parts from a slice of bread made me sick. But I did it. I can still feel myself forcing down clumps of bread that supposedly didn't have mouldy parts, but in my mind, it was still mouldy. And it was always stale. I hated it.

Nothing was ever fresh. Bruised and soft bananas, soft mushy grapes—that is, when we had even those. Our fridges were always as bare as anything. I had a habit of opening them non-stop; I think I was hoping that something good to eat would magically appear in them. Like, oh, there's nothing in the fridge. Close it. Open it. Presto! Now it's loaded! My mother hated when I looked in the fridge.

"What the hell are you looking for in there? Did you put anything in it?" she would say. "Close the goddamn fridge. You're wasting electricity." Or if someone would come over to visit and they opened the fridge without asking my mother's permission? She'd lose it. She caught a friend of my father's snooping. It was like he had breached Fort Knox. "What the fuck do you want in there? Did you put something in that goddamn fridge? You might be a friend of my drunken husband, but you've got no business in my fridge. Now go sit the fuck down or get out!" You didn't mess with her fridge. Sometimes I think she was just embarrassed about having nothing in it. She often reacted to things in ways that seemed unreasonable or out of proportion to me.

My mother, unlike my father, never threatened. She liked to shake me when she got really mad at me.

"Oh, I could just shake you, you're so stupid!" she would yell at me as she grabbed my shoulders and shook me violently like a crazy person might shake a human-sized snow globe. I used to get shaken from the time I was about five until I was about thirteen. Then after that, she only threatened to shake me.

When she shook me, I used to imagine that my brains were getting all mushed up and I wondered if she knew or cared that she was making me retarded. She told me that if you shook a baby it would become retarded or die. What was she trying to do to me? Why did I make her so mad? Why did she hate me? Was it because I was like my father and she hated him? "You're just like your goddamn father!" she often said. The whole time, though, her words were what hurt me the most and are what left the most scars.

I WAS ABOUT SIX YEARS OLD when I realized that my mother didn't like me very much. I'd had about two years' worth of shaking and plus the endless verbal abuse. I tried to stay out of her way as much as I could. We seemed to get along best when she could ignore me, the way she ignored all the stray dogs I brought home. But when I popped onto her radar, that's when the problems would start. So I preferred being invisible, which is why I tried to always be outside the house whenever possible. At least I didn't get into trouble that way. I think I even tried to get out of the house when I was three, although I don't remember why.

I was three years old when I almost fell out of our upstairs window.

Somehow I made my way onto an open window ledge on the second floor of a house we rented on Niagara Street. I was perched on the ledge, feet dangling over the edge, just sitting there. My father came home and saw me sitting on the ledge from the street. He ran into the house and yelled to my mother, who was on the main floor.

She ran upstairs and grabbed my dress and pulled me into the room.

I wonder what would have happened had my father not walked by at that moment.

MY MOTHER ALWAYS dressed me in long drab dresses. Like a fussy old lady.

I always envied those kids whose mothers dressed them in cute dresses with crinolines and bright colours. I never had new clothes. My mother always made my clothes or I wore whatever she could find at second-hand stores.

I never had toys either. In fact, I don't remember having anything except one Barbie doll my Auntie Helen bought for me one Christmas.

Apparently I was a quiet baby and wasn't any trouble at all. My mother always told me that I never touched or broke anything in the house—that is, she said, until I got older. I could never figure out how a baby that was pretty much stuck in a crib and at the mercy of another human being could be "no trouble." A baby had no choice; it had to be no trouble! "When you got older you were a bloody holy terror getting into everything!" So, I was perfect until I was able to walk around. I was perfect if I was sleeping or in a crib, I guess. I was perfect until I started to become me.

She used to rain down on me endlessly how bad I was as a child with scribbling and writing on everything. Not like when I was a baby in the crib.

I used to get paper that I would find in the house and then dig for a pencil (a contractor's pencil—those thick, flat pencils that are used in construction, because my mother didn't let me have access to pens or pencils) from my dad's tool box and pretend that I was writing, even when I was too young to know how. So I used to draw wavy lines on paper, page after page, endlessly. I used to talk out loud and then pretend that I was writing what I said.

My mother would walk into the room I was playing in and grab the paper and crumple it up and throw it into the garbage, shouting at me for wasting paper by writing on everything and making a mess.

"Goddamn it! What a dumb kid! Do you have to make a mess out of everything!"

When all the paper was gone or hidden—I suspect she hid everything—I would find black-and-white photos that my parents had taken, because they were blank on the back and that was good enough for me to write on. So I'd get that contractor pencil again and I would scribble on the backs of all the pictures, pretending I was writing a book. Well, my mother lost her mind over that. I got smacked and tossed around and yelled at worse than before and eventually I gave up trying to write. But she never threw the pictures out. Believe it or not, I still have photos from the 1950s and early 60s with my scribbling on the back of them!

During my first years at school when I was encouraged to draw, I didn't like to. Oh, I wanted to, but I didn't understand why I couldn't at home but I could at school. My Grade 1 teacher, Mrs. Cameron, came by my desk looking at the blank page in front of me when we were supposed to draw our family. All the other kids had finished drawing their pictures and she saw that I hadn't even started mine. She crouched down to be on my level and said, "Cathy, why aren't you drawing?"

"I don't want to make a mess. You won't like it."

"Well, why don't you try?" she said, encouragingly.

"I don't know what to draw," I replied.

"Well, how about you draw your family, like the other kids are doing? Do you have a sister or brother? Show me what your family looks like." I thought about that for a bit and then I picked up a black crayon and drew. I was finished in about thirty seconds.

"That's your family?"

I replied that it was. On the paper was me, just me, in pure stick form with a head, two eyes, a nose, straight black lines for hair, but without clothes or a mouth. I had no hands or feet either. She walked away not saying anything else to me, and I thought that she was the nicest teacher I would ever have. Playing at home that night I asked my mother if I could draw after having had such a good day at school.

"Can't you just bloody well sit still for five minutes?! You're always running around, or touching things ... Oh, I could just shake you!" It was always five minutes that I was told to sit still for, when really she was asking me to sit still forever.

For years she would say, "Sit still for five minutes and I'll give you a nickel!"

If it wasn't my chattering that bothered my mother, it was my antsy feet. If it wasn't my feet, then it was my hands. I never remember her taking me for walks or encouraging me to play. When I went outside to play, she insisted that I not get dirty. "I don't understand how other mothers let their kids play in the sand and get all dirty!" she would say. I would watch other kids play in the sandbox and never join them for fear of angering my mother. One time I collected all the empty sardine and vegetable tins from the neighbourhood garbage cans, and I set up a store front consisting of these empty cans. While putting the merchandise on display, which happened to be all along our front fence, I sliced almost the whole tip of my finger off. I ran into the house crying and screaming; my mother shook me while yelling at me, all upset that I got cut. She had to get the neighbour to call a cab and take me to the hospital, where I got stitches. When we got back from the hospital, she threw all the store merchandise in the garbage and warned me to never play that game again.

Once I broke her prized, hand-carved wooden jewellery box. It was the only thing she ever owned that was close to being something nice and that my dad didn't manage to sell on her. She used to polish that jewellery box and keep it all gleaming and shiny. However, she did take it to a pawn shop a few times. My dad would sell her belongings but she pawned them. She had a few pieces of jewellery in that box, but everything was costume-type stuff except for her wedding ring—it was a quarter-carat round diamond set in white gold. She rarely wore it but she pawned that too. I don't know why my dad never sold it on her.

When I was six years old and bored one night, I decided to go try on my mother's ring and costume jewellery. I wasn't going to be running around, and I wasn't going to be trying to write and I wasn't going to be talking too much. I was just finding something to do in the house by myself that I wouldn't get in trouble for. My parents were in their usual place, in the kitchen arguing and drinking. When I got older, I thought, You know, if they had argued in Polish or Ukrainian for all those years, maybe I would have learned a second language. Mind you, I did learn all the Polish and Ukrainian swear words.

I walked into my parents' bedroom and saw my mother's jewellery box on her dresser. She always told me to never touch it, but I still did when she wasn't watching me because I liked it. I wanted a jewellery box of my own. I stood on tiptoe and got the box in my hands. I took it off of the dresser and started inspecting it. It was beautiful. It was either carved out of a chunk of black wood or stained black, and it had carvings of birds and nests all over it. I opened up the top and tried to find the ring when all of a sudden the box slipped out of my hands and crashed to the floor. Part of one of the birds' heads broke off, and one corner of the box was chipped. I immediately started crying because I knew I was in big trouble. Hearing me in her bedroom, my mother walked in and freaked out. She picked up the jewellery box.

"What the hell did you just do? Why are you in here anyway? Didn't I tell you to never, ever, touch this again? Didn't I?! Son of a bitch!" She shook me so hard I thought my arms would come loose from their sockets. "I can't have anything good around this goddamn place! Why do you have to touch everything? Get the hell out of here!"

It was about that time that I started kicking uncontrollably when I slept and wetting the bed. My cousins refused to sleep with me when we were over at their places trying to escape my dad's drunkeness and violence because I was so physically violent when I slept. They would wake up with bruises all over them from me kicking and lashing out in my sleep. I remember often waking up in a cold puddle of my own pee.

For years my mother would bring up how I broke her prized jewellery box. You would have thought I had stolen a car or robbed a bank.

She used to tell me that when she was a kid, all her sisters and brothers played with their friends but she never, ever, left her house or her front porch if her mother told her to stay put. "I used to stay on that porch for hours, not doing anything. I was perfect. My mother didn't have to worry about me running around or touching things that I shouldn't be touching or going somewhere that I wasn't supposed to be going. I did what I was told. I was the perfect child."

I learned early—and often—that I was far from being the perfect child.

Picture this: My mother is inside the house, which we have just moved into from our previous house down the street. We were always moving. We moved down the street, up the street, over to the next block, or across to the next neighbourhood every few months. I used to look forward to moving, hoping with all my heart that the next place would be better than the last. But that never happened. I never gave up hope, and I was always excited until I walked through the front door of the new place and saw that it was just as crummy as the one we'd left. Maybe worse. Even back then, I was very much aware of how little we always had.

Whenever we arrived in a new neighbourhood I would play with whoever lived nearby that liked me and I never thought of the few friends that I'd made and left behind. I never had a huge pool of friends to choose from, so I couldn't be picky.

Anyway, the girl next door has wandered over and is sitting beside me on the steps. After we learn each other's names she says, "Wanna have a 'wearing contest?" She is missing her front tooth and can't pronounce s's.

I figure I can do pretty well at a swearing contest. I don't do many things well but I know some bad words. Plus, I will take any opportunity to talk. So we get started, and I intend to win.

I start. "Shit," I say.

"Bath-tard," she says.

Then we're really rolling.

"Asshole."

"Fuck."

"Cocksucker."

"Cunt."

"Whore!" I yell. I'm having fun and my new friend is laughing when I hear the cover of the metal letterbox on the front door rattle and slam shut. Somebody has been peering and listening through it. I know, because that's what I do when I'm watching the kids play when I'm stuck inside because my mother says that I can't go outside. She never tells me why I can't go outside but I know it's not because I did something bad. I know she just doesn't want me to play and have fun. She says the ground is dirty. Other kids can get dirty, but I can't. She loves to tell me how clean I always manage to stay and she seems impressed with that.

I'm thinking about somebody listening to our swearing contest—and I know it's my mother because nobody else is home—when the door flies open and my mother swoops me up by my hair and shirt with one hand and drags me into the house, where she lifts me off the floor and then pounds me back onto it again, over and over.

First I feel terror, then I feel nothing, because I am beyond terrified. She throws me to the right and I fly that way. Then she picks me up and throws me to the left, and I fly that way. After doing this for a while, she leaves me in a heap and I lie there on the cold floor. It's colder in the house than it is outside. It's usually like that. It's always darker in the house too than it is outside because my mother is always turning off any lights that happen to be on.

I don't know how long I remain there before I feel my mother grab my arm and put me in a sitting position on the floor. The floor was getting warm but it's cold again because she moved me when she sat me up. I feel the goosebumps creep up my legs. The piece of soap she pushes into my mouth is as cold as the floor. I bite down on the soap, trying to get it out of my mouth, and my mother holds my mouth shut. My spit is making the soap sudsy and suds are seeping out of the corners of my mouth and nose and the soap is burning my throat. I can't breathe. She is an inch from my face now, bending over me and saying, "Who taught you to say those goddamn dirty words? You little spoiled brat. Son of a bitch!"

She lets go of my mouth and the soap falls out, along with pools of drool and suds that spill all over me and onto the floor. My mouth won't stop drooling. My mother tells me how rotten I am over and over before throwing me into the crib in the living room of the house. I don't know why I still sleep in a crib, but there I stay until the next day. I am in the crib so long that I even pee in it. I just lie down in the drool, which is warm on my cheek, and the strong soap taste doesn't go away. It seems like forever until the taste of soap is gone. Without moving, frozen because it's cold and I am still terrified, I start thinking about the wet bed, and I realize I will be in trouble yet again. I may get a spanking—even a beating—but I pray all night that I don't have my mouth washed out with soap again. My mother always said that I was nothing but trouble. The trouble with trouble is that it always starts out as fun.

WHEN I WAS ABOUT TEN YEARS OLD and old enough to venture into stores on my own, I would visit the nicer department stores, the ones displaying dresses with beautiful buttons. They had to have beautiful buttons.

Nobody paid attention to me, even with my second-hand dress and shoes. Sales clerks don't worry about ten-year-old girls admiring expensive dresses. They thought it was cute when I would take a grown-up dress from the rack, carry it to a full-length mirror and hold it up to my scrawny body, pretending I was about to waltz off to a party or a dance, or just act as if I were a child in a real family, where parents bought nice clothes for their kids.

I would move out of sight, walking among the rows of dresses on the racks and touching the fabrics—the velvets and linens and silks—with my fingertips. I loved the bright colours, especially if they were velvet or bold prints, and I would imagine buying those dresses and taking them home.

Then I would take a few dresses, those I loved the most out of the whole store, and I would hang each of them on the end of a rack so I could see the dress in its entirety. I would stand in front of the rack and just stare at the dress. I would feel the fabric and the buttons and check if the dress was lined or if you had to wear a slip under it and think about what gorgeous accessories would go well with it. I would hold the dress and smell how new and fresh it was. Not like at home where everything reeked of cigarettes and I was told not to touch anything.

I would sometimes ask the sales clerks what fabric a dress was made of if I had never felt or seen anything similar before. I learned about all the different types of materials and how you were supposed to cut or sew certain fabrics, and it made me wonder why my mother made her dresses of cotton all the time when she could have had so many other choices.

It was important that I burn the image of each dress perfectly and permanently in my mind before I left the store.

When I was sure no one could see me, I would remove scissors from my pocket and snip two or three buttons from each dress. Sometimes I thought the buttons were more valuable than the whole garment. Some buttons were made of mother of pearl, some of brass or other metals; some were made from the same material the dress was made of; some had two holes and some had four—I mean, every button had a real special place and role in the context of each dress. Someone did a lot of thinking and planning about those buttons, just like the planning that went into making the dress. I could have spent all day in those stores thinking about the whole dress business.

I used to wonder where the dresses were made and who made them, and I imagined women seated at sewing machines in row after row in a factory that buzzed away constantly as they worked happily making all those dresses. At the end of the work day, the women would all get paid in cash as they walked out of the factory on their way home to their families, but not before they stopped in at the grocery store, spending all their earnings on fresh food. A lot of good feelings and ideas came to me from spending time with those dresses and buttons.

Sometimes I even talked to the mannequins that wore the dresses because I could swear they were watching me and knew what was going on. I felt as though their eyes followed my every move. But when I would quickly look their way, their eyes weren't moving at all. I think they kept my secret. Sometimes I imagined that the mannequins would get down from their display boxes and help me pick out the prettiest dresses with the best buttons. I often envisioned interacting with statues or mannequins because it was fun and I was lonely.

I'd leave the store with a pocketful of beautiful buttons and memories of the lovely dresses they came from. On the way home, I would look for cardboard boxes or discarded newspapers or paper of any kind, and I would take it all home. I loved paper, probably because I could take what was in my mind and make it come to life on paper in so many different ways. Once I found a pile of tissue-type paper, except it was a bit heavier and wouldn't easily tear, and that was the best find in the garbage I ever had—well, as far as paper went. At home, I'd select some paper and draw pictures of the dresses from memory. I'd use crayons to reproduce the dresses as accurately as possible. Then I'd mix up flour and water for glue and stick the buttons into place on my pictures.

Every night I would pull those drawings out from under my bed or closet or wherever I hid them and I'd dream about where I would wear each of the dresses and how I'd accessorize them: That one I'll wear to mass on Sunday with the pearl necklace, white gloves and pink satin pumps. That one I'll wear to the racetrack with the big straw hat and high heels and—oh, I hope I don't forget to wear a slip too! That one I'll wear to my wedding with a big crinoline and white patent leather shoes and white tights with a pattern in them. Some day, I promised myself, I would be able to buy any dress I wanted, whatever the price. But for now I just had the buttons.

ACCORDING TO MY MOM, almost everything in life would lead to trouble. Sitting on cement would give me hemorrhoids; eating food containing sugar would give me worms. If the food was hot it would loosen my teeth, and drinking something with ice in it was to be avoided at all times because it made you sick. Showering or washing your hair more than once a week was bad, flossing your teeth was bad, breathing cold air was bad. Eating meat was bad for my kidneys, as was drinking too much water, and milk was unnecessary. Lifting my arms over my head made my heart work too hard; exercise was bad for me.

One day as she drank a beer and smoked a cigarette while reading the newspaper at the kitchen table, she lifted her head to watch me walk by on my way into the bathroom. I was twelve.

"How many goddamned baths are you going to take this week!"

Taking a bath when I had my period was a big no-no. She used to cover her face with a Kleenex if we walked by a certain type of tree on the street, saying that those trees smelled bad because they were the same type of tree that Jesus's cross was made out of. The list of what to avoid or never do was endless. Mom said she had a tapeworm when she was a kid and when it was hungry it would slither up her throat and almost choke her. That terrified me. I saw tiny white worms coming out of my bottom one time and I was scared they too would come up my throat and choke me. I was happy to learn from her that they preferred the other end. "Eat some more sugar!" she'd berate me, insisting that that was how I got the worms in the first place.

If I was sick with a cold or flu, she might place a bowl of vinegar and garlic cloves cut up into small pieces next to my bed while I slept—maybe to keep the vampires away, who knows? My parents believed in vampires and ghosts and aliens, and they were pretty sure that either the mob or the crooked government controlled everyone and everything. My mother said that being a communist was ideal. At least that way, everyone had food available to them. I thought maybe being a communist would be better too. Let's face it: if it had to do with increasing my chances of eating, I was game.

All my mother told me about our family was that they were

from a long line of Bulgarian gypsies on my grandmother's side. My dad used to tell me my fortune sometimes when he was drunk. He'd get me to cross my left palm with a silver coin and tilt his head slightly to the right, away from the puff of his cigarette smoke so he could better see my palm. He would stare at my hand and he would tell me my future. Usually he was too addled to think, and it was stupid, drunken crap. Then he'd just let go of my hand and take a sip of his drink.

One time, however, he seemed really lost in thought.

"Well, what is it? What do you see?" I asked excitedly.

"You are going to be something very important one day, Cathy. And don't worry about your mother. Your mother is your mother. She can't help the way she is and she doesn't mean anything wrong. I'm going to die first and you will both be okay."

WHEN I WAS THREE YEARS OLD, I had a fever so high that my parents took me to the hospital, where the doctors decided they would place me in a tub of ice water to lower the fever. Hearing that, my mother elbowed the doctors aside, lifted me out of the hospital bed, yelling "No goddamn ice!" and she took me home and wrapped me in thick blankets.

Later I was diagnosed first with rheumatic fever and then scarlet fever.

My mother told me that that was why I could never donate blood, because I could pass the disease onto other people through transfusions. Besides, transfusions were bad for people, she said. If everyone ate raw liver the way they did when she was a kid when people got sick, no one would need transfusions. Later when AIDS became an epidemic, she told me that I could get the disease by swimming in an infected swimming pool.

MY MOTHER HAD A PART-TIME JOB at the post office, where she worked sorting mail. She said that she loved that job and that she did it faster and better than any of the other workers on her shifts. She showed me how she did her job by flicking her right wrist as though she were showing me how to deal cards. She moved her hands up and down as she did this to indicate the various stacked boxes that the mail would be sorted into. She often worked nights and didn't come home until the morning.

She was business-minded I guess, because she started making egg rolls from a recipe that my Auntie Nellie gave her, and she'd sell them to people at the post office. Egg rolls were very exotic then. My Auntie Nellie had lived with an Asian family for a while and they taught her how to cook Chinese food. Auntie Nellie could cook anything and it would be fabulous. Sometimes she would fry me up smelts and they were the best thing I had ever tasted. My mother, on the other hand, was not a good cook—she boiled everything possible in a few inches of water. But she followed Auntie Nellie's recipe to a T and the egg rolls were the exception. Well, I *think* the egg rolls were amazing, but I only got to eat one or two during the months that she made them. The problem was, eating something so delicious only made me more hungry.

When my mom was making eggrolls, the aroma drove me crazy. I could hardly stand the smell of the bubbling oil and perfectly squared egg dough frying to a light crispy brown, which meant they were ready to take out of the fryer and placed on a towel to let the oil soak away. She was meticulous in the way she made them and I used to love to watch her. I'd focus intensely on every step of the process, sort of like the way the stray dogs I would bring home used to look at me when I ate something without giving them some fast enough. I did try to beg for more egg rolls, but I was told to be quiet, that I was spoiled and always wanted what I wanted and I ate too fast and, no, I couldn't have another one. I was just like my father, she would tell me, bothering her all the time. The egg rolls were to be sold and not to be enjoyed by people like me who weren't paying for them.

My mother also had a part-time job at Eaton's department store. She told me she was a sales clerk. She always made these jobs sound as though she worked very hard and remained in them for decades. But usually they lasted only a few months.

"When I was ten," she said, "I had to go to work in the tobacco fields to buy my own shoes and clothes," and she was very angry telling me these stories. When I asked why she was mad, she said, "Why the hell do you think? A ten-year-old kid has to go to work to buy their own shoes and clothes!"

When she had that job as a kid, she fell off the machine with blades that was cutting the tobacco. She said that she almost died and when she went home crying to her parents, they didn't even care. In fact, they just sent her to work again the next day, even though she was terrified.

It was a bizarre story and I was always struck by how angry she was telling it. It was as if she was lashing out at everything and everyone—her parents and my father especially—who had cheated her or done her an injustice. Her point in telling me stories about how hard she worked was to remind me of the injustice she endured not only as a kid, but also even now as an adult married to my father.

"I had to go to work to put food on the table because your father is a lousy husband who can't support us!"

"So why not just leave him?" I wondered out loud.

"And where the hell am I supposed to go? Who will support me?"

It was at times like those that I promised myself I would never put up with anyone or anything in my life that wasn't exactly the way I wanted it to be, regardless of the consequences. Nothing could be as bad as the way we were living.

Easier said than done, I would learn.

MY FATHER PAID no attention to me when my mother went to work. He was always too drunk. Usually he would occupy himself tinkering with the TV antenna (the wall above the TV was pockmarked with hundreds of holes from his nailing the bent-wire-hanger antenna). I never remember him wondering if I had eaten dinner or when I went to bed or if I had clothes for the morning or anything at all. Sometimes he would be drunk and do nothing except drink; he would sit at the kitchen table and talk and sing to himself. I hated that, especially when I would come into the kitchen and he would think I was someone else or think he was somewhere else and start yelling at me or whoever he thought I was.

When he did this and got angry, it would terrify me. I would have to scream at the top of my lungs, "DADDY! STOP! PLEASE!" until he would collect himself as best as he could. My mom used to say that he hallucinated. He claimed he saw giant rats and felt as if bugs were crawling all over him. "It's the drinking," she'd say.

Well, I used to see rats running around those apartments too. It made me wonder if I was sick, like my dad.

"You inherit the alcohol disease. It's a sickness. He's a sick bastard."

I never thought about his drinking as a disease. I just thought he didn't give enough of a shit to quit or—more likely—that I didn't mean enough to him to quit. If I were a better daughter, my parents would quit drinking and fighting. That's what I thought for years. That it was all my fault.

A few times my mother came home from work to find the place looking like a disaster. Not that it didn't look like a disaster all the time, but there would be extra dirty glasses and ashtrays from his friends visiting and partying it up with him, and that made the place look worse than just having one dirty ashtray and one dirty glass. Anyway, she came home really pissed off one morning and she woke me yelling and screaming. I thought she was screaming at me, but it was at my dad. She said, "I can't even keep a goddamn job because I can't rely on you to watch that goddamn kid of yours! You are such a bloody drunkard and whoremaster and you can't watch that kid?"

On my seventh birthday we invited over my cousins Diane, Richard, Janice and Michael and my Auntie Nellie and my maternal grandmother. We had hats and balloons and a cake with candles and even food, and a camera to take pictures. (I don't remember the birthdays before that. And the ones after were attended only by my parents' drunk friends; no kids came.) My Auntie Helen sent me a dress that year for my birthday. It was navy blue with a crinoline and it was short and beautiful. My cousins bought me slippers and my grandmother bought me socks and made some amazing cabbage rolls.

It was a happy day because my dad had won big at the track a few days before. Usually he lost and that always cut into the food budget. Booze came first, birthday or not. But mid June 1963, Dad won on number five at Woodbine. So I knew I would be getting a present from my parents. I didn't know what it was until I saw it there on the street right in front of our house: the most beautiful big tricycle I had ever seen. It even had red, white and blue handlebar streamers. Right there I named her Sally. It didn't matter that I had an ice cream cone in my left hand; I was sure I could jump on and steer with one hand while pedalling as fast as I could. I had just blown out the candles on my cake and now the kids were playing inside the house and starting to come outside too. I wanted to ride Sally as soon as I could. The cake could wait to be eaten.

I remember the sun glaring in my eyes, making me squint while I ate the ice cream cone and pedalled along the sidewalk. To avoid the sun I closed my eyes for just a second while taking a lick of my ice cream. At that moment my front wheel hit a crack in the pavement and I fell forward and landed on my chin. My ice cream went flying, I tore my new dress and my chin throbbed with unbearable pain. The party ended with me being taken in a cab with my mom to Sick Children's Hospital's emergency room, where I got twenty stitches. When I got back from the hospital there was a big mess left in the kitchen from the party, and then one hell of a fight started between my parents.

"You always get that kid what she bloody wants. Now you see what happens? You think she needs a goddamn bike? How much did that cost? Like I have nothing better to do than go to the fucking hospital!"

Dad didn't say anything back. I cried myself to sleep listening to my mother smash Sally to pieces. Every birthday after that was pretty much the same: my parents' adult friends showed up and got drunk, and I was left alone at the end of the night while they all headed for the nearest bar.

Birthdays meant shit to me.

CHAPTER THREE

Trust

I WAS FIVE when my Dad brought a buddy home with him to watch television.

Our cheap little black-and-white television never worked properly, mostly because Dad kept trying to use a coat hanger for an antenna. Both he and his friend had been drinking. I could tell he wasn't getting anywhere with the TV set because when he was doing his Johnny Cash imitation he kept swearing, sometimes in Polish, sometimes in English.

My father's friend, keeping his eyes on Dad, started sliding his hand up my pyjama leg and slowly started tilting his body close to me so he could get higher and higher up my leg. At first, I froze. Nothing was spoken between the man and me. My father, not ten feet away, kept his back to us and his attention on the television set and his drink. His friend kept watching my father and exploring my thigh with his fingers, making large circles that progressively got smaller and smaller as he got closer and closer to my private parts. I sat in silence, wondering if my father would catch his friend doing something I thought might be wrong, and what he would say if he did catch him.

I didn't dislike it. I didn't know what to think. My dad brought this man into our house and sat him down on the couch beside me. My father's friend was showing interest in me and he was smiling and being gentle and even tickling me a bit. I figured I must mean something to him. He must like me. He must care about me. I enjoyed the attention and I enjoyed the feeling of being touched.

The experience planted something in me. It planted the awareness that men and boys were attracted to me, and knowing this made me feel good. Dad never knew what his friend did to me that day. But I would tell my mother when I was much older.

A few months after that incident, we moved a few blocks away to a house two doors from the neighbourhood pervert. I was now six. He was just a local slob, about two hundred years old, I thought, who lived alone. I never knew his name, I only knew his smell.

People in the neighbourhood called him a slob because he always wore a dirty T-shirt over his big gut and you could smell him across the street. He would stand in his doorway and crook his finger at children, promising them goodies if they came to visit him. A lot of kids in the area went into his house. I counted seven one day, all of them girls. It was exciting to be there, partly because we knew it was dangerous. We would all be giggling and running around his house. He liked watching us play. Eventually he would say he wanted to "talk to us."

He would call us into the kitchen, say, where there would be a big bowl of gum and candy on the kitchen table. We would all pipe down because playing wasn't the priority once everyone saw that bowl. Then he would select a girl to sit on his lap, and if it wasn't me, I used to get upset. I was the one that wanted to sit on his lap. I wanted the candy.

When it was me, he would play a game with me that was fun. He used to put candy in all his pockets—in his shirt and pants—and then he would tell me to find the candy. I could have whatever I found, he promised. I would go from pocket to pocket and he would laugh and so would I. Eventually one by one the other kids were called home for dinner and would leave, but I never was called home for dinner, so I stayed behind. After the other kids left, he would tell me I was his favourite of all the girls in the neighbourhood. He gave me candy. Lots of candy. As I ate away to my heart's content—and it was a big content—he would sit me on his big fat knee and start to bounce me up and down while I munched away, smiling at having so much candy—and a ride too! He would then undo the zipper on his pants. He would place one hand inside my panties and place one of my hands on his thing and tell me to move my hand up and down. When he was done he would put me down and I knew it was time to leave.

I could smell his body odour and feel his sweat all over me after I left. When I got home, I would stand in front of my parents and wonder if they knew what had happened to me. Couldn't they smell that horrible smell? Couldn't they just look at me and know what happened?

We lived in that house for about a year, and for about a year I visited the smelly old man and his fat thing and ate enough candy to keep me full.

It was a week or so after my seventh birthday party that I spent a hot summer afternoon with a boy named Carl.

Carl and his parents had moved into the neighbourhood and across from us on Cameron Street a few months earlier. This was our second move to Cameron. When I asked my mother why Carl looked different from me, she told me that he was "part native Indian." She said that "Indian men were good lovers." I wasn't sure what that meant at the time, but I knew from the way she said it and the way she smiled that it must have been a good thing. Carl's mother was very fat. She always looked a mess too, just like my mother. But his father was very handsome, I thought. None of them ever talked to me.

My parents had gone to the racetrack and I was left alone and I was mad. I wasn't mad at being left alone as this wasn't unusual, even though I was usually left alone at night, not during the day. I was mad because when my dad took me to the racetrack at night I sometimes got to eat hamburgers. Today, I figured I wouldn't get to eat.

I put on a pair of way-too-short, denim cut-off shorts. They were also so tight that I had to lie down on the bed in order to zip them up. I could hardly breathe, they were that tight. A little of my butt cheeks also popped out and the pocket lining for the two front pockets hung below the edge of the shorts. I put on a T-shirt and running shoes without socks. I never wore socks or underwear or shoes if I could help it, but the pavement outside was hot so I wore shoes that day.

While wandering the street looking for something to do, I eventually walked in front of Carl's house. He was sitting on his porch. He was around seventeen or maybe a bit older, with big brown eyes and longish, straight dark-brown hair. He was wearing jeans without a shirt. I'd thought he was cute from a distance, but now I saw that he was beautiful. His chest was hairless, unlike my dad's, which was very hairy.

I stopped in front of his house and asked him what he was doing. "Nothing," he said. I asked him why he was doing nothing and he ignored me. Kids ask the stupidest questions sometimes and I knew this was one of them.

I stayed where I was, just looking at him, feeling the heat of the sun beating down on me. He got up and walked across the grass to the other side of the fence. He looked down at me and squinted because of the sun and asked me about my Band-Aid. I told him about the party and I lied, saying it was the best birthday ever.

"Where's your bike?" he asked.

"Oh, my mother smashed her."

"Her?" he repeated. I told him about Sally and my mother smashing her. We were quiet for a while. "My parents went to the racetrack and if they win, they're going to buy me another bike."

He got really quiet. "Hey," he said finally, "do you want a glass of milk?" I preferred Coke, but I replied, "Yeah, okay!" So he opened the small white gate and told me to come into the house. I followed him into the kitchen, where it was dark and cool and the lights were out. "Does your mom make you turn the lights out all the time too?" I asked.

"No, it's just that it keeps the house cooler since it's so hot outside." It was a really clean house. I sat down at the kitchen table. He got me a glass of milk and I drank it so quickly he asked me if I was hungry. He offered a bologna sandwich. He was taking such a long time to make it that it was starting to bug me. He would get the bread and then stop and come over and touch my ponytail. Then he would get the package of bologna and come over again and touch my arm, saying that I had really soft skin.

"It's from not washing too much," I said. He looked confused.

"My mom says that washing too much ruins your skin. That's why my skin is soft."

"Oh," he muttered. Then he came over and touched my chin and said something about that being too bad but at least it was in a place that wouldn't show when I went out with boys. "Boys?" I asked. "No, not me." My mind was only on him hurrying up and making that sandwich. He touched me again. I laughed and told him that he was like the witch in the Hansel and Gretel story who kept feeling all over the little boy and girl to see if they were fat enough to eat. Carl laughed at that and said that he wasn't going to eat me and I was silly to even think that, because I should look at the sandwich he just finished making and I should eat it while he made one for himself to eat.

I took one huge bite of my sandwich and before I could swallow it or take another bite, he took my hand and led me away from the table. I looked back at the sandwich wondering what was going on since I really wanted to eat it. Eventually it was out of sight when we turned a corner and walked into a bedroom. I saw a single bed and a four-drawer dresser and a couple of rock band posters on the wall. The bedroom was at the front of the house. There were sheer beige curtains covering the window, but they were pulled open. I stood in the middle of his room while he let go of my hand and closed the curtains. I knew what he was going to do. I didn't run even when he took off his jeans. He had underwear on and he jumped onto the bed smiling. I smiled back and he patted the bed, inviting me to join him. I lay right down on my back beside him. He had one elbow propped up and he was on his left side. I was staring up at the ceiling, staring at the light fixture, not making a move.

Carl started moving his hands all over my body. His hands were cool and soft and I wondered if he also didn't wash too often. I had my shoes on and he left them on. He took off my T-shirt and I saw that his chest looked similar to mine, but larger. He kissed me on the mouth and then he kept kissing my face. This was the first time that I recalled my face and mouth ever being kissed by anyone except my grandmother, who sometimes kissed my cheek when she saw me. My grandmother's breath always smelled really bad, but Carl's breath didn't smell bad at all.

Then, he undid the button on my jean shorts and unzipped the zipper. I could finally breathe and I laughed. Initially he was very gentle trying to remove my shorts, but then he became rougher because the shorts wouldn't come off. They were so tight and he was trying to peel them like a banana. He got up over me, straddling my thighs, and used two hands to jerk my shorts down but they still didn't budge. He tried to get his fingers up the legs of my shorts and then inside the waistband and then in where the zipper was, and then finally he just stopped and stared down at me. After what seemed to be a long time, he told me to get my shirt back on and get out. I asked him why. That was another stupid question and this time he told me it was. "Don't be stupid," he almost whispered. "Get out before I do something that I shouldn't be doing. You're just a kid."

I had to get him to help me zip my shorts back up and after I put my T-shirt on, he lay there on his back with his arm up over his eyes. I said, "Uh, Carl? Do you think I could take that sandwich with me?" He didn't answer. I walked into the kitchen and picked up both halves and had the sandwich eaten before I walked out the front gate.

When I got home, my parents weren't there. I found a pair of scissors and I went into my room and I cut my shorts off. As they dropped to the floor, I thought, 'Carl would have really liked me if not for my stupid shorts.'

When I was seven, we moved into a house that had a family living next door to us comprised of two teenaged boys, two younger sisters, an African American father and a white mother. We hadn't been in that house for a week when the two teenaged boys invited me to their house for dinner. I was all excited because my parents wouldn't be home and I was desperate not only for a meal, but for some conversation too. I thought I would be able to make new friends. When I walked into the house, I immediately noticed that the house was very quiet.

"Where's Sandy and Trina?" I asked.

"They're not home right now."

"Where's your mom and dad?" I then asked.

"Mom's out. Dad's on his way home from work."

I guess they were making idle conversation. I don't know what happened to dinner, but I was dessert. They took me upstairs to the bedroom that they shared. They both took me onto one of the two beds in the room. One of them took off my pants; the other took off my panties. I asked them what they were doing, but I knew. I didn't fight them or try to run or scream. I just lay there letting them both do what they wanted with me. And what they wanted was to put things up inside me. One boy kept getting different things, like a pen, a pencil and a stick attached to a long elastic that was then attached to a stuffed toy dog, and I don't remember what else. One boy kept bringing things over to the bed while the other one inserted whatever it was into me. They would both watch as the one boy put the items into me and then once in a while they would look up at me to see my reaction. It felt uncomfortable and some things hurt. But I didn't say anything. They didn't touch me anywhere else like Carl did.

This went on for about half an hour or so until they heard their father's car pull up in front of the house. They told me to hurry up and get dressed and get downstairs and ran off without me. A few minutes later, I walked down the stairs. The father and the boys were in the kitchen, talking and laughing. I think the boys were trying to distract their father from seeing me walk down the stairs. I knew there was going to be no dinner, so I walked out the door. I went home and stayed the night by myself. We lived in that house for less than a year and I never went into the boys' place again. Every time they saw me after that, they ignored me.

That's what made me feel good: getting attention and feeling wanted regardless of who it was or how long it lasted. Even when it was a friend of my father's doing something I knew was wrong. I was a lost little kid looking for someone—anyone—to love me.

The thing is, if you aren't sure what love really is you can't be sure where you'll find it or what it looks like if you do find it. And so maybe you find yourself looking in a lot of the wrong places. I didn't know I was being abused. All I knew was that someone was being nice to me. And those experiences had a lot to do with my sexual promiscuity later on in life because by the time I was twenty-five, I had slept with a couple of hundred men.

CHAPTER FOUR

Hello, God? It's me.
No, Cathrine ... *Cathrine*

WE WERE CATHOLICS.

Well, my parents were born Catholics, but they never went to church. I do remember my mother taking me to midnight mass on Christmas Eve a couple of times when I was a kid, but that was it. I used to wonder why they couldn't just go to church on Sunday morning like most people in all the neighbourhoods we lived in. I guess the odd Christmas Eve would have to do. It used to annoy me going to those midnight masses anyway, because I could hardly stay awake long enough to hear the sermons, although I really tried to. It was just as annoying being kept up by a loud priest as it was by my loud, drunk parents.

Church represented something to me. It represented truth and hope and comfort and security, all those things that people have looked for in a church for centuries. Sometimes when he was drunk, my dad used to tell me things about God and Jesus.

When my mother tried to make me behave, she would quote the Bible. Her favourite word for me—besides "phony"—was "obstinate."

"Oh, you are so obstinate! Do everything I ask you to do without complaining or arguing, like it says in the Bible." I wondered how the heck she could quote the Bible when I never saw her read it even once. I don't even remember owning a Bible until my First Holy Communion.

My father taught me how to pray: "Kneel down on the floor each night beside your bed and talk to God," he said.

I had lots to say to God, so big surprise that after a while my knees started to hurt. At one point they hurt so bad I used to cry in pain. My mother took me to the doctor, and he said it was growing pains. He told her to give me baby aspirin and she did a couple of times, but that didn't help. When I was seven and I had been left alone while my parents went out to the bar, I was starving. I prayed for some food. I waited. After a while I figured God had other things on his mind and decided to eat whatever I could find. I started eating baby aspirin. There weren't enough to get sick on. Then again, there weren't enough to get filled up on either.

Anyway, when my dad was showing me how to pray, he never really told me what to say. He just told me to talk to God. I had a bit of an idea who He was, but I wasn't told too much. You know, baby Jesus at Christmas and the manger, and there was a book called the Bible and God created people and ... hmm ... okay, I guess I was told very little. But praying was still something I thought I should be doing anyway. Okay, so I sort of had to fake knowing prayers. I also wondered why I couldn't pray in the morning instead since my knees hurt the most at night. Plus, what was it with this family that everything had to be done at night anyway?

So, I prayed every night as a child, sore knees or not, hungry or not, but God just didn't listen to me. My dad told me that everyone would "negotiate" so I tried to negotiate with God. "God, if you make my dad stop drinking, I will become a nun," or "God, if you fill our fridge up with food, I will pay you back when I get older," or "God, if you make my mother like me, I will say one hundred prayers, no matter how sore my knees get." Nothing.

I didn't think that I ever asked for too much or for too many things from my parents, but my mother said that I did, and this caused a lot of confusion for me. I started feeling as though I was bad and then because of certain things my parents did or said to me I started feeling even worse. I wanted to go to the source, God, to find out if I really was bad or not. My mom said that I should fear God, that everyone feared Him. But I would risk being scared if I could be forgiven.

When I was eleven, we moved into a small two-bedroom apartment on a second floor and I again transferred schools. We lived next door to the Regans, an Irish Catholic family with seven kids including Donna, whom I got to know pretty quickly, and she told me that her family all went to church every Sunday. This was a Saturday, so she asked me if I wanted to go to church with her and her family the next morning. I told her that I only prayed at home at night by myself and that yeah, sure, I would like to go with her. Maybe that would make my parents like me. I wanted to be seen as good and part of something good, and I was looking for a deeper connection with, or maybe even validation by, someone who really mattered: God. Someone who might know more than my parents did. I was also excited about this opportunity for other reasons: I was desperately looking for a friend and I was trying to grow a soul.

Our new landlords happened to like booze as much as my parents did, so now I had four drunks keeping me up all night instead of two. They all partied downstairs in the landlord's kitchen, not in ours upstairs, but I could hear them as though they were right next to me. There was no door at the top of the stairs leading to our apartment. You walked up the stairs into a small hallway that led to a kitchen one way, a bathroom in the middle and two bedrooms, one at the side of the house and one at the front.

I went downstairs before I got into bed that night, and announced to everyone that I was going to get up early in the morning and go to church with the Regans next door. Everyone stopped drinking and looked at me.

"Church?" my mother repeated. "They don't want you bothering them and tagging along."

"Mom, they invited me. Please, can I go?" She never really gave me permission, she just kind of lost focus—or interest.

I wish I could say that I hardly slept that Saturday night over the excitement of going to church the next morning, but the real reason I was up all night was because of my parents' drinking and fighting. I hardly slept. At daybreak I got myself up and dressed in the best dress that I owned—from the second-hand store—and then left the dead quiet house where everyone was still passed out. This was going to be a Sober Sunday anyway, I could tell, so it was best that I found something to do by myself and church would be perfect. I could kill half a day at least if I went back to the Regans' place afterwards too.

I went next door at seven, an hour early.

Donna and everyone else were still in their pyjamas, all having breakfast around the table. I stood in their kitchen doorway, watching them all eat and laugh and play and I wished that I was part of their family instead of mine.

After everyone got up from the table and into their Sunday best, we all left the house together, including Mr. and Mrs. Regan. I was surprised that they were coming with us kids. Even the youngest kid, Kelly, came. We started our walk up the street to St. Helen's Parish with Donna and me trailing behind, and we were laughing and talking until we got to my house and I suddenly grew quiet. Donna kept talking to me and walking, not realizing that I was no longer listening to her or beside her. I had stopped walking and now stood in front of my house, looking at the front door from the sidewalk, and my mind started to wander the way it always did. I imagined my mother standing on the porch, all dressed up wearing a nice hat and white gloves just like Mrs. Regan was wearing, coming toward me with open arms, hugging me and saying that she'd decided to come with us— and how silly it was that another family was taking her daughter to church without her. I wanted that to happen, but it didn't.

"Hey, Cathy!" shouted Donna, "are you coming or not?" I ran to catch up with her, turning my head a couple of times just to be sure that my mom really wasn't coming with us.

Around this time my parents were operating a bookmaking and bootlegging business. My parents told people that they had a "store" at home. What kind of store?

A "none of your goddamned business" store. They were selling booze and taking bets on horses. Both my parents loved to gamble.

One Saturday night my dad had a few men over and they were all playing craps in the kitchen, tossing the dice against a wall, where they would land on the floor. They were drinking and having a good time and I don't know where my mother was.

I couldn't go to sleep so my dad told me that he would teach me how to play craps with everyone. Over the course of the next few hours, I learned what snake eyes was and about blowing on the dice for good luck and what loaded dice were and cocked dice and what a dime bet was versus a nickel bet, and all sorts of things that I wouldn't be able to teach or show Donna. I even collected all the bets for every game and handed the winnings over to whoever won, less my dad's share, and he'd tell me exactly how much that would be. It was a fun night, especially when Arlene, the landlady, came upstairs and brought us all sandwiches. I rarely had sandwiches. But every day I would go to the local store wherever we lived and I would eat a bag or two of chips and drink a couple of Cokes.

Sometimes my parents let me stay up all night and gamble with strangers along with them, and sometimes I had to go to bed. That alone was a crapshoot—whether I got to stay up and play or not. Most times though, I just went off into my room by myself and listened to everything happening in the kitchen as I lay in bed, unable to fall asleep until the parties ended. Other times, the whole night would be quiet when they went out to the bars and I would be able to fall asleep. But then they would come home and that's when the fighting and screaming would begin and I would be woken up.

Usually between the two of them the fighting would end in a draw. But sometimes my dad would turn crazy wild when he was drunk. Or else there were times when I guess she had just had enough. But she would take me into the bathroom with her and lock the door. I would sleep in the tub with a blanket and my mom would sit on the toilet and smoke cigarettes, waiting for my dad to pass out. Then, when it was quiet, she would wake me up and tell me to go to bed.

For years after, whenever I went into a bathroom that didn't have me facing the door when sitting properly on the toilet, I would sit so that I always faced the door, and that usually meant that I sat on the toilet sideways. I was so terrified that at any second some drunk would start pounding on the door trying to get in that I made sure I was at least ready to react. Even in the bathroom there was no peace for me. I realize now that I was a pretty stressed-out kid.

I LOVED THE SMELL inside a church.

It was so pure and clean, as though the air inside was better somehow than the air outside. And the little bowl filled with holy water that I blessed myself with? I was so thirsty one day after running to church on a hot July morning, late yet again, that I first blessed myself, then realizing how cool the water was, I cupped my hand and drank it as well. I thought that maybe in addition to having a drink, I would get a good soul-cleaning at the same time.

In church, I would be warm and safe. I was fine with God sort of ignoring me when I prayed to Him. But when I visited Him in person, He couldn't. I used to stand in front of the huge statue of Jesus hanging on the cross at the front of the church and stare into the blank ceramic eyes. I could swear sometimes that the statue looked right back at me or that its eyes would move to the side, ever so slightly. That made me think that God did hear me and know me. And now that I was right there in front of Him, maybe He would know that I was serious about wanting to talk to Him. One time after standing there staring for what seemed like forever, I got the idea that He was saying, "What the hell do you keep looking at? There's nothing to see here, now move along!" just like my mother said to me when I used to stare at her sometimes.

What was really important about church was that it was one house that I never got kicked out of. I remember churches staying open really late or all of the time, like later on in life when I needed a place to sleep or escape to. Only I wouldn't stare the big statue of Jesus right in the eyes. I would sit at the very back of the church or lie down in a pew, staring at the ceiling like a cast-out angel, still trying to figure out how to get back into God's good books and, more importantly, wondering why I wasn't in them in the first place.

Before the Regan clan left for church, Mrs. Regan used to put money into a small white envelope that she then dropped into a basket that everyone passed around during the service. People used to give me a dirty look when the basket was passed around and I figured it was because I didn't put money into the basket.

The Regans had lots of fun together. They also had more food in their pantry than I had ever seen in my whole life. I figured

Mr. Regan must have made a lot of money in his job as a sales manager. Mr. and Mrs. Regan never fought or argued or drank either, not that I ever saw. The kids would cartwheel or somersault down the hall, holding a peanut butter and jam sandwich in one hand, laughing all the way, or they'd ask me to hold it for them for a second and then I would laugh and take a bite while they chased me around the house, trying to get their sandwich back.

My mother always rolled her eyes when I said anything nice about the Regans. I shouldn't believe everything I saw, she said. I didn't quite understand what she meant. She told me that Mr. Regan was as bad as any other man, a guy who slept with other women and tried to look like some kind of hero, going to church with his family every Sunday. I was shocked. My mom told me that every man fooled around and couldn't be trusted.

When I told her Mr. Regan wouldn't be going to church with us one upcoming Sunday because he'd be away on a business trip, my mother said, "Like shit he's going on business trips. He's screwing around!"

Maybe she was right. Then again, maybe she was jealous. After all, she and my father had been up all the previous night fighting about his screwing around with Arlene, our landlady.

I thought those Regan kids had everything. I used to tell people that Donna was my sister. She had a deep red birthmark all up one arm and people used to stare at it. I never did. I asked her once what happened and when she told me that she was born that way, I never mentioned it again. My mother told me that her mother must have been beaten by Donna's father when she was pregnant because that's how babies got birthmarks: the redder the mark, the worse the beating. I checked myself over thoroughly after that, because my mother said that my dad beat her up when she was pregnant with me. I found only a faint brown mark on my right shoulder and figured I must have blocked his blows pretty good.

It was a great year living next door to the Regans, but of course it had to end. My mom and Arlene started arguing and then we moved again.

AT MY NEW SCHOOL, my teacher told our class that it was time to take First Communion. I was as excited as though it were Christmas. Not that Christmas was ever that great for me personally, but I had seen others girls at church making their First Communion and I loved the dresses that they wore. They all looked beautiful and happy and white and clean. They walked down the aisle with everybody's eyes on them, and when they took their First Communion they were on their way to becoming adults. They received presents too, our teacher said, and had people over for dinner and a celebration. Usually the presents were little white Bibles, which I wanted so badly, or a silver or gold cross that, if I got, I would put around my neck and never take off. But I would have settled for just a little party. And maybe, just maybe, I'd get a dress with beautiful buttons for the first time in my life!

I dreamt about it for weeks. Just once in my life I wanted things to be perfect. I wanted a fancy white dress with crinolines. I reviewed all of my drawings of the dresses that my parents could never afford to buy me and I tried to pick out which type of buttons might come on my dress. I decided that I wanted mother of pearl buttons because they would go best with bright white. I wanted white leotards and especially black patent leather shoes, the kind with the strap over your instep. And I wanted curly hair. I hated my fine, straight black hair. I wanted curly thick hair like Renee, the prettiest girl in my class and maybe in the whole school. Renee's blond hair was always perfectly curled. She looked gorgeous every day I saw her. I wanted to look pretty for just one day, the day of my First Communion.

My mother agreed to buy me a white dress and I was ecstatic. I expected it would come from one of those stores where I went to steal all the beautiful buttons, but this time I would be with my mother and we would walk out with a dress.

Then she changed her mind. Two days before my communion, I started panicking because I still didn't have a dress. I had been to all the stores and seen so many dresses that I wanted but my mother never came with me to see any of them. She'd always say she was too busy. Instead, my mother said she would sew me one and that I'd still have the dress I wanted. That's all she had to say for me to get sad and a bit depressed. I never saw her sew anything except unattractive dresses for herself. I didn't even want to take my communion any more. I wasn't excited and I started getting scared. What would I look like? This was not going the way I thought it would. Why couldn't she just buy me one dress?

My mother said that she'd got some material from Auntie Sophie and it would be perfect to use for my dress. She went into her bedroom and came back with a brown paper bag. She took the material out of the bag and held it up for me to see. Stained and discoloured, it reeked of cigarette smoke. I touched the fabric; it was rough and scratchy like wool. I was heartbroken. I wanted to cry, but that would have only made my mom angrier.

There was also no hope of wearing crinolines or white leotards or patent leather shoes with little straps across the instep. When I protested, when I asked to have something special just this once that would make me feel proud and pretty on one day of my life, my mother started getting mad at me, saying, "You're a spoiled brat! I'll make you a dress and it will have to be good enough!" I knew better than to speak when my mother didn't want me to. I couldn't win the argument about a yellowish, stained dress. My veil was not what I expected either. I'm not sure where the fabric came from, but I do remember that it was bright white, which made the yellowish dress appear even yellower. I felt like a clown and I hated clowns. They scared me and now I would scare the whole church.

If I couldn't have the dress I dreamt of, maybe I could at least have curly hair like Renee. Unless, of course, she was born with it. "How do you get your hair so nice and curly all the time?" I asked her in school one day.

She looked at me with a perfect smile and said, "With curlers, stupid," then turned and walked away.

I knew what my mother would say if I asked for curlers so I figured I would work on my father. I waited for him to get home from work, brown paper bag in hand. He walked straight to the kitchen for a glass. I followed him, just watching. He carried the glass to the fridge, where he got a bottle of 7Up and sat down at the kitchen table and poured himself a drink.

He lit a cigarette and then looked at me. "So, what do you want?"

It wasn't really a question because he just sat there smoking and drinking like I wasn't there. I fussed around looking through cupboards as if I was looking for something and waited for the warm glow to kick in. Then I sat down across from him at the kitchen table. "Daddy," I said sweetly, "can I have some curlers?"

"Oh, my million dollars," he grinned, "you can have anything you want."

Just then my mother walked in; her hair still was in curlers after several days. She pulled a cigarette from a package in her dress pocket and lit it. "What the hell's she want now?" she growled as though I weren't even there.

I ran from the room to find some pages I had pulled from a magazine at the corner newsstand. I showed them pictures of girls and young women in bridesmaid, wedding and communion dresses, their faces polished, their smiles wide, their hair shiny and curly. "Can I have curly hair like them?" I asked. "Can you please get me some curlers?"

My mother said, "We have curlers."

"But you're always wearing them," I replied. "Anyway, I need new ones. Special ones."

She hissed, "Spoiled little brat!" and walked out of the room.

Dad watched her leave and then said, "Go get me a couple of brown paper bags and a pair of scissors." I knew that we had lots of brown paper bags because my dad came home with one every night.

Between long drinks of whisky, he cut the paper bags into strips. Each strip was different from the one before. He was getting drunk. I wanted him to finish before he became so drunk he'd start fighting with my mother or just pass out there at the kitchen table, which would mark the end of my dream of curly hair.

With the brown paper strips piled in front of him, he told me to get my hair wet. I dunked my head in the bathroom sink, which I'd filled with warm water. I gave my hair a quick dry with a towel and then ran back into the kitchen.

I sat at the table for hours, inhaling my dad's whisky breath while he tried to make his drunken fingers work, rolling strands of my hair around the paper strips and tying them in place. A few strips would tear here and there and this was a real test of my patience. Between that and his taking breaks for regular cigarette puffs and doing a poor impression of Johnny Cash every once in a while, it was after midnight when he finished. He finally sent me off to bed after dinner, which was a can of pork and beans, and told me to undo the twists in the morning. The knots in my hair hurt and my wet hair felt cold all night long. I didn't care. In the morning I would look like Renee.

The next morning when I woke up I reached to touch my hair, which was finally dry, and started pulling the paper bag twists away. When they were all out, I felt my hair with my hands. Curls! I had curls! I ran to the kitchen to show my parents, who had already been up for hours, smoking up a storm.

My dad was stirring his hot tea and I made sure not to get too close to him because he had a habit of whacking the hot spoon on the top of my hand. I put my hands behind my back and walked up to him.

Both of them stopped talking and looked at me. They smiled and then they began to laugh. My dad started choking and turning all red from laughing so hard. When he stopped coughing, he lit a cigarette and stood up and walked toward me. In between trying to talk and laughing, he actually reached a hand out to steady himself against the table. My mother was howling away by the stove, cigarette dangling from her lips.

I hardly ever saw them laugh together. I realized they weren't laughing with joy. They were laughing at me. I asked them what was so funny.

When he got close my father said, "Jesus Christ, you look like a bloody Sambo!" and he exhaled a big puff of smoke right in my face.

I coughed and was more annoyed at the smoke than the comment. I didn't know what he meant. "A what?" I said squinting and fanning my face with my hands, which were no longer behind my back. "I look like a what?"

"Like an African," my mother said. "A nigger. You have an afro!"

I ran to the bathroom and looked in the mirror to see what they were talking about. No, I didn't have curls like Renee. I had a frizzy bird's nest on my head. I grabbed the scissors from the shelf and began to cry while chopping at my hair, cutting it to get rid of all the frizz, feeling like I would never, ever achieve anything I dreamt about. I cried more loudly with every piece of hair that fell into the sink while my father shouted from the kitchen, "Keep crying like that and I'll really give you something to cry about!"

I took my First Communion in a homemade, knee-length cigarette-smoke-stained dress wearing thick beige tights and ugly brown winter boots over ugly shoes, with hair that was short and cut lopsided and partly straight and partly wavy and a brilliant white veil that was better suited to a bride, not a kid. They took a picture of all the kids at their First Communion that day. I'm standing among the others girls with their short, beautiful white dresses with crinolines and patent leather shoes and white ankle socks with little pink bows on the sides. The boys are wearing white shirts and ties with their hair all slicked back. I'm actually smiling. Or grimacing. I don't know. Either I was just trying to make the best of what I had been handed or I was being that phony girl again.

I didn't get a white Bible either. My Auntie May—not really my aunt—gave me a black rosary she said was a present from her daughter, who was a nun. *Had been* a nun.

"Auntie May's daughter got pregnant," my mother explained. "Nuns aren't supposed to get pregnant."

I understood from my mother's look the daughter had done something really bad, but she was still nice enough to give me a rosary so she couldn't have been that bad. Later, I learned that she left the convent. My Auntie Helen sent me a rosary—blue—that had been blessed by the Pope. I guess people thought that I really needed to pray a lot.

I LIKED THE WAY the communion wafer used to stick to the roof of my mouth. It was weird, though, thinking that this thing stuck to the roof of my mouth was the body of Jesus Christ. We had been taught that we weren't supposed to handle the wafer ourselves so I always tried hard not to get it off by using my fingers and used the tip of my tongue instead to wedge it off but that didn't always work. Usually I had to stick my fingers into my mouth. I never saw anyone else in church have the same problem, and I thought maybe my mouth really was as big as everyone said it was because I had to dig pretty high up there.

One Sunday morning an extremely skinny old lady wearing a high hat with circles of small plastic flowers caught me with my finger up high in my mouth trying to free the wafer. She was sitting a few people away to my left in the same pew. Our eyes met and she immediately got this look of outrage on her face. In a loud whisper over the three people sitting between us, she said, "Young lady, get your fingers out of your mouth! Have you no manners?" I winced at the smell her stale old lady's breath.

"No," I said and pointed at her hat, "just like you have no taste!"

CHAPTER FIVE

Death and pets

I LOVE ANIMALS. From the time I was about seven, I started finding stray dogs in every neighbourhood we lived in. I loved dogs especially. I like animals because I can trust them more than people. I like them so much that the only ambition I had as a child, besides getting away from my crazy parents, was to become a veterinarian. I would dream about being surrounded by animals that no one loved or wanted because I felt exactly like them.

Animals needed me. People didn't. People could do anything they wanted to me and I wouldn't feel anything most of the time, even when they did bad things to me. If you did something bad to an animal, it might bite you. I was too afraid to bite. So instead I went somewhere else in my mind.

When you were a child, did you have something, one thing that you absolutely loved? Something that made everything all right, no matter how bad it really was? Something that in your mind became magical when you had it with you or wore it, or maybe made you invisible or gave you super powers? And of course nobody could understand why the hell you had to take that stupid blankie everywhere you went, or why you insisted on wearing those ratty shoes.

I felt that way about dogs. Wherever we were living at the time, I would find stray dogs and bring them home. I would be playing by myself and if I saw a dog going through someone's garbage or sleeping in a cardboard box, like magic I would find a piece of rope that I could use for a leash and collar and walk the dog home with me.

You really didn't have to do much to get a dog to love you and want to be with you, and I never did anything to them they didn't like. On the other hand, I got fleabites and ringworm from them, but I didn't care. Once I was bitten by a stray dog and when I ran into the house, displaying my bleeding fingers, my mother told me I could get rabies that way. She said if I got rabies, I would become crazy and foam at the mouth and bite people just like a dog, although I didn't think that biting people would be such a bad thing to do. But then when my parents went out and left me alone, I heard sirens in the middle of the night that sounded like they were heading my way. I was convinced that the ambulance was coming for me because I had rabies. When the sirens faded, I figured it was because I was going to die and no one could help. I was terrified.

I began to fear dying when my grandfather died. I was around five years old. We went to his funeral; I don't remember anyone else being in the funeral home except me and my mother. Taking me by the hand, she pulled me to the casket but I couldn't see, so she picked me up. She put me too close to my grandfather's face and I panicked.

"What happened to grandpa?" I wailed.

"He was a dirty rotten drunkard bastard and he died!" my mother replied.

"Why did he die?" I sobbed.

"Because everyone dies. When God wants you, he takes you. You're going to die one day too."

I calmed down after a while. "When God wants me, I'm going to hide under my bed so He can't find me."

My mother frowned. "Don't be stupid."

That was one of the first times I really felt the terror of dying but also the terror of not having any control over my life. That feeling haunted me. It still does.

I DIDN'T KNOW WHY my mother didn't like me, but I kept trying to figure it out so I could try to be more like someone she would love.

"Oh, your cousin Diane is PER-FECT! Auntie Sophie is so

lucky to have a daughter like her. Oh, she is WON-DER-FUL! And Auntie Sophie treats Diane so badly, that's awful! I wish I had a daughter like Sophie. She is one in a million!"

My mother would say this while we were in the same room, but it would be as though I weren't there. She wouldn't look at me. She would just say it into the air as though magically I would turn into Diane.

But then Diane used to get the shit knocked out of her and maybe that had something to do with it. Still, I was so jealous of Diane at the time.

WHEN I WAS SIX YEARS OLD, I met a kid in the neighbourhood named Janet. She was a few years older than me and my mother usually left me with her when my parents and hers went out drinking. My mother said that Janet was a spoiled brat, just like me. One day I walked out of the house and saw the neighbourhood kids playing on the other side of the street. It was a narrow one-way street with cars parked on both sides. Janet was playing with her new puppy.

I was still scratching the bedbug bites that I got from sleeping at Janet's place the previous night. Every wall in Janet's bedroom was full of little red splotches that were squished bed bugs full of blood. Her house was even dirtier than mine. I used to sleep at Janet's house all the time while we lived in the neighbourhood. She and I used to stay alone; although she had an older brother and sister, they were rarely home, and when they were home, they didn't talk to us. Janet and I used to watch the bedbugs run all over the room and she showed me how she squished them with her thumbnail. Those bedbugs were pretty smart, we figured, those that didn't end up getting squished, that is. Mind you, there were so many of them, we could never squish them all, even if we tried. Janet said they could hide in books and wallpaper and come out to bite you when you were sleeping.

Anyway, Janet's puppy was the smallest, cutest puppy I'd ever seen. Janet was throwing a ball and the puppy would run and get it and bring it back to her.

I stopped scratching my leg. I could see a car coming up the street, and I could see where the puppy was on the other side of the street from me. I called, "Here, doggy doggy." The puppy looked at me, wagging its tail. Then it started running toward me. I stood there, stone cold and frozen, and kept calling the puppy. I couldn't feel the bedbug bites anymore. I didn't feel anything. But I saw the car out of the corner of my eye, and the puppy kept running and the car kept coming.

I heard the horrible thump. Suddenly, Janet was screaming and kneeling beside the puppy. I knew what I had done. I started to feel the terror inside. Janet was screaming so loud that my father ran out of the house to see what the commotion was. Janet told him what I had done. I froze.

My father turned to me. He was drunk. Red in the face and full of rage.

"You stupid son of a bitch!" he roared. "What the hell did you do? What did you do? You evil goddamn son of a bitch. You brat. You little WHORE!" He punched me in the face, hard, with his clenched fist. I fell over from the blow, and he lifted me up by my sweater and tossed me around as if I were a rag doll, still punching me. Hard. My nose was bleeding and the blood was spewing all over me and my father and the sidewalk, and I focused on the bright red of my blood so that I wouldn't feel the pain of the blows.

He hit me over and over and I just didn't feel a thing.

I didn't remember anything for a very long time after that.

I DON'T KNOW WHY I DID IT. I loved animals. I liked Janet. Her parents were a lot like mine. I suppose I was jealous of her. I have always been protective of helpless things. But that hasn't stopped me at times from lashing out at what I love most. That incident haunted me; it still does.

Anyway, a few weeks later I remember finding a stray in the neighbourhood nosing around some garbage cans. She spotted me and ran. It seemed as if I chased after her for a week. When I ran to the right she would run to the left. When she ran onto a main street

I followed her, car horns honking and people yelling out of their car doors, "You're going to get yourself killed!"

Eventually I couldn't run anymore. I was breathless and on the verge of tears. All I could think about was the dog getting hit by a car. I couldn't let that happen. Not again. I started crying. She turned around, ran back to me and stood there looking up at me. I had a rope dangling in my hand and I cried out to her, "If you don't stop running and let me put this rope on you now, you're going to die. Do you want to die? Do you? Please, please, come to me ... Peanut, please come."

I don't know where the name Peanut came from. It just seemed to fit. She took a few steps toward me as if to ask, "Do I know you?" I stopped crying, reached out to put the rope around her neck, tied it and walked her over to the sidewalk. I sat down right there and picked Peanut up and hugged and kissed her. When her tail started wagging it was the happiest day of my life!

We walked home. I really wanted to keep her. But I started to feel really guilty. I knocked on Janet's door and her dad, Dawsie, answered. I asked to speak to Janet and he gave a loud yell over his shoulder.

I heard Janet yell back, "WHAT DO YOU WANT? LEAVE ME!" She was always yelling for people to "leave her" and I don't know why.

Dawsie walked away from the door, leaving it open, and I saw Janet at the top of the staircase. She stopped walking down the stairs when she saw me and gave me a dirty look. Then she looked down at Peanut, who was scratching her ear. Janet started running down the stairs and went right to Peanut. Handing Janet the rope leash, I told her that Peanut was for her. She said, "Really?" and ran into the living room with Peanut, calling to her dad to come see what she had. Janet and I never discussed her puppy. Peanut stayed around for a few months and then disappeared. Janet and I never talked about Peanut either.

WHEN I WAS EIGHT, I found a big dog eating out of a Dumpster. I knew he was a nice dog because when I started to pet him while he was eating, he didn't growl or bite me. He just wagged his tail. He was fine with me touching him. I named him Rexie.

I used to stay away from Dumpsters because my father told me rats lived in them, and they would run up your skirt or pant leg or go for your neck, so you had to be careful when you were near a Dumpster. I never saw a rat in a Dumpster, but I saw them at home all the time and they never jumped at me. If I'd known stray dogs hung out in Dumpsters, I would have been in them more often.

Anyway, I brought Rexie home. I loved all the dogs I brought home, but Rexie was special. My parents didn't pay any attention to the other dogs, but for some reason my mother paid attention to Rexie.

As soon as Rexie and I came through the door my mother said, "Where'd you find that mutt? You can't keep him here. Who the hell is going to feed him? We don't have enough food for ourselves!"

I told her that he wasn't a mutt, and his name was Rexie. I didn't know what a mutt was, but it didn't sound like a good thing.

"Whatever his name is," she said, "we can't afford a dog."

I explained that Rexie ate from a Dumpster. "He finds all kinds of things in it," I said. "You don't have to feed him anything."

This was enough to persuade my mother that Rexie wouldn't be a problem, meaning he wasn't another mouth to feed. So every day Rexie and I would visit the local Dumpsters, and he would eat. When the pickings were slim, I would find Rexie something to eat, and he ate whatever I gave him. He wasn't fussy, like my father said I was. True, I got fussy about eating pigeons and brains and pigs' feet and mouldy bread and rotten grapes. Better things were found in the Dumpsters and with fewer problems, and Rexie ate better than I did. And, yes, sometimes I ate right along with Rexie. Do you know that stores sometimes throw out fruit that is in better shape than what they sell in the store? And do you also know that bakeries throw out warm bread ends?

One day I came home from school and couldn't find Rexie. I ran from room to room calling his name louder and louder, and finally asked my mother if she knew where he was. "How the hell should I know?" she snapped.

I started to cry and ran to my father, asking if he had seen Rexie. He had been home long enough to have a drink. In fact, long enough to become drunk, and when I asked if he had seen my dog he said, "I don't know. Who's Rexie?" He started singing a song he made up. "Oh, Rexie, oh Rexie, did you pack up and run away to Mex-i ... "

I walked and ran and walked some more for hours through the neighbourhood, searching every yard, knocking on every door, and asking everyone I met if they had seen Rexie. No one had seen Rexie. It was as if he never existed.

I walked back to the house. It was fall and the house was cold. I cried about him for weeks.

CHAPTER SIX

Mommy's perfect angel

ONE YEAR MY MOTHER mentioned that she thought she had gotten my birthday wrong, that it might not be the fourteenth I was born on but rather the fifteenth.

"What?" I cried. "You don't know what day I was born?"

"Oh, for God's sake! What does it matter? You're here, aren't you?"

Birthdays were like that. Holidays? They were even worse.

For me, Christmas was over well before December 25 every year. It had to do with the present that Auntie Helen, who lived in New York, would send me: from the time I was five until I was ten, it was always a beautiful dress, and when I was seven she also sent me the only doll I ever owned, a Barbie. I didn't really play with dolls, but I loved my Barbie. In fact, I don't remember having many toys around at all. Lttle girls are supposed to love playing house with their dolls. I used to play with empty food cans. Auntie Helen's Christmas present would arrive in a gorgeously wrapped box with a huge bow and a little card saying that it was from "Auntie Helen, Uncle Frank and Frankie XO."

When I was thirteen, Uncle Frank told me that girls like me who wore miniskirts deserved to get raped. He said that it wasn't a man's fault that they got tempted by women, that it was our fault for not covering ourselves up. What did we expect? he asked.

My Auntie Helen used to listen to that crap and neither she nor my mom ever contradicted him. When I once asked my mom why

Uncle Frank was so fucked up, she first said, "Stop swearing!" then added, "Helen's married to a fucking asshole just like everyone else in my family is. If she needs a dollar, he'll lend it to her and then put a note about it on the front of the fridge until she pays that dollar back! What a goddamn jerk he is!"

Uncle Frank was always screaming, "HEL-LEN! Come here!" the way someone would call a dog they hated. But she acted as though she was the happiest person alive, saying that he was Italian and Italians always screamed when they could talk instead. When she died, in her seventies, I called her doctor in the United States. He said that my auntie sort of lost her mind and it was in part due to the horrible abuse she'd endured from her husband. I told my mother this and she said, "She had Alzheimer's, for God's sake!"

"No, Mom, I spoke to the doctor myself. Plus, you always said that Uncle Frank was an asshole, remember?"

"I'm telling you she had Alzheimer's!" she insisted. "Now stop with that bloody stupid shit!" As I said, *denial* ...

Anyway, Auntie Helen's gift would arrive about two weeks before Christmas. Whenever my dad had some money in December, he'd buy a tree. Sometimes it would be way too early in the month and sometimes it would be about three days before Christmas, but anyway the gift would go under the tree. Also at Christmas time, a ham, some nuts and a few other food items would also appear, and this would be the most food I would see all year in one sitting—and it wouldn't be rotten or mouldy food either. My dad would eat non-stop. As he ate, my mom would say to me, "He'd eat shit on a stick if he had to. He's gotta eat every goddamn thing like a pig!" I would think, Well, he's eating like crazy because this meal is as far away as possible from even being close to shit on a stick; she must be thinking about the pigeons that he caught on top of the roof, or pigs' feet or beef tongue or that type of shit on a stick.

The tree would be decorated with strung popcorn, coloured lights, tinsel, ornaments and candy canes that would get eaten by me and my dad five minutes after we finished decorating the tree. The quality of the decorating would be directly related to how drunk he was at the time. The tree only ever got decorated on the visible parts, like the front and partway around the sides, never the back or the whole tree. My mom said it was a way to save on the decorations. Plus, she said, you can't see the back of a tree when it's up close to a wall. But that bothered me because I could see from the side that the tree wasn't fully decorated and I thought that was just dumb and I told my parents. Mom said, "If a tree falls in the forest when no one is around, does it make a sound?" I used to think this meant that I should expect the tree to come crashing down at any time, and I was sure that it would because of all the decorations being on the front of the tree and weighing it down.

Sometimes I thought that grown ups said and did stupid things all the time yet they were still so sure of themselves being right and that annoyed me. I knew some other poor kids in the neighbourhood who were smart yet they were full of doubt like me, and I wondered if I would get stupid when I got older too. Anyway, when I tried to insist on decorating the whole tree, my mom said, "Nothing is ever good enough for you! Who gives a damn about the back of the tree. Just be quiet!"

So I would concentrate on the smell of the tree instead of the way it looked. I loved the smell of the fresh pine. Every day I crawled under the tree, taking my time and breathing in really deeply, and then giving it a daily drink of water like my dad said I should, because this was something that I could be in charge of and do right. That one present from my Auntie Helen would sit under the tree and I would sit on the floor and stare at the present for hours. I couldn't stand it! It wouldn't be long until I caved and gave in to the temptation of that gift beckoning me to tear into it. I would never, ever as a kid have anything to open on Christmas Day. Well, except for the presents from my mom, which were cans of peas and corn and other canned goods wrapped in Christmas paper. It didn't take me too many years before I could pick up these "gifts" and quickly ascertain exactly what was in them. Yet I would always open them and act as though I was happy to receive the cans. I guess I didn't want to seem even more spoiled or ungrateful; besides, those cans would get eaten even if they weren't very creative as gifts. No one cared that I opened Auntie Helen's gift early. So every Christmas morning, I would wake up in a freezing-cold house, go to wherever the half-decorated tree was, look at it and feel disappointed that I'd done what I always said I would not do the following year. It was a very lonely feeling, just me and the tree, and I would sit down on the floor to open the few wrapped "gift" cans. I would then take them into the kitchen, put them in the cupboard, thank my parents when I saw them and wonder what type of dress my Auntie Helen would be sending me next Christmas.

My mother always bitched at me for being impatient. She said that's why I got crap for Christmas, because Santa knew what a lousy kid I was and always instructed Rudolph to fly over our house. It was a pretty depressing lesson every year. Was I really that awful?

I guess my Aunt Olga felt sorry for me. One Christmas she crouched down in front of me and looked me straight in the eyes: "Don't worry, Sassy"—I told people my name was Sassy when I was a kid because I couldn't pronounce Cathy—"there's really no Santa Claus anyway. It's all a lie."

ONE DECEMBER my father took me to see the decorated windows at Eaton's. The following year the whole family rode the streetcar together to go see the display; I was seven and so excited. But instead we went to a pawnshop, where my parents hawked my mother's engagement ring for money for food. On the streetcar an old man in dirty clothes with dirty hands was playing a song on his harmonica for everyone. I was the only one who clapped. The man got up from his seat and, smiling, gave me a formal bow. I kept clapping and laughing.

"Oh, so do you know what song that was?" my mother asked. There was an edge to her voice. The man and everyone else in the crowded streetcar looked at me and waited. My smile disappeared.

"No."

"How can you not know that song?" she shouted at me. "Everyone knows that song! It's 'I Saw Mommy Kissing Santa Claus,' for God's sake!"

On the infrequent occasions when my parents did pay attention to me, I would have preferred that they hadn't. Like Halloween when I was seven years old.

That year my father said he was going to make me a costume. He sewed as well or better than my mother did, and she made all her clothes. He didn't ask what I wanted him to make for me. He just called me into the kitchen a few days before Halloween and showed me a pink bunny costume that looked as if it came from a real store and was expensive. I stared at that costume laid out on the kitchen floor, and then I got down on my knees and touched it. It was the most beautiful costume I had ever seen. I wouldn't be able to wear this to school after Halloween, which is what I had done with the Halloween clothes from last year, purchased at the secondhand store. I didn't care. I would have the best costume around. I imagined myself going from house to house loading up my pillowcase with candies and chocolate. I hoped I wouldn't get any apples. I hated it when someone gave me an apple.

My father told me to try the costume on, so I picked up the one-piece body and the one-piece head with long, fabulous ears, and handed both pieces to him. He was sitting at the kitchen table sober. That was a bad sign. It was Sunday and a Sober Sunday to boot.

A cigarette dangled out of the corner of his mouth and he didn't look happy. He smoked non-stop to the tune of about two packs of Player's Plain cigarettes a day. Then mom added about another pack or more to the perpetual cloud that hovered in our kitchen. I hated waking up to the smell of cigarette smoke every morning. You would think, from the way I coughed, that I was the one smoking.

Dad watched me slip into the body portion of the bunny costume and I turned around for him to zip me up. I was laughing. This was going to be so much fun!

He put the headpiece over my head and tried to zip it up at the back, but it was too tight, and when he finally got the zipper closed I couldn't breathe. I panicked and started pulling at the bunny head, trying to get it off, screaming and jumping around and flapping my arms and legs, feeling as though I was trapped in a coffin like Grandpa at his funeral. My mom had told me that everyone dies and I was going to die one day too, and I thought this must be my day—if not from rabies, then surely by suffocation. My mother said she wished my dad would suffocate while coughing, and now I knew what that would feel like.

Suddenly I felt myself being lifted off the ground by the bunny ears, and my head started hurting from being punched and slapped. It was my father, punching and slapping me, hitting me harder to compensate for the thickness of the material I guess. I was trying to get the bunny head off, and he was beating me up. When I finally ripped the bunny head away he continued to beat me, angry at me because the bunny suit didn't fit or because I wasn't giving up and just letting it suffocate me, or maybe simply because I was his kid. I don't know.

I wasn't a bunny for Halloween. I needed something darker than my cuts and bruises to be part of my costume so I covered them with black powder from a cork I held over the gas burner and I went as a tramp. I wore the tramp clothes to school after Halloween because the coat and dress were like the clothes I wore to school anyway. Without the black on my face I looked like the same old Cathy in her old second-hand clothes.

WE HAD A COUPLE of family vacations that I can remember. They both centred around my dad winning big at the track again. How big, I don't know, but it was big enough to pay for a cab to and from Beeton, which was where one of my dad's half-brothers, Stanley, and his half-sisters, Mary and Jenny, lived with their families.

My mother, my dad and I would get into the cab late at night and drive all the way to Beeton. I think the drive took a couple of hours and I could see how much money that cost on the cab's meter. It seemed like all the money in the world and, even back then, I knew that it was a dumb thing to do to take a cab all the way to Beeton only to do something they could have walked across the street to do: drink. And maybe we could have bought some food instead. Shit, I was always hungry on that drive to Beeton and I knew there'd be two chances of eating once we arrived there: slim and none. Maybe the Beetonia Hotel offered my parents something different, but Beeton sure didn't offer me anything better or different than what I had at home except maybe a bit more company.

My Uncle Stanley and Auntie Teresa's house offered all the conveniences that mine did except I could now share the experience with my cousins. There was still little or no food, lots of alcohol and cigarettes and a freezing-cold house to shiver the night away in when we visited in the winter and were all left alone because our parents went to the bar together.

This was no holiday for me. But I remember the house having train tracks behind it and I used to think that was pretty special. I liked to walk on the tracks with my cousin Googish (real name, Karen; I don't know why we called her Googish) and my cousin Stanley Jr. In the summertime we used to pick gooseberries, which grew dangerously close to the train tracks. We would eat the berries right there, only stopping when a train's loud whistle would get our attention. Then we'd back off the tracks until it whizzed by us, almost blowing us over. When the train passed, we would continue picking again, laughing at how we almost got smacked. We went out on a limb because that's where the fruit was.

I knew my cousins were poor too. They were a lot of fun to be around, but they had about as little as I did. One night I couldn't sleep because I was freezing, so I walked around the house trying to keep warm by putting my wrists under hot running water the way my Auntie Olga showed me how to do when I was cold, until the 'rents got home from the Beetonia. All my cousins were sleeping, and my mother, my dad, Uncle Stanley and Auntie Teresa all arrived well after the bar shut down and were now in the kitchen talking loudly and smoking and drinking. While I had been waiting for them to return, I spent two hours writing a play. It was about a man who fought with his wife and destroyed their house in a drunken rage. I played both the man and the woman in the play. I found my auntie's makeup in the bathroom and I had half of my face done up like a woman's and the other half like a man well before they all got home.

While the other adults drank it up in the kitchen, I got my dad to sit in a wooden chair in the living room to watch my performance. When it was time to play the man, I would turn to the left. When it was time to play the woman, I would turn to the right. My dad could hardly hold his head up to watch me perform. It upset me that he couldn't even watch me when I'd worked so hard at putting this all together. At the schools I went to, we often had plays and concerts, but my parents only ever showed up once, when I was eleven and got to sing "Those Were the Days" along with about twenty other kids. I never tried out for anything else because either the kids in the school didn't want me in their plays and performances or I figured my parents wouldn't come to see me anyway. So I figured my father could at least watch me this time. I had an empty whiskey bottle and pretended to take drinks from it as I stumbled around, first yelling at the wife and then switching roles to then drink and yell at the husband. When I finished the play, my dad was passed out cold so I had the imaginary audience, who did manage to stay awake and was clapping for me, give me a standing ovation. I then curtsied before leaving the freezing stage to go to bed. He just didn't care and neither did my mom.

I will never forget one Halloween when I was twelve. I was again, a tramp. After the bunny costume incident, I didn't mind the lack of creativity in my costume designs every year. This time though, instead of my going trick or treating alone as I usually did and randomly joining a group of kids as they made their way from house to house, my dad said that he was going to go with me. I didn't expect my dad to actually dress up, but he did: he dressed up as a woman. He wore my mother's pantyhose, shoes, flowered cotton dress and old brown winter coat with its fur collar, along with makeup that made him look freakishly scary, more like Red Skelton than a woman. After he'd polished off a bottle of whiskey, we left the house together, with him weaving from side to side and his eyeballs rolling around in his head as he tried to see straight. We both had pillowcases for the treats and decided to have a contest to see who could collect the most candy. He loved candy more than any kid, especially when he was sober.

He started trick or treating with me but before I knew it, I was alone again. I wasn't surprised to find him gone, so I kept going from house to house on my own, thinking that I still had to collect the most candy to win our game. Next thing I knew, I heard a bunch of sirens that sounded as if they were getting closer and closer. Kids and parents started to move toward the edge of the sidewalk to see what was happening. I was curious too, but I had a game going on and I didn't want to stop, especially because if all the kids were drawn to the sidewalk, I would keep getting candy.

As I was walking away from a house, a cop car drove by very slowly with its interior lights on. I could see two male police officers in the front and my dad in the backseat. My mouth dropped open and my pillowcase, now full of candy, fell to the ground. My dad looked sad and I wondered what had happened. I picked my pillowcase up and walked home. I found out the next day that my dad had decided to go trick or treating by himself instead of staying with me. He got to a single woman's house and when he knocked on the door and called out "Trick or treat" she screamed at the top of her lungs and phoned the police.

The police arrested my dad and he spent the night in jail. I went home and told my mother what happened. "Oh, what a stupid goddamn bastard he is!" was all she said. It was a quiet night at home and, frankly, it felt a bit odd. I wondered what was wrong with my wanting exactly this sort of thing—my dad to be taken away so that my parents wouldn't fight and drink— and now that he was gone, it felt weird. He came home the next morning, all sobered up, still wearing all the makeup and clothing from the night before. He didn't say one word to me as he walked by on his way into the bathroom. My mother, who was sitting at the kitchen table smoking a cigarette and reading the newspaper, said, "They should have kept you there where you belong!"

CHAPTER SEVEN

School daze

SCHOOL WAS A BLUR and just one more place that I felt afraid and alone. Not only did nothing stick in my head in class, the kids were always able to assess that I was the poor one by the way I dressed, and my gawky appearance didn't help me win any awards for most popular kid in the class. I'm not exaggerating. My nose was over-sized with a hump in the middle. I was flat chested when all the other girls were wearing bras and my butt was bigger than every-one else's. My hair was too thin, I felt as though my ears were way too big for my face and when I looked really carefully, I could see that one eye was a bit lower than the other. Thank God I didn't also have "cankles," my dad said. That would have made me even uglier. That was the only thing that was okay about me, I guess: I had thin ankles. I liked nothing about myself and I liked everything less when I found out that everyone pretty much hated me.

No one wanted to be my friend although I kept trying. I tried to have a birthday party and I invited the kids in my class. I saved money for months—change that I got from my dad—and I bought balloons and a cake from the corner store, without candles because I didn't have enough money for the extras. No one showed up—ex-cept my parents' drunk friends, as was pretty much the norm. But I still tried to get kids to like me at every school that I went to. Even-tually, I found one kid in each neighbourhood who was as unpopu-lar as I was and we would become friends. But they were rarely from the same school I was from, so I could only play with them on the weekend. Unlike me, they usually weren't allowed out on a school night.

At every one of the seven or eight schools I went to before I started high school at fourteen, it always started off the same and I would do the exact same thing. At first I would sit right up at the front, hoping to become teacher's pet. But that never happened. What did happen was that I always asked too many questions or cut off the teacher or other kids in my excitement to try to learn and be part of a group, and I would piss everyone off. The teacher would sometimes tell the kids to ignore me, or my hand would be up for eons and I'd never get a chance to answer something that I thought I knew the answer to. And before you knew it, I'd be told to move to the back of the classroom where I pretty much would give up on trying to learn.

When I was in Grade 4, another teacher complained to my mother that I talked too much. "Cathrine is always trying to monopolize the conversation" was the way she grumbled about my habit of speaking out and interrupting her and the kids in class. This teacher wrote a letter to my mother and told her that she had to show up for teacher-parent night. This was the only one that I remember going to with my mom. After the meeting my mother said, "Why can't you just be quiet? What's wrong with you?" I didn't know, so I didn't answer. I just liked to talk.

In every school, some girl or group of girls regularly beat me up and called me things like "dumb," "ugly" and "stupid." The teachers were as bad as the kids. One teacher called me a liar, just like my mother did. Another called me a creature. Creatures were ugly things that lived in caves and under rocks. They were things that people wanted to avoid or kill, and apparently I was one of them. This teacher was tall with short, thick, curly blond hair and black-rimmed glasses. She was from eastern Canada.

"Come here, creature!" she would command. I didn't even have to look to see who she was talking to, I knew it was me. But just because she called me that didn't mean that I had to answer. So she would stomp over to my desk, pull me by the ear and, with a scowl on her face, lift me off of my seat and drag me to the front of the class. I would hang my head down low and stand before everyone waiting to hear what I'd done wrong. I prayed for God to take my life on the spot but, as usual, He ignored me.

"Ya were talkin' in the cloak room this mornin', weren't ya? Creatures never do what they're s'posed to be doin', now do they?" On the last day of school, she said, again in front of the class, "You won't be gittin' far in life talkin' all the time, Chatty Cathy. Good riddance, creature!" and she gave me a little salute, the way I'd seen my dad do and which he told me he'd learned in the army.

Kids get nicknames. Some kids like theirs. One girl in my class was called Cookie and another Baby. Who wouldn't enjoy being called that? I didn't have one until I was twelve in Grade 7 and I hated it. I was called Seahorse. I don't know who came up with it, but somebody thought it fit to give me at St. Veronica School. I grew tall for my age: five feet eight inches by age thirteen. I was skinny and pale with straight, scraggly hair, but my most noticeable feature was my nose. Maybe that's how I got the nickname Seahorse. The doctor said it must have been broken at some time. I couldn't remember when it might have happened, except for the time my dad beat me up after the incident with Janet's puppy. But my mom told me that I broke it in a swimming accident that I don't recall happening at all.

Anyway, I was Seahorse.

I DIDN'T DO WELL in this school, sort of like the rest of them. E in arithmetic. C in spelling. C in writing. My clearest memory of school was being all excited at first and then losing all my enthusiasm. I became tired and hungry and eventually I spent a lot of time in class thinking about what all the kids would be eating for lunch. I would sit watching the teacher draw numbers on the blackboard and ask us to add them up, or talk about something that happened in history and expect us to remember it, or write words that we had to learn to spell correctly, and all I could think about was how I didn't want to go home after school or what to play at recess or how hungry I was or whether my mother would surprise me and show up at school with something for me to eat. Once in a while she did that. It was a crapshoot. I'd be in the school yard all by myself during lunch as the other kids ate and then all of a sudden I'd see my mother standing behind the fence with a brown paper bag, I knew what was in it and I'd be so happy. I didn't care what kind of a sandwich it was, I ate it, because I knew it was one that was bought, not homemade. I never had a homemade sandwich. It was either nothing or something she bought from the store. And when there was no lunch brought by my mother, I sneakily went through the gym or lunchroom garbage pails and found my own.

I was twelve years old when we moved next to the liquor store—I think Dad smiled for a week after we moved in—and transferred to St. Veronica School, which was some distance away. I went to one school dance and never went to another one after that. My Auntie Helen had sent me the most amazing dress (short, bright orange, very happening for the time) the past Christmas and I planned to wear it for the upcoming spring dance at school. I walked into the gymnasium, where the dance was being held, and stood in the corner all night by myself. I watched all the popular girls get asked to dance and felt a fool when one boy walked by me and I immediately smiled and said, "Yes, I'd love to dance!" and he just shook his head and walked by me to ask another girl. One girl walked by me and said to her friends, but meant for me to hear, "Hey, is this supposed to be a Halloween dance?" and they all broke out laughing. I walked home alone in the dark, wishing that I'd never gone to that stupid dance.

At St. Veronica, my two teachers—a man from Wales was my Grade 7 teacher and a woman from England was my Grade 8 teacher—were not like any other teachers I had. They didn't call me names the way teachers did at other schools I attended, but they did pretty much ignore me. Or maybe they felt that I was getting a rough enough time already. Who knows? I still got beaten up on a semi-regular basis by other girls, but I didn't get grief from the teachers.

The prettiest, but also the meanest, girl in my Grade 7 class, Linda, told me that a boy liked me when in fact he didn't exist.

For two months, she handed me little notes all folded up supposedly written by a "Donnie Robinson" in a barely legible scribble. She told me that Donnie broke the hand that he writes with, so he had to write with his other hand, and that's why the notes were messy. Wow! I thought, somebody actually liked me at school! I was in love and I didn't even have to see Donnie in the flesh. (I can see how Internet dating works!) Anyway, this girl told me that Donnie was away from school while his hand healed and I believed her. I did nothing except dream about Donnie and how we would fall in love and get married and he'd take me away from everything that was going on at home. Linda described Donnie to me; he had blond hair and blue eyes and he was a bit shorter than me. Oh, well, two out of three wasn't bad, I figured. I just didn't want to look odd beside my husband the way my mother looked beside my father. Then, on the day that I was supposed to meet Donnie, Linda handed me another note while a bunch of her friends stood behind her watching all this in the school yard. I opened it up, but it was a blank piece of paper. Do you really think, she said so the other girls could hear," that someone like you, who wears second-hand clothes and is ugly and poor, could ever really get a boy to like you anyway ... SEAHORSE?!" The girls all broke out laughing. I dropped the blank note and just walked away. I went into the bathroom and cried until I heard the school bell ring for class. I felt like a fool. But as I was walking to class, something deep down inside of me thought, Hey, maybe she's just jealous and Donnie Robinson really does exist. He didn't.

The trip to St. Veronica meant a long walk there and back, alone, which included entering a dark underpass for trains. One day I noticed a man, maybe about thirty years old, walking toward me in the underpass. I remember thinking, Gee, he's good-looking, and as I passed him I thought, And he smells good too, because I walked through a cloud of his cologne.

In the middle of this thought, he grabbed me from behind. In one motion he gripped me with one hand while his other hand slid up my short skirt and began tearing off my panties.

Nobody was around. Trains roared on the tracks above. Nobody would see what was about to happen. Nobody would know about it except me.

I dropped my books and started fighting and flailing my arms, kicking and scratching the son of a bitch, who punched me back and kept trying to keep me from running out of the underpass. Pinning me to the concrete wall, he tried to grab my wrists. I started screaming and, after what seemed like an eternity, I managed to get away and run faster than he was chasing me. I ran out from the overpass and into the street, yelling my head off and pounding on front doors, my lungs on fire, feeling as though they were going to burst at any second. None of them opened.

The guy kept following me until I gave up on the neighbours and ran like crazy to the school and into the principal's office. The school called the police and the staff calmed me down until two female police officers arrived and talked to me. Meanwhile, the school called my mother, who arrived to find me sitting outside the office, my clothes ripped, my body covered in bruises and scratches, my face still wet with tears and patches of my hair missing. She stood listening to the cops tell her it was very important for her to walk me to and from school every day. Her expression was one of real concern, and for a moment or two I was actually glad about what had happened, because it made my mother worried about me.

I liked the idea of my mother worrying about me. I *wanted* her to worry about me because then I would know she cared. Sometimes I would tell the kids that I had to get home right after school ended because I was grounded when in fact I was never grounded. I could usually come and go when I liked.

The next day my mom came to school with me, and the day after that as well. By the third day the look of concern she had worn when listening to the police officers had changed to an expression of annoyance. Walking me to school was eating into time spent at whatever else she had to do, but I was excited. My mom was walking me to school. Wow! As if she was any other mom. We didn't talk. I never expected her to discuss a thing with me. I just felt safer being with her until I realized how much it was bothering her.

On the fourth day, when I was dressed and ready to leave, she looked at me and said, "Do you really need me to walk you to school any more?'

I told her no, I didn't. It was no problem. That's what I said.

Inside, I didn't know if I was going to cry or be sick to my stomach. In a way that was very different and yet so very similar, it was as though the good-looking, nice-smelling man in the dark underpass was attacking me again.

So I walked to school alone that day and for another week until one morning, while walking through the underpass again, I saw him standing at the top of the hill ahead of me, the same good-looking guy in the same dark suit. I froze on the spot, unable to keep walking and afraid to run back into the darkness of the underpass. The guy began walking, then running toward me, and before I turned away from him I saw him smiling as if he'd been waiting for me all this time. When he got close to where I was standing, paralyzed, I heard a woman's voice shout, "Police! Get down on the ground!"

It was the two women cops. They had been watching me go to school every day from a distance, waiting for him to show up again. After they forced him to the ground and handcuffed him, one of them approached me, put her hand on my shoulder and said, "We knew your mother wouldn't walk you to school every day."

This guy, this perverted creep, had been arrested seventeen times for rape and sexual assault, and if there is any justice, which I often question, he is still rotting in a jail cell somewhere.

I told my mother about it when I got home from school later that day. Her only response was to say, "Tsk tsk," or something along those lines. We never talked about it again. But I was always impressed that the two women police officers knew my mother would break her promise to walk me to school within a few of days of the first assault.

During the summer holiday between Grade 7 and Grade 8, I had an incident with my teeth really hurting. Not long before, I'd met a neighbourhood girl, Terry, and we became good friends. Terry always had money on her from her mother. She hated her stepfather, who was really mean and treated her like a slave. He scared the hell out of me too. Terry and I used to spend all of her money every weekend on nothing but potato chips and Coke and complain about our miserable lives at home and at school. Ketchup chips were all the rage and she and I ate them until our entire mouths, teeth, lips and hands were dyed bright red. She had to stay in during the week so I really looked forward to being with her on the weekend. But for the next three weekends when she came over to hang out with me, I'd have to send her away because I had a really bad toothache. I couldn't eat or talk.

The toothache gradually became worse and worse; I missed school and I cried non stop about the pain. I told my mother, but she didn't do anything about it. Then, after hearing me moan and cry for what must have been long enough, my father got some cloves, boiled them, crushed them up and told me to put the mixture on my teeth because cloves stopped toothaches. This did squat for my pain.

Terry came over another weekend and I was still in pain from my tooth. She told me that I had to go to the dentist right away. She said she always went. So I took her advice and on Monday when I should have been at school and my parents were out, I went looking for a dentist all by myself. I found one that was right on Queen Street, on the second floor over a store. The dentist was older and not too friendly, and I didn't like the smell or the feel of the clinic. I was scared. He asked me if I had an appointment. I told him no, but that my teeth were really sore. I started crying, partly because of the pain, partly because I was hoping he would help me out. Without saying too much to me, he told me he would take a look. Then he said, "Very rotten. Gotta come out. Now." I saw a huge syringe and needle in front of my face and before I knew it, he pulled out four of my back teeth on the spot.

I didn't even have a baby and I was already losing my teeth! The dentist's receptionist took my name and address down and I don't know who paid the bill, but if my parents were billed for that visit, I'd have to guess they didn't pay. My parents never saw my teeth as a priority; that's just how they were. In fact, that was the first time I had ever been to a dentist. We had checkups at school, but I can only remember one or two of those. It didn't stop me, though, from continuing to eat crap again with Terry again the very next weekend.

The next year, in Grade 8 at the same school, my class had an art assignment: each of us had to draw or paint a small mural. The best one would be displayed on the corridor wall right next to the front doors and principal's office. Well, my first thought was that my creative genius had been squelched years ago, never to return, but I thought I would give it another try, since I was older. But I didn't have any ideas on what to paint. On the way home, I stopped at the store across the street and flipped page after magazine page, looking for inspiration. I finally found it about an hour later, in a beautiful photograph of the mountains and setting sun in a lush, tropical paradise with birds flying high. I loved it. I would draw that picture. I quickly tore out the page when the storeowner wasn't looking and ran out the door, eager to start my project. With a few dollars from my dad I bought all the supplies I needed. Two days later, I brought my work of art to school and when it was my turn to show what I had created, and in front of the whole class, I held the drawing up for all to see. I heard gasps and oohs and ahs and I knew that I'd done great job. So great in fact, that I won the contest!

A few of the teachers congratulated me and so did a couple of the kids. I can't tell you how proud of myself I was. I was in heaven for a whole week.

The next day a girl walked up to speak to the teacher and they both turned my way while the girl smiled and pointed. I smiled back. I could see that she had the same magazine I had used for my mural.

"We have a liar among us!" the girl announced. Everyone got quiet. Opening the magazine to the page I'd copied, she held it up I'd found for the whole class to see. Then she walked up and down the aisles. The teacher just stood at the front of the class with her arms folded disapprovingly and stared at me.

The girl stopped at my desk. "You copied this photograph right here! You're a cheater! We all knew you couldn't have done something that well on your own. You're too ugly and stupid!"

Finally the teacher interrupted and for a second I felt that she was coming to my defence. "She's not that ugly," she said.

At recess I walked by my mural. It had been torn down and the pieces were scattered on the floor. A teacher walked by.

"Is this your mess? Better clean it up."

I wasn't sure exactly what she was referring to—the mural or my life.

CHAPTER EIGHT

Food

FOOD WAS ALWAYS IN ISSUE with me. Still is. First I didn't have enough, then I had too much, then not enough again. I went from being a skinny kid to a fat, unhealthy adult to, finally, a healthy older adult in my fifties.

For me, food was an obsession. Growing up, I could hardly handle the mostly awful smells that sometimes emanated from our kitchen. At our house, the menu had two items: take it or leave it. Have some fried brains, pigs' feet, beef and pork tongue, liver, pigeons that my dad caught himself in wooden boxes at all the places we lived—or don't. No one cared. Dad would eat it all anyway.

One time we lived above a restaurant. It was called the Marianna Restaurant and I used to wonder if Marianna was the owner's daughter. I also wondered if Marianna could eat all the food she wanted in the restaurant. If so, Marianna was a lucky girl.

I saw people eating in the restaurant all the time; the smells from that place drove me crazy. I ate in the restaurant once and had French fries and gravy. My mother left me at the counter seated on a round stool that I spun around and around on. I grabbed one French fry as I spun around and passed the plate. On the next spin I dipped the fry into gravy, spilling a bit on the counter every time. I stopped spinning only when nothing but drops of gravy were left on the plate and the counter, and I didn't hesitate to lick the plate and the counter until every one of those drops was gone.

An old man behind the counter was watching me and I asked

where Marianna was. "There is no Marianna," he said. I refused to believe this and preferred continuing to imagine his daughter being able to eat all the food in the kitchen whenever she liked. In fact, this imaginary daughter had my face.

One day in our apartment I was sitting under the kitchen table at my father's feet. I used to do this a lot. My father was eating cheese. He cut a clean chunk of cheese for himself, a clean chunk for me, and a chunk of the mouldy part. He ate the first chunk himself and dropped the other two pieces to the floor. I ate the good piece of cheese. I threw the mouldy stuff into the corner where the rats were peeking at me out of a hole. I didn't care about the rats. They never bothered me. In fact, I wondered how I could catch them and keep them with me all the time. My mom said that they were ugly and that their tails were disgusting. I thought they were cute and funny and smart. The roaches were disgusting and ugly but the rats weren't so bad. The rats scuttled out of their hole and took the cheese in their little paws. They didn't care about the mould; they seemed thankful to have anything to eat.

I could never stop thinking about food.

When I was about seven, my mother enrolled me in a school program run by nuns that provided food to poor kids who didn't bring a lunch. We were hungry little kids whose parents were too poor or too drunk or too something to make sure we had a lunch to eat and the sisters acted as if we came to jail every day at noon. They should have been recruiting souls or something, but instead they sent a few of us to the dark side, I'm sure. They never smiled, never laughed, and they made me think that Heaven was not worth wanting to end up in after all.

The nuns often served tapioca pudding. I hated the stuff. Who the hell can eat tapioca pudding anyway with those balls of white cement going down your throat? Tapioca reminded me of the cockroach eggs I used to see at every place we lived in and that made me sick, sick, sick. When I refused to eat a bowl of that crap during one lunch, one of the sisters smacked me on the side of the head until I swallowed a few spoonfuls, which I instantly threw up. This made the nun even angrier and she insisted I eat the stuff I had just thrown up along with the tapioca still in the bowl. All of it. As my tears plopped into the mix, I ate it.

Considering how obsessed I was with food I guess I should have been grateful. But I wasn't.

At school I learned the trick of hanging around the garbage can in the far corner of the cafeterias, or if one of the many schools I attended didn't have a cafeteria, then it would be the lunchrooms. Maybe I'd have a book in front of me, a book that I never read but used for cover instead. I remember one time a kid walked by me and noticed that the book I was "reading" was upside down. Our eyes met and I gave her a look that said, "What the hell are you looking at?" since she ignored me in class all the time.

She stopped and said, "Stupid Seahorse. So stupid you don't know the book is upside down!"

"Yeah, well, I can read upside down too, so you're the stupid one!" I retorted, and she huffed off. Book accidentally upside down or not, I would peer from behind and watch the other kids carefully to see what they were eating, when they were finished eating and what they were about to throw away. Sometimes they would complain about the sandwiches their mothers made for them in their lunches—"She gave me salmon again! I hate salmon!"—and I would wait until they dumped their salmon or egg salad or baloney or whatever sandwiches they hated, the spoiled rotten brats, into the garbage can. When their backs were turned I would toss the book aside and dive into the big green or black bin and grab the sandwiches and maybe a half-eaten apple or whatever I could find and scoot back to the table, where I now ate behind the book's pages.

We never had anything like a food budget. I never remember my mother coming home form the supermarket like other mothers, weighed down with shopping bags filled with food. Whatever money we had for food was basically whatever was left after from my dad's paycheque after buying booze.

On rare occasions—if my dad won at the horse races, for instance—we might splurge on a T-bone steak. I would watch hungrily as my mother cut it up: the right side went to her, the left side went to my father, and the bone in the middle was left for me.

Mostly I ate a lot of bread on those nights. My dad used to threaten to give me a backhand swat across the face if I didn't eat bread. He would bare his teeth like a mad dog and raise his arm and yell, "Don't think you're going to get full stuffing your face on the good stuff. Eat the goddamn bread ... son of a bitch!"

To this day, when I have steak I prefer to eat the meat that is close to the bone. Filet mignon doesn't do it for me. But a T-bone with just a bit of meat around it is heaven.

THE TIME WE SPENT living above the restaurant was hell. Having to inhale the aromas of a kitchen practically all day and all night drove me nuts. Without doubt, though, my parents' favourite apartment was the one over a Kentucky Fried Chicken and next to a liquor store. All my father had to do was fall down the stairs and roll to the right a few feet, pull out a couple of bucks, and he had another bottle of booze. All the while we lived there I hoped that one of my parents would take me there or at least bring back a meal so I could taste what I had been smelling. They rarely did. I saw the inside of the liquor store on many occasions, but I think I set foot inside the KFC three times in the year that we lived there.

My mother told me that all the restaurants served cat anyway and that's what I would be eating. She said that the Chinese people walked the streets at night catching people's pet cats and then they'd take them back to their restaurants and cook them up for us dumb white folk who didn't know any better. She told me that there were articles in the newspapers all the time warning people to not let their cats out at night.

I tried to not want to eat fried cat. But one time after my dad won at the track they took me to a "chicken" joint. I have to admit I didn't care what I ate when I was starving. I just sat at that restaurant table and took a bite, closed my eyes and tried really hard not to think about what the cat that I was eating might have looked like. Being hungry as a kid was bad enough; now I was made to feel even worse about eating cat.

CHAPTER NINE

Trust ... again

I CAN UNDERSTAND now why my mother never trusted my dad. Hell, I didn't trust him either.

My father liked sex; I don't think she did. Then again, they had some very complicated ideas about sex.

She called him a whoremaster and I called him a promise breaker. We both had our reasons. Hers wasn't so obvious to me at first. But then as I got older, I began to see her point. I didn't like her calling him names, but then I didn't like him calling her names either.

When I was around twelve or so I remember my mother was out somewhere for the evening and my dad called me into the kitchen. I noticed that about a third of the whiskey bottle was gone. He was just butting out a cigarette into the ashtray as he stood up and then downed the last of what was in his glass before saying, "Do you want to make some money?"

"Sure," I said. I didn't have to ask how, because he volunteered the information.

"I want you to come with me and babysit this really nice lady's kids," he said.

"How many kids?" I asked.

"A couple. But she's very nice and she needs some help with her kids. I'll give you five dollars for the night, okay?" and with that he started walking out of the apartment telling me that we were going to get a cab on Queen Street. He took cabs everywhere when he had money. He would rarely phone for a cab, if we even had a phone or if the phone wasn't disconnected as was the norm, just like anything else that came along with a monthly bill. I followed him down the stairs and after locking the front door, we walked the short block to Queen Street. I didn't ask where we were going and he didn't volunteer any more information than I can remember. I do know that he had on a clean white shirt and looked nicer than if he were just going to be home drinking all night, but he wasn't really done up either. He whistled as an available cab drove by us and the cab pulled over.

My dad gave the driver the address and we headed toward the Dundas and Bathurst area to a rundown townhouse area. It was around dusk and there were a few kids playing here and there and they looked just about as poor as I did. My dad told the cabbie where to pull over and he looked at me and said, "We're here!"

After paying the cab driver, I got out and waited for my dad to lead the way. We walked up to a townhouse and my dad knocked on the door. A boy around the age of seven answered the door. My dad said hello to this kid like he knew him and the boy grabbed onto his leg, all excited to see him. I really didn't think much about this whole thing. I was a bit confused, but I thought I was going to babysit and I trusted my dad. The inside of the apartment was a bit better than the way we lived, but it was pretty messy too. I don't remember being introduced to the boy by my dad. Then I saw a younger girl running around the apartment and then a woman appeared seemingly out of nowhere.

Now I started thinking. Probably because she was pregnant and I don't mean a few months either. She was huge. About to pop any second, I thought. She was wearing black pants and a short-sleeved cotton maternity top that had all kinds of food spills and stains on it. When I looked at her face, she didn't look normal. Something wasn't right about her. She smiled at my dad and I don't remember if they hugged or kissed hello because I was too busy trying to figure out about what the hell was going on.

This woman yelled to the kids to sit the hell down and shut up and I was like, great, another place where kids can't be kids. I joined them on the couch. I was starving. I saw the fridge and figured by the mess of her top, it probably had some food in it and I was already planning when I would be able to get over to it and get something to eat. As soon as I sat down on the couch, my dad and this woman went into a bedroom that was just off the living room. They laughed and giggled a bit together and the two kids started watching TV. I figured this was my time to raid the fridge. I got up and opened the fridge and it was as bare as ours was. Closing it, disappointed, I glanced into the bedroom and saw that my dad and that woman were under the covers. My dad was on top of her and they didn't even care that the door was open or that we could all see in. The kids weren't watching them. They weren't watching us. I was upset there was nothing to eat.

I sat back down on the couch more concerned about the rumbling of my stomach than the banging of the headboard. I knew I wasn't supposed to be watching them, so I tried hard not to. The kids started jumping all over me and I welcomed the distraction. Soon after, my dad walked out of the room all dressed but the woman stayed in bed, by herself. I'm not sure how long we stayed, but it wasn't very long. My dad said a few words to the kids, gave them each a few bucks and we left. While hailing a cab, I asked my dad if we could get something to eat.

"Don't tell your mother about this, okay?" he said. If I was going to eat, I would have to promise that I wouldn't.

"Are we going to eat before we go back home?" I asked.

"Cathy, we need to have a pack." He meant pact. We were standing outside of the townhouse complex and it was getting dark. "What's a pack?" I asked.

"Where you and I can't lie to each other. No matter what, we have to tell the truth and we have to keep secrets from your mother. You won't tell your mother anything that I do and I won't tell her anything that you do. Okay? Do we have a pack?"

"But you're a promise breaker," I said.

"Not if we have a pack," he replied. I thought about it as he limped away quickly and whistled for a cab that was passing by. We got into the cab and he said, "Waddaya think. Can we shake on it?" and he held out his right hand.

I looked at it and shook it saying, "Okay, as long I get something to eat." He laughed and I knew that that meant we had a deal. We stopped in front of a restaurant on the way home and my dad got out and I waited in the cab. My dad came back with a brown paper bag. I opened it up and inside was a hamburger. I ate it on the ride home. Hamburgers were a real treat. The couple of times my dad took me to the racetrack reminded me of hamburgers. They had the best ones and this one wasn't too bad either. My dad would have to win at the track before I ate. This was a better deal. From the way he always touched every woman's knee with his hand when they were visiting and drinking with him when my mother was home or when she wasn't, and with how these women would drink and laugh along with my dad like big phony balonies, I'd say more burgers would be coming my way through our pack than at the track.

My mother came home later that night and it was as though my dad and I had been there all night waiting for her to come home, for all she knew. When I walked into the kitchen about fifteen minutes later and my mom was in the bedroom doing something, my dad looked at me and whispered, "We have a pack, just you and me." I nodded remembering the burger I just ate so I tried to forget what happened earlier on at the townhouse. As I walked by my mother when she came out of her bedroom, I said hi and then wondered if she too was out visiting a friend. She never bought me any burgers.

There was another time I came and I walked up the stairs to dead quiet and when I got to the top of the stairs I heard some murmuring. The door to my parents' bedroom was ajar. The light wasn't on, but who knows if that bill was paid?. But it was light outside and the room wasn't dark. On the floor I saw a pile of my dad's pants and some other clothing. Then I saw my dad's friend Certainly sitting on the edge of the bed, and he had no clothes on.

The door then slammed shut and I could hear my dad say, "Shit, Cathy's home!" and then all kinds of hustle and bustle went on behind the closed door. Oh, my God. Did I just see what I think I saw? I doubted it. Of course not. But mom did always say that dad would screw anything. In fact, one of their worst fights was because my mom found out that my dad had screwed Certainly's teenaged daughter.

Frankly, at the time I could care less who he screwed. What mattered mostly to me was whether they brought anything to eat when they visited.

I remember Mona. She always brought me something like a piece of cake that she made. Mona wore a foot-high beehive hairdo and only wore black. I mean like Johnny Cash all black. But a skirt instead of pants. Black everything. Mona "liked women" and I remember her as being fabulous to me. It turns out that lots of my parents' friends were gay.

I suppose I had an easier time understanding my father's whoring. It was my mother I could never quite figure out.

One day I remember I had just finished cleaning my room—I don't mean just tidying it up, but actually cleaning it. This is not the kind of thing you expect a twelve-year-old girl to do on her own, but it's something I did regularly. I would wipe the beaten-up furniture with a damp cloth, sweep the floor with an old broom from the kitchen, and do whatever else I could to make my own little corner of whatever apartment we were yet to be thrown out of as neat and clean as possible. Once I scrubbed the floors with Listerine mouthwash. The bottle claimed it killed germs, although that's not the reason my father and his friend Certainly drank the stuff. But if it was good enough for him to drink, it was good enough to clean our floors, right? Sometimes I couldn't tell if the Aqua Velva aftershave lotion was on my dad's face or down his throat. Certainly always smelled good, but I know he never used it on his face.

I was lying on my bed, listening to a record on the record player that my father had found at the dump. I didn't have anything to hold 45 rpm records on the turntable so I'd centre the 45s as best as I could. I had records by the Lovin' Spoonful and Herman's Hermits and a couple of other ones that my dad got for me from the dump. The album covers had a bit of old dried food on them, but the vinyl was pretty much in near perfect condition. I loved listening to my records over and over again, holding my hairbrush in front of my mouth like a microphone and mouthing the words, pretending I was a famous singing sensation. When my mother walked in I quickly pulled the hairbrush away from my face and stopped singing. I looked up to see her standing with her arms folded, her foot tapping the floor and her mouth tightly pursed. She was wearing a look on her face that I had often seen; it meant she was totally pissed about something.

"What's this?" she said, and she pointed at the wall behind my bed.

I walked over to my bed, trying to stare at what she was pointing at. She was so damned angry that her head was shaking quickly from side to side. "I don't see anything—" I started to say.

"What the hell is *that?*"

I looked closer. I practically pressed my nose against the wall, trying to see what she saw. All I could see was an old scratch on the wall. It had been there for years, long before we moved in, I figured. Anybody could see that. Anybody but my mother.

"That's a penis!" she screamed.

"A what?" I answered. I had heard her say "cock" before but never "penis."

I began to explain it was some old scratch, but she shouted even louder, "You drew a penis on your wall! Are you that boy crazy that you have to draw a picture of one on your own wall, you dirty pig!? You are sick!"

The hand that had been pointing to the scratch on the wall swung around and punched me in the face, knocking me onto my bed, where I huddled while my mother screamed and shook me over and over again, calling me a liar and a little bitch and whatever other names she could think of. She was great at discovering everything except the obvious. Cowering under her blows I wondered what I had done to deserve being treated so badly, as the 45 rpm record skipped over and over again while I cried along to its crazy beat: "Do you believe in magic, in a young girl's heart ... how the music can free her ..."

Now and then my mom would ban me from doing something without rhyme or reason. Like the time I went to an afternoon matinee with my cousin Janice, and my mother pulled us out of the theatre, yelling and screaming at the manager for letting two young girls alone into a movie. "I'm going to take you to court and sue your goddamn ass!" my mother yelled, not two inches away from his face. "What kind of a person are you to let two young kids into the theatre without an adult?" Janice and I just rolled our eyes at each other over what was happening because we'd just spent the previous night alone when both my parents went to the bar, leaving us without an adult.

At other times I could stay out all night without question, so I never knew what was right and what was wrong. Until I was about twelve, I was usually home at night because my parents wanted me home before they left me alone to go to the bars. Around the age of thirteen I started staying out past nine or ten o'clock at night, and at this age, my parents didn't wait around to tell me they were going out. I'd simply come home to an empty house. Around fourteen I started staying out all night. I felt as if my parents wanted me to grow up fast.

One Friday night when I came home around ten o'clock, I was surprised to find them both there. They were in the kitchen drinking and they'd run out of cigarettes. My dad told me to go to the store and get a couple of packs and he got a few bills out of his wallet and tossed the money onto the kitchen table. I was their errand girl, always getting the cigarettes and the pop and usually I didn't mind because I usually got to buy a chocolate bar or a bag of chips or a Coke with the leftover change. But that night I didn't want to go to the store, so I reached into my purse and pulled out my own package of cigarettes. Tossing the pack on top of the bills I said, "Why don't you two just smoke mine instead?" and I waited for their reaction. Without flinching my dad got up, took the pack, pulled out a cigarette for himself and then offered one to my mother. They both lit up and didn't say a word to me. I left the pack on the table and went out again. I couldn't believe they hadn't even pretended to be surprised that I was smoking.

MY DAD COULD BE pretty entertaining. When he wanted to be.

He took me to the Canadian National Exhibition (CNE) twice, once when I was about ten and again when I was about twelve. That was the time I learned about hot dogs on a stick. Oh, my God, I had never tasted anything so fabulous in all my life. After I smothered mine with mustard the way I saw everyone else at the concession stand doing, I looked over to see that my dad was keeping himself amused by taking a swig out of the mickey-sized whiskey bottle he had in a brown bag in his jacket. As long as he was drinking, I could spend all the cash he had won at the track. That's why he took me to the CNE in the first place. I planned on having a hundred hot dogs on a stick, but he caught a glimpse of the Zipper ride while his head was tilted back drinking. I looked up to see what he was staring at.

"Les go 'n that!" he slurred, pointing up toward the ride with the hand that was holding the mickey.

I had been on that Zipper ride once already the previous year, with my cousin Janice. After making sure she and I had no loose change and after getting satisfactorily strapped into the car—or so I thought—we looked down and saw the earth getting farther and farther away. As soon as the car began going over the initial big loop at the top of the ride, I realized I was not strapped in. Before I knew it, I was being thrown all around the car. Janice, who had been laughing gleefully, immediately stopped and realized what was happening. She held onto me as best as she could while I envisioned getting tossed right out of the car and banging into the ride's metal support structure all the way down to the ground. That didn't happen. But I sure never wanted to go on that ride ever again, that's for sure.

As my dad and I lined up for the Zipper, the guy who strapped us into the ride told us to make sure our pockets were empty. I told him to make sure that he goddamn strapped us in properly and to leave the chump change situation to us. He slammed the ride door closed and put the security pin into place. Well, at least I wouldn't splat to the ground, I thought. My dad had his pockets full of coins and as we flew around and around the car, we were literally bombarded by coins whacking us in the head and face and all over and hurting like hell before they worked themselves free and fell to the ground. I knew that the growing group of screaming kids gathered under the ride were collecting our—no, *my*—next hot dog on a stick and I got pretty depressed about that. My dad was laughing his head off. Until he turned pale as a sheet and said he was going to barf. He retched a lot but he never tossed his cookies, thank God! I guess it's because he had lots of practice drinking so much and keeping it all down. He once told me when he was drunk that barfing was just wasting good alcohol and no one should ever do that.

Point is, my dad was always doing something stupid—whether it was Halloween or most any other time. Trouble loved him and, I guess, so did I some of the time. But there was only one time in my life that he let me know he cared about me too.

My dad and my mom socialized with a lot of the same friends over the years. One of my dad's friends that we sometimes visited was a man named Bob. I don't remember Bob's wife's name, but they had a son a few years older than me named Robbie. I used to like talking to Robbie when we visited his place, because our parents got drunk together and we were sort of forced into either ignoring each other or talking. So we became friends despite his being a bit older. When I was twelve, Robbie and I were together at a kids' Christmas party held by my dad's union. Santa was there, and Robbie and I laughed at how there was no such thing as Santa. We ate candy and the lunch of turkey and all the trimmings and shared a great afternoon. That was probably one of the best Christmases I ever had, because I was around kids my own age and there was a ton of food. We even got one gift each. I forget what mine was, but all the gifts were under this huge tree decorated by someone who wasn't drunk, that was for sure.

So Robbie and I weren't really close, but we did see each other once in a while because of our parents and kept in touch with the odd letter. I would write to tell him what I was doing—going swimming sometimes, hanging out doing nothing, and so on. One day my parents told me that Robbie was dead; he had drowned in a boating accident in Honey Harbour. He must have been around sixteen or so. I couldn't believe it—I was shocked. He'd been drinking alcohol in the boat late one night and he fell into the lake. Apparently in the dark and with his construction boots and clothes on, he didn't stand a chance. I remembered Robbie being really nice and good looking and I sort of had a crush on him. Anyway, there was a wake at Robbie's parents' house. All the adults were drunk, of course, as they would be at any event, be it a wedding or a funeral, and my dad was crying uncontrollably.

In front of about twenty people he sobbed, "I don't ... know ... what ... I ... [break to blow his nose] would do ... if ... that [break to wipe his tears with his hanky] ... was ... Cathy ... dead."

I sat on the landing of the stairs in the house listening to this going on in the kitchen and I decided to talk to Robbie in heaven, since that's where everyone said he was.

"Hey, Robbie. It's me, Cathy. Did you kill yourself? Did you want to die, or was it really an accident?" I think I thought that Robbie wanted to get away from the drunks as much as I did since all our parents did was get drunk together and Robbie seemed less happy about it than even I was. I couldn't believe he was drunk himself when he died. I told Robbie that at least he didn't have to listen to this crap where people pretended to care about you but really didn't. I spent the next few hours on the staircase landing thinking about what Robbie must have gone through in that cold lake by himself, and it terrified me. First my grandfather and now Robbie.

By this time, things hadn't changed at home much compared to when I was younger, except there may have been a bit more food around. I remember eggs and kielbasa popping up in the mix, in addition to the same menu of stuff I didn't like to eat. There was also head cheese for lunch if I wanted it—yuck! I'd stick to the garbage bins at school. The bread was still bought when it was old and the fruit when it was just about throw-out-of-the-store quality. My parents hadn't changed much either. They still fought like crazy, although they didn't go to the bars and leave me alone as much as they had in the past. It was now pretty much a drunken party night every night at home.

I don't know why I watched my parents fighting day after day, year after year, because I hated watching. But I did. I'd always become the referee, screaming and pushing them apart when things got too violent, when someone might get really hurt, which was usually me. Once, in a drunken rampage, my father hurled a construction boot at my mother but hit me instead. I was positioned behind the kitchen door. The boot smashed the dangling light bulb and, before I could duck, crashed through the glass pane in the door. There was an explosion of shattering glass. I started crying. "Enough already!" I yelled. "You need to stop before you kill each other!"

One jagged piece of glass sliced into my ankle like an icicle and cut it open as cleanly as a scalpel would. I was bleeding and screaming and I didn't know what to do. My dad just walked away and my mother stood there looking at me.

"Mom, help!" I yelled.

She went and got some towels and I wrapped them around the largest wounds, but the blood was quickly seeping through. I needed to go to the hospital, so she called a cab. Luckily the phone was hooked up again after having been cut off for the last month or so. We took a silent cab ride, except for my whimpering, to the emergency department of some local hospital. My mother stared out the window on her side. By this time, I didn't expect her to do anything more. There would be no holding me or telling me that everything would be okay or calling me poor baby ... none of that stuff. When something happened to me, it was pretty much my own fault.

At the hospital, the intake nurse asked my mother what happened and she replied that I'd run into a glass door. The nurse took me into the back area and my mother followed. A young male doctor stitched me while trying to make conversation with me, again asking me what had happened. I looked over at my mother before answering and I got the evil eye. That meant *Better not tell the truth or you're in trouble!* In my head I heard, "What goes on in the house stays in the house!" So I said that I ran into a glass door. Protect the drunk. Screw the kid.

In the cab ride back home, my mother didn't say anything to me. I had a mouth full of glass shards, bleeding over my entire body, and neither parent ever apologized to me. In fact, a few hours after I got back home, all stitched up, the fight was on again, but I was in too much pain to play referee anymore. I went to bed and prayed, *Please God, let them fucking kill each other before they either kill me or I kill them.*

CHAPTER TEN

Self-esteem issues

ONE EVENING IN NOVEMBER, 1970, when I was fourteen, a snowstorm hit and there was fresh deep snow on the ground. My mother and I had just moved again, to a house her brother Johnny owned. We shared the second floor with one of their sisters, my aunt Olga, and her two kids, Janice and Michael. My dad wasn't living with us then. That was the way it went: one day we were living with my father and the next we weren't. I wasn't sure if he had left on purpose or had just never got around to coming home. He'd be gone for days or weeks at a time. Then he would be there again. The thing is, they fought so much and so often it was hard to know what might have happened.

Anyway, my mother and I shared a single bed, sleeping head to foot next to each other like two Lego pieces while Janice and her brother and mother slept in one bedroom. We all shared a small kitchen and a bathroom.

Everyone was out somewhere and I wanted to go play in the snow. Bellwoods Park was practically around the corner, and kids rode their sleighs and toboggans down a hill there. I didn't have a toboggan, but I wanted to find or make one. While walking the neighbourhood, I noticed a metal sign advertising tea or something, hanging by one screw from the brick wall of a grocery store that had gone out of business. I could ride that down the hill, I thought, and I tried jumping up to pull the sign off the wall.

"What're you tryin' to do?" somebody behind me asked. At

first I got scared, but then I realized it was just a homeless guy, wrapped in a filthy blanket and pushing a shopping cart filled with plastic bags and junk he had found. The snow covered the wheels of the cart and he was having a difficult time pushing it.

I told him I was trying to pull the sign off the wall to use as a toboggan.

"That's a good idea," he said, and he grabbed the sign and twisted it away from the wall.

"Wow! Thanks! You wanna ride with me?" I asked him.

He smiled, showing me a mouthful of really bad teeth. "I ain't been on a toboggan since I was maybe your age or younger," he said.

We crossed the road and headed toward Bellwoods Park. I had been there with Janice, so I knew the first hill we would come to would be the steepest. As I looked down, I realized it was not only steep, but it was scary steep. I got excited about riding that sign down the hill, but first, I had to bend it a bit in the front to put my feet into it and make it look a bit less like a sign and more like a ride. The old man helped me bend the sign back just enough.

I dragged the sign as close to the hill's edge as I could without letting it slide down without me. Seating myself carefully on it I said to the man, "Get on and push," and he did. He was behind me, holding my waist and laughing and I smelled the liquor on his breath. I screamed and he kept laughing while we slid down the hill, over the sidewalk and across the road, landing smack into a house on the other side of the street, where we finally stopped., Laughing so hard I couldn't stop, I rolled off. He jumped up faster than I thought he had it in him to do.

"You all right?" he asked, looking down at me. I couldn't answer because I was laughing and gasping for air. When I finally told him I was fine he stood up and said, "Goodbye, crazy girl," and he walked back around the hill with a limp he didn't have when we met.

Somebody was glaring at me from inside the house we had crashed into. I waved to them and walked away, hoping they wouldn't come out and give me hell. The sign was now all bent and I realized that would be the only ride I'd be able to take on it. No matter, it was an awesome one.

But I wouldn't have too many happy experiences living on Bellwoods Avenue that year.

I had started high school in September. I was always changing schools. I figured by the time I moved out for good I had lived in at least eighteen different places and had attended at least as many different schools. Since I had no money for a bus I always had to be walking distance to whatever school I attended.

Anyway, school mornings at Bellwoods would happen the same way almost daily. I would get up for school at the same time my cousins Janice and Michael got up. Janice would leave the house first because she had to go to school the farthest away. I would go into the kitchen and watch my cousin Michael eat a big bowl of cereal that my Auntie Olga bought for her kids. My mother and I never shared their food. Plus, my mother said I was old enough to feed myself. "See, Michael has beautiful teeth because he doesn't eat anything hot," my mother would say. "If you eat hot food, you'll lose your teeth!" she added. Well, what's going to happen to my teeth when I'm hungry all the time? I used to think to myself.

Sometimes my Auntie Olga would feed me too. But first, she would have me peel all the potatoes or prepare the food for her family and my mother and me before she cooked it up. She told me that I was the best potato peeler she ever saw and I used to feel so proud of that.

"Oh, Cathy, you are just so fast and perfect at peeling all those potatoes!" she would exclaim. Later on, my cousin Janice told me that my auntie just said that to me so I would do her dirty work in the kitchen. In any event, I got to eat whatever my Auntie Olga prepared, but my mother told me their food was not our food and I took care to respect that rule. Auntie Olga and my mother slept in and rarely got up with us in the mornings. Sometimes my mother was hungover and sometimes she just slept in for no good reason. Auntie Olga on the other hand would be out all night with her then boyfriend, Hub. My mother actually used to say that *she* felt sorry for Janice and Michael because *their mother was never home.*

Anyway, I would get dressed for school and leave the house, running down the stairs out the front door. You see, I loved the idea of going to school. I didn't know what to expect at high school, but I was hoping it would be better than any other school I'd gone to. How could it be worse? I'd heard that this school, Central Commerce, was an easier high school to graduate from than some of the others, and that kids who couldn't become anything really special went there. I'd also heard that becoming a secretary was easy for people who had a hard time learning, like me. Even so, I loved the idea of going to school. My mother didn't give me any career counselling, and I didn't know what all my options were, so I went with secretarial training.

My Uncle Johnny, unlike his sisters, was an early riser. Every morning when I ran down those stairs, he would be standing at the bottom landing with his arms folded and a scowl on his face.

"Goddamn it. What the hell is wrong with you, eh? You sound like a fuckin' baby pony, you're so fat and loud. Look at you!" (I weighed about 130 pounds but I was larger on my bottom half.) "Why don't you try cleanin' those goddamn stairs that your big ass runs down every day instead of trying to break 'em? Eh?"

I would be perched on the second last stair, gazing at him pretty much eye to eye and wondering when the hell he was going to get out of my way so I wouldn't be late for school. Well, if I ended up going, that is. I felt like shouting in his face, "Why don't you go read all those porn books you've been collecting for a hundred years that are all hidden under your bed, you loser?" Okay, so I sometimes got bored and went snooping through his stuff when he wasn't home, but that ended when he put a lock on his bedroom door.

A few weeks later I had some French homework and I really loved trying to learn a new language. My mother was in our bedroom napping and I didn't have anywhere to practice my French. So I sat at the top of the staircase with my books out and was happily chirping the words in French for dog, then cat, then the colour red, then ...

"WHAT THE FUCK ARE YOU DOING?" yelled my Uncle Johnny from the bottom of the stairs so loudly that I swear my hair flew back from the wind coming from his breath. He was furious.

"I'm speaking French," I replied. He ran up the stairs and stood there looking down at me.

"There'll be no fucking speaking French in this house! You understand? I hate that fucking language." His face was all distorted. "Those fucking bastard frogs, I hate them. Yeah, yeah, French, eh, you stupid bitch fat baby pony ... stupid." Then he walked back down the stairs, leaving me frozen, unable to move, and he turned his head around as he kept walking, saying, "You better never talk that shit again—ever! Fucking frogs ... stupid goddamn language ... got it?" and then he was gone.

So much for my desire to learn French.

In music class, I decided to learn the clarinet as my instrument of choice, but only because Janice brought one home one day to practice on and I wanted to be like her. I played fabulously. Just kidding. I faked playing the clarinet, just like I faked my prayers as a kid. When playing, I simply made a lot of noise that the rest of the band, playing in tune, covered up very nicely. I couldn't read the notes. Oh, I knew how to read and play three or four notes from sheet music after a while, and thank God the teacher didn't isolate me and ask me to play something by myself as he sometimes did with a few other students. I was more terrified of what names I'd be called in front of the class than I was of being revealed as a phony. But Janice was doing pretty well. I'd bring my clarinet home too, but I don't know why, because I just made a bunch of noise. Just like the books under my arm as a kid, I guess. I wanted people to see and think that I was smart or talented or anything that I thought I wasn't. Well, my uncle wasn't impressed and he told me to cut out the bloody noise because I was giving him a headache. I was giving myself a headache, but the point is, everything I did seemed to bother somebody. I never brought my clarinet home ever again.

I can still hear him calling from over his shoulder to me, "Big fat ass big baby fuckin' pony breakin' my goddamn stairs."

CHAPTER ELEVEN

The "budding" entrepreneur

NOBODY WENT HOME for lunch in high school. Everyone brought something to eat in the cafeteria, or brought money to buy food there, lining up with a tray and filling plates with fries and hamburgers and macaroni and cheese or whatever the special was that day. I rarely brought or bought food. I had worked at the Canadian National Exhibition that summer at Nobett Tavern as a waitress, so I had a bit of money saved. I also did some work for free at the CNE. I used to befriend all the guys who put the rides together each summer and they would use me as their test dummy. By that I mean they would let me ride for free in order to see if the rides would kill someone or fall apart or otherwise malfunction before the exhibition officially opened. I was happy to be a test dummy because it was a lot of fun. Janice and I also volunteered as lifeguards at Woodgreen Community Centre's summer camp for kids. I felt good about helping out kids, but it didn't help my pocketbook.

I was at Central for less than a year. Janice went away to another school in another part of town and I felt abandoned and alone. I really loved her; we did so many things together and being around her made me happy. I even used to call her my sister. One summer when we were both thirteen we met an old lady on our way to Centre Island. The woman said, "You two young ladies are lovely. Are you sisters?" I beamed and said, "Why yes, we are. How did you know?" I was happy because I thought Janice was beautiful. She had thick, long, straight dark hair, beautiful blue eyes and a sweet smile; she was as tall as me but had a nice chest and slim hips.

So, when Janice went to another high school, I did what any neglected kid might do. I sold drugs. It was my first venture into business, and I picked up some practical lessons on the basics of being an entrepreneur, including the need for venture capital, the value of setting a decent profit margin, the law of supply and demand and most importantly, the fact that if someone liked you, you could get most anything for free.

At the time, hippies were everywhere. I became a sort of pseudo-hippie, looking for anyone or any group that would see me as their own. I bathed in stinky patchouli oil, carried a colourful hemp bag with a jute-rope shoulder strap at all times, wore peasant blouses and bell-bottom jeans and told everyone I had attended Woodstock and it was really far out, man. Peace and love, baby.

Anyway, there was a new eighteen-storey apartment building that was a co-operative student residence and an alternative education facility not far from where we lived. It was called Rochdale College and it was open from 1968 to 1975. I heard you could buy a BA degree for twenty-five bucks, no questions asked, and a PhD cost $100. I wish I'd bought one at the time, because years later I realized one of those degrees would have come in pretty handy, but for now, I just wanted to buy some hash.

I didn't really understand that the place was a college or what "alternative education" was. I knew two things: adults in our neighbourhood smoked a lot of hash and marijuana, and Rochdale was the biggest source of the stuff in the city, maybe in the whole damn country. I hitchhiked to Rochdale and simply pressed a gazillion intercom buttons until someone buzzed me in; then I started knocking on every door until someone answered.

He was a typical spaced-out, thirty-something hippie dude. He had a joint in one hand and used the other to steady himself against the door frame. His eyelids were at half mast.

"What's shaking, dudette?" he said as he inhaled the joint deeply and then coughed while sizing me up. The whole apartment was full of smoke that seeped out into the hallway. I heard voices in the background; it sounded as if there were three or four other people in the apartment, if I had to guess.

"Hi. My name's Cathy. I'm looking to score a dime of hash or grass. Can you help me out?"

He continued puffing away as though he hadn't even heard me.

"Sorry for bogarting this hippie lettuce, but you look too young, so beat it." He was about to close the door, but he was so stoned he sort of fell backwards. I stepped forward a bit.

"I'm not a pig. I only have five dollars." I reached into my hemp bag and pulled out the bill.

He looked at it. "Bummer, man."

I figured he or anyone else had more money than me, but I was hoping that didn't mean I was out of luck. He took another toke and inhaled so much smoke that he had huge chipmunk cheeks. I laughed. He blew out the smoke and I started to cough. We smiled at each other. I thought, Bingo. I do believe I am going to score after all. I learned that you just need to find a way to connect with people when you want something. Or you trade. I heard my dad's voice saying, "Everyone negotiates."

"So, like, you live in a pretty cool pad," I said.

"Yeah, we got everything we need here. Okay, I dig ya. Wait here and I'll be right back." He offered the last of the joint to me. I shook my head no. As I held the door open with my foot, he went away and I heard him tell the people inside that some chick was at the door wanting to score and he was going to help her out but he didn't know why because she was really young.

When he returned, I asked him what his name was. He said, "Oh, no name, man. You just need to know that I like to play the banjo."

"Fine. I'll just call you JoJo then."

"Oh, that's far out crazy, man," he laughed.

JoJo handed me a small square of aluminum foil. "Here's a dime and, like, I don't want your bread, man, if that's all you got." I told him that it was. "At least you won't freak out with this like with acid, you dig? Okay, I didn't need a lecture, but he was rambling on about all kinds of things now and I just wanted to leave. I stopped talking and just smiled, looking at him. Finally, he said that he had to go and with a two-fingered peace sign, he told me to make sure I didn't do something stupid like get busted. I took the elevator down when the doors closed. I said aloud, "Holy shit. That will never be me!"

That was so easy I knew I would be back. In fact, I went back about twenty times. I usually sold what I'd scored on the way home, but sometimes I'd go to the Toronto Islands, where it seemed everyone went on the weekends to get stoned.

For the record, I rarely used drugs. It didn't interest me then and never did later. I got high a few times on marijuana and hash and once on acid, and the one time I snorted coke didn't count because I can't say that I "got high." I always stayed away from mainline drugs. I suppose if I'd wanted to use something it would have been heroin because I heard it relaxed you. I could have used some relaxation. I was sure as hell too hyper for meth; I didn't try that either, because I didn't like the idea of losing control over my actions. For all the crap in my life, I still believed that the best way of dealing with everything was to have as much control as I could over my situation, which meant staying sober. I did drink when I was a teenager and later on when I went to clubs, and I smoked cigarettes right up until I was forty. Still, I think if I'd gotten heavily into drugs or drinking, that might have been the end of me, given what I saw that stuff do to other people. Instead, I turned into a control freak, and sometimes I'm not sure that was any better for me.

My little business lasted about a year and basically I made enough to keep me in some food and clothes. Naturally I hung out with the local druggies at school and around town. But only for business or because they were the ones that accepted me. My mother, of course, accused me of being a dope fiend and didn't believe it when I tried to tell her otherwise. "Mom, I'm wearing patchouli oil," I told her, when she said that I smelled like grass. "You goddamn dope fiend. You're doing drugs."

"Mom, it's patchouli oil!" I said again.

"You're a goddamn liar! You lie about everything!"

IT WAS AN HOUR'S WALK to Central Commerce. I went to school diligently for a little while, carrying my books with their handmade paper book covers, which were so easy to make but which made the books look extra special. I used to get as nicely dressed as I possibly could, considering that some of my clothes were still bought at second-hand stores. I'd gone to Woolworth's and bought all of my school supplies and I was so excited about starting high school. I was still often late for school, but I'd show up all positive and ready to make up for the learning I hadn't done in other schools. But soon enough, I found out that high school was just as difficult for me as junior school. I still didn't learn anything. Well, not until my cousin Diane told me her plans to become a private secretary one day. Then I started taking my typing class much more seriously. I didn't need any sort of background to learn how to type. Everyone in my class was starting from the same place: the bottom. Unlike math and science, where the previous four years of school came into play, no one had taken a typing course before high school.

My typing teacher, whose name I've forgotten, had a hard outer shell and a really soft inner core. I liked her right off the bat. In my first typing class, I again sat right up front as I had done in all the junior schools I went to. But this time, I was never moved to the back of the class. I would rush into that class—when I attended, that is—so I could grab the desk and typewriter closest to her. She was about five feet five inches tall, with short black curly hair and glasses. Always very prim and properly dressed, she usually wore a cardigan over her simple dress and maybe one strand of pearls—nothing too flashy.

I would hand in my typing test to her when I was done and she'd look at it and read, "Hmm, thirty words per minute." Then she'd look at me sternly and say, "Cathy, you can do better!"

She always said I could do better, and you know what? I could and I did! Eventually I was typing over sixty words per minute and that was good enough to make her break into a very small smile when she passed by my desk. That was about the most any teacher ever mentored me. So I became the typing queen of the class, even though I eventually missed more than half the sessions. A, S, D, F

G, space, semi-colon, L, K, J, H, space and so on. At least I didn't have typing homework because I am sure Uncle Johnny would have had a problem with that too: tick, tick, click, click ... "BABY PONY!" I imagined him trying to stop me from learning how to type too. Anyway, in class I typed endlessly as the teacher walked up and down between the desks, arms folded, peering over her glasses, glancing at the crisp white bond paper that each person in class was typing on. Slowly she moved her head left and then right—return—and then left and then right—return.

I thought that by taking typing I would make my mother proud. But since we never talked about what happened at school, I never told her what courses I was taking, although she did tell me I should pay attention in home economics class so that I could learn how to sew and cook for my husband one day. I made sure I didn't attend even one home economics class.

I really wanted to graduate. I was making progress.

But then I met Eddie.

CHAPTER TWELVE

Eddie

A COUPLE OF YEARS AGO a news story out of Toronto had people everywhere shaking their heads over one man's stupidity. In his fifties, the man had been stopped by a female police officer while driving a pickup truck. When the officer asked to see his driver's licence and ownership papers, his response was to roar off in the truck while the officer's arm was caught in the door handle, dragging the woman cop seventy-five metres before she managed to get free, run back to her cruiser, call for backup and start pursuing him.

The guy drove like a madman through the city, trying to get onto the main highway leading out of town, until he lost control of the truck and struck a minivan carrying a man, woman and their three little kids. The van rolled over, injuring members of the family, and when the pickup truck spun into a pole, the police pulled the driver out of the wreckage and arrested him. The driver was drunk and the truck was stolen. When they added up all the charges against him it sounded more like the city had been invaded by six gangs of Hell's Angels than one fifty-year-old loser: criminal negligence causing bodily harm, dangerous operation of a motor vehicle causing bodily harm, three counts of assault with a weapon, two counts of failure to stop for police, leaving the scene of an accident, possession of property obtained by crime over $5,000, possession of property obtained by crime under $5,000 and driving while disqualified. I'll bet he wasn't wearing his seat belt either, but I guess they overlooked that one.

Just another day in the big city, right? Then the rest of the story came out. He was on parole from prison, had been banned from driving for life four times, had 158 criminal convictions for theft and assault on his record, and faced a national warrant for his arrest on a long list of other offences.

People who read the story in the media were ready to lynch this loser, or at least toss him behind bars and bury the key. I understood that. I felt the same way. I had my own reasons to agree with them when I learned his name was Eddie Skotnicki, my first love and the father of my son, Michael.

Every time I hear people almost excuse some criminal's actions because he suffered a lousy childhood, I want to tell them about Eddie Skotnicki. Compared with just about every other person I have met, Eddie's childhood was golden. His father was a tailor who worked hard every day at Primrose Garments in what is now the fashion district of Toronto, made good money and brought it all home to his family. Mr. Stanley Skotnicki walked from Grace and College streets to his workplace at Spadina and King streets and back every day, rain, snow or shine, to save the bus and streetcar fare and give Eddie a better life. Hell, Mr. Skotnicki never spent money on vacations or other indulgences, all to save money for Eddie's sake.

I met Eddie Skotnicki just after I started high school. I had decided to go for a walk around dinner time and it was a mild evening. I was wearing a purple dress I had picked up at a second-hand store, and by this time, believe it or not, buying from second-hand stores was starting to become fashionable. Lucky for me, I guess, but I still hated second-hand anything.

Eddie was walking on the north side of the street when he saw me, and he dodged and weaved his way between speeding cars to get over to the south side of the sidewalk where I was. Just like Superman, dodging speeding bullets, I thought. I had no idea who he was or where he lived. But he was a pretty good-looking package, two or three years older than me, and he could talk a good line. I was still skinny and flat-chested and still starving for everything, but mostly for the attention of a boy.

And that's what Eddie gave me. He had money to buy me things, thanks to his parents' scrimping and saving. He made me laugh. He kept me company. And he was half-Polish like my dad while the other half was Ukrainian like my mom.

And he wanted me. *Me.*

Before I knew it, he would show up at my school, trying to get me to play hooky. But I told him that I wanted to go to school and he should go to school too. He would disappear for a few days or a week and then he would show up again. Eventually, he was at my school most mornings, leaning up against the brick wall, smoking a cigarette. Finally I broke down, reasoning that here was someone who was actually waiting for me and who wouldn't give up until I saw things his way, so he must really, really care about me. Then I would see everyone walking into the school and I'd think that I'd better go to class and tell Eddie to come back after school was finished for the day. But, sure enough, I eventually believed that although school was waiting for me too, it didn't look as good or need me as badly as Eddie did. Besides, the only thing I was good at was typing and since I could type faster than anyone else in the class, I could afford to take the day off. If only it had been a day.

"Hi there!" he would say with a slight lisp—the result of a bottom lip that was a bit bigger than the top one.

We started dating, although what that meant was that Eddie would tell me to be available 24/7 and he would decide when—and if—he would show up. Usually we would go to his parents' house when they weren't around, and he would paw me over in what went for sex and that would be it.

He often told me to come to his place, but then he wouldn't be home. Sometimes I walked up and down his street for hours waiting for him to come home. Or he'd tell me to meet him somewhere and he wouldn't show up. I never got used to it.

"Hi. What happened to you last night? I waited for hours."

"Yeah, I had some business to take care of."

Eddie's notion of business generally meant he had scored with another girl or, increasingly, that he was pulling a B & E—break and enter. Those jobs could last all night. When it came to being a night owl and hating the sunrise, Eddie was like my mom and Auntie Olga.

I realized that Eddie was unreliable so I'd tell him that I really had to get to school and that's what I was going to do starting tomorrow. He'd say something like "You're going to be late anyway, like you always are, so why not just play hooky?" Or he'd give me some other lame reason to not go to school and I always gave in.

Eddie was enrolled in vocational school but he never went. So we started hanging out together every day and I stopped going to school. Eddie was my new school. If anyone at Commerce ever tried to contact my parents about my "attendance issue" I never heard about it.

Then again, we never had a phone.

THE FIRST TIME WE HAD SEX I was fourteen. Eddie took me to his sister's apartment one day to babysit his nephew Anthony. That in itself might say something about Eddie's judgment. Anyway, after Anthony was sleeping, we got naked in his sister's bed.

Ever since we'd met, Eddie had put a lot of pressure on me to have sex with him, but I always put him off. I knew he would eventually win. It wasn't as if I had a phobia about it or crazy expectations about what the "first time" might be like. I wonder now if maybe I had thought having sex with Eddie might make him stop paying attention to me. I mean, that had been my experience with people who had had sex. It didn't seem to make them happy. In fact, they seemed miserable as shit.

Eddie told me that having sex was something that he needed from me or else he wouldn't be my boyfriend. I didn't want to lose out on the first person that I thought loved me.

After a few short kisses on the mouth, he turned me onto my side and got really close behind me. I felt something painfully pushing into me. After a few minutes he lay back, breathing heavily as though he had just run a mile.

He had a big smile on his face and told me I wasn't a virgin anymore. I asked him what he meant and he showed me some drops of blood on the sheets, which he made me wash before his sister and brother-in-law got back home. And that was that.

HE TOOK ME TO HIS HOME and introduced me to his father, Stanley. From his reaction you would have thought Eddie was the greatest son ever born. Nothing was too good for Eddie; he was always buying Eddie expensive hockey equipment and he'd leave money in Eddie's pockets every night for his son to find and spend. Eddie's mother dressed like a middle-class immigrant clotheshorse in pillbox hats and brocaded jackets, which made her look wealthy. Most of the clothes Mr. Skotnicki made himself; he was very talented. I may have been impressed with Mrs. Skotnicki at the beginning, but she was clearly unimpressed with me and that never changed. When Eddie introduced me to his mother, her only response was to look me up and down, then turn to Eddie and say, *"Ona nie ma zadnego titski!"* Eddie laughed and translated: she doesn't have any tits. Like I didn't know. At least she didn't say I had a huge nose. But then again, maybe she did because she always spoke in Ukrainian when I was around. My grandmother did the same thing. Then someone would have to translate. I thought it was because they couldn't speak English. But when I heard Mrs. Skotnicki speaking English a few months later, I realized she just didn't want to speak to me and I wondered what my grandmother's excuse would have been. I never asked her.

Eddie's mother kept a sparkling-clean house that was always warm and peaceful, with a refrigerator stocked with food. And Eddie had a smart older brother, Stanley, who worked at GM in Oshawa and who was married to Emilie; they had two fabulous daughters, Sandy and Debbie. Sandy became a dermatologist and Debbie became a happy housewife. Point is, if Eddie needed anything, he only had to ask. Well, I guess he didn't ask, because he started stealing from them all and taking what he wanted and they did nothing about it except yell a little at him here and there.

AROUND THAT TIME, Eddie gave me two amethyst rings. They were the most beautiful rings I had ever seen. I guess someplace deep down I knew Eddie had stolen them. But it didn't matter. I wore one on the ring finger of each hand.

Sometimes when Eddie's parents used to fight with him about "not following the rules," Eddie would splurge on a hotel room for us. Like Eddie could follow rules. It was a joke. He used to stay away for a night here and there and then go back home. His mother would be so happy to see her baby return that it was okay if he broke the rules again. I thought it was funny that Eddie's older brother wasn't allowed to even smoke cigarettes or stay out late. But with Eddie it was pretty much, "Eddie, don't leave your crack pipe on the coffee table" type of rules. As for me, I never remember my parents asking me where I had been all night. It just didn't matter.

One night at a motel I took the rings off and put them on the night table by the bed. When I woke up in the morning and wanted to put the rings back on, they were gone! Eddie was still fast asleep. I woke him up, asking him where my rings were. He threw off the bed covers and walked naked over to where his clothes were on a chair and got out his pack of cigarettes. He smoked just as much as my parents put together and he couldn't do anything, not even speak, without a lit cigarette in his hand. He kept the cigarette in his mouth as he put on his pants, took a puff of his cigarette and then kept it in his mouth while he buttoned up his shirt, closing one eye to shield it from the smoke. I watched him, trying to figure out when I could start yelling and accusing him of stealing what he'd already stolen.

"Eddie, what did you do with my rings?"

I was still in bed, propped up on a pillow against the cheap imitation-wood headboard. "I put them right here on this night table and now they're gone." My voice grew louder. "You must have taken them!"

"What? Are you some sort of fuckin' detective, eh? You lost your rings and you think I took them? Why would I take them? Close your head, you talk too much!" With that, it looked like he was going to walk out and leave me so I backed down the way I always did.

"Okay, okay, I'm sorry, Eddie. Please don't leave me. I don't know what happened to them and I thought you took them."

He said that he didn't take a thing, especially not something he'd given me, and now he was pissed off and my snatch and me could just go fuck ourselves. He said he'd be waiting in the car for me. About a half hour later, while trying to ignore the gazillion honks of the stolen-car horn that Eddie seemed to be leaning on the whole time while waiting, I scoured the entire dumpy motel room. I found lots of stuff under the bed and behind the door and in the closet, including a pen, one earring, a used lipstick in a crappy colour and a small used makeup brush, but not my rings. I left everything on the bathroom counter below the large mirror, which had a huge horizontal crack in it, and with the tube of lipstick I wrote, "YOUR HOTEL STEALS SHIT, SEE!" with a downward arrow pointing toward all the crap I'd found and put on the counter. I tossed the lipstick into the pile and left.

Once I was in the car, Eddie gave me shit about making him wait so long because didn't I know the bent car was a heat score for fuck sakes?

I DON'T KNOW IF I LOVED EDDIE. I wanted Eddie because he was the only alternative I had to my battling parents and the dumps we lived in. Plus my parents kept telling me I had to stay with him and get married to him one day.

He had so many things going for him, including his appearance. Blessed with thick blond hair, sexy blue eyes, a great physique and a sense of humour, he attracted girls easily, especially when they learned about his talent as a hockey player. He may not have made it as a professional in the NHL because he wasn't a big guy, but he had been chosen to play Junior B hockey in Ontario. He might have moved up to Junior A and had at least a semi-professional career in hockey. Instead he got nothing—except a few girls like me knocked up and maybe one of the longest criminal records in history.

Eddie's family were strict Catholics, with crosses and pictures of Jesus and Mary on every wall and big Sunday lunches after church, which made Sunday my favourite day to see Eddie. Eddie even used to be a choir boy when he was a kid. When it was Sober Sunday at my house, at Eddie's it was eat until you're as stuffed at the cabbage rolls in front of you.

Mrs. Skotnicki might have believed she was a good Catholic, but she was a lousy Christian. On Sunday afternoons after the services at the local black Baptist church, the congregation would leave singing joyfully and clapping their hands. They did this all the way down Grace Street, passing by the Skotnicki house. Mrs. Skotnicki, wearing her pillbox hat from church, would call me over to the living room window to see them pass. Standing there laughing at them, she'd say they believed they were children of God and they were going to heaven, but they were black and black people weren't allowed in heaven. "Won't they get a surprise!" she'd cackle.

Mrs. Skotnicki got her own share of surprises from Eddie. One of the biggest concerned her false teeth. Like many Europeans of her generation, she believed that gold fillings in your teeth indicated you were wealthy and sophisticated. Anyway, her false teeth had gold fillings, and one morning she woke up to discover her upper plate, which she had left in the dining room cabinet, was missing. Eddie had taken it and sold the gold for enough money to get high that day. I was there when Mrs. Skotnicki realized what had happened and I was torn between shock that Eddie could pull such a stunt and laughter over Eddie's mother screaming at him, unable to pronounce her words properly with no upper plate in her mouth. "Eddju, Eddju, why you take my teeth?" She tried to act all sad and hurt, but Eddie didn't care. He knew that she'd have a new plate in no time, and she did. But she never got gold fillings again.

EDDIE WASN'T STUPID BACK THEN.

He did a lot of stupid things without being stupid, if you know what I mean. What Eddie was, I think, was a kind of natural survivor. He had no sense of morality, fair play or ambition. If he saw something he wanted, he took it. If he could find somebody to take the blame for anything he had done, he used them. And he obviously never learned anything from the punishment when he was caught. To Eddie, rules and laws were jokes. Sometimes the justice system proved he was right.

Eddie was also a first-rate bullshit artist. His stories were outrageous and of course I believed most everything he said. The thing is, I'm not sure I knew the difference between a lie and the truth. Sometimes all that mattered was what worked. Anyway, I wanted to believe him.

He told me he had had his home address changed to 52 because 52 was the jersey number of one of his favourite hockey players. He changed his phone number to include the number 27 in honour of his hero Frank Mahovlich. I mean, stupid boyish stuff. But he really seemed to want it to be true. The fact is, I found this crap kind of endearing.

On the other hand, I remember the time he was out all night on a "score." Eddie was a petty thief. I believed him. Later I found out he wasn't out on a job. He was with a girl.

That was Eddie.

EDDIE WAS ALWAYS TRYING to get me high on drugs. Things to swallow or smoke or snort or inhale or lick—I could take my pick. Except for a couple of times I smoked pot with him, I always declined. Well, almost always. It was a hot July day in 1971, and I had just turned fifteen. Eddie told me we were going to a concert in High Park, on the west side of Toronto. Nobody had taken me to a concert before and Eddie and I didn't do things like that together, so I was all excited. I knew I was going to look good for him that afternoon, especially because my boobs were getting bigger, which made me look sexier, I thought. I didn't know why they were growing, but they were, and it was obvious enough that the boys who hung out at the Grace Street schoolyard across from Eddie's house noticed too.

"Hey, Cathy, your tits are getting really big!" a kid cracked one afternoon after a tip to toe inspection. I had been wearing a top that showed as much of my expanding chest as possible but then realized that my ass was expanding too because my jeans were way too tight. I got Janice to help me zip them up and we had a good laugh about how at least I was balanced now, not like before when I was flat-chested. I guessed I was a late bloomer and I figured better late than never.

Eddie and I took the streetcar to High Park and it looked like it was going to be a huge concert because more people than I had ever seen in one place were flocking in from every which way, all following the same path to where the concert would be held.

Mid walk, Eddie stopped and pulled something out of his pant pocket. He unfolded some paper and showed me something that looked like tiny pieces of broken glass.

"What is it?" I asked.

"Windowpane," he said. "Acid. Take some. Take lots."

I looked closer at what he had and figured that it would take about six of those tiny squares to fit on one penny. Something that small couldn't possibly do much to me, I thought. So I picked up a few of the tiny squares and put them in my mouth, where they pretty much instantly dissolved.

We entered the huge park and sat waiting for the concert to begin. I must have blacked out because I woke up and I was lying on my back on the grass, staring up at the sky. And what an amazing beautiful sky it was! The clouds were whirling and twirling around, making a soft whooshing sound as they did. I was sure that everyone could see and hear what I was experiencing. The clouds became colourful pastels all mixing into one giant cloud; I don't know how long I watched them dance but when I sat myself up, no one was staring at the sky except me. Eddie was sitting beside me and he was watching the band, which had just begun to perform. At first the music sounded fabulous. But then, it got faster and faster and faster and I started getting more and more anxious. Then, when I thought I was going to scream out for it to all stop because the music didn't sound much like music at all at this point, it was playing a gazillion times too fast, the whole park became quiet. I mean dead quiet. No music, no voices, nothing. I looked around; everyone turned to face me and they all pointed at me and starting laughing. I thought I was going to lose my mind. Somehow I managed to leave the park on my own because Eddie had left me by myself. I watched the cars and buses go by in big colourful waves and was pretty intrigued by my hands, which had amazing trails of colours coming off them every time I moved them.

I realized I couldn't go home in the state I was in, so I went to Eddie's house hoping he was there and he was. I went up into his room on the second floor because his parents weren't home and lay on his bed wondering what was going to happen to me next. I didn't have to wait too long. On the wall facing his bed, there was a huge poster of Smokey the Bear holding a shovel and pointing right at me with big black bold letters at the bottom of the poster that read "ONLY YOU." Well, Smokey started growing fangs and salivating and took on a deeply menacing look. Then he climbed over those two bold black words, one furry leg at a time, hell-bent, I was sure, on whacking me over the head with that shovel and killing me.

I didn't wait around. I grabbed my shoes from the floor and went screaming and crying out of the bedroom, tumbled down the two flights of stairs and ran all the way home, where my mother was drinking beer at the kitchen table. Ah, home, I thought. Somewhere I could be comfortable and safe knowing exactly what I got with drunks as opposed to not knowing what to expect from those crazy fucking druggies.

IN JUNE 1971, I went into the washroom at school before class and I overheard some girls discussing how they had to go to the bathroom more often when they had their period, and that's why they were in there for the fifth time that day and it was still morning.

They laughed together and it got me thinking. I couldn't remember the last time I had gone. I was badly constipated.

I hadn't paid attention to my periods, either.

A week later, I found out that I was about five months' pregnant.

CHAPTER THIRTEEN

The joys of motherhood

THAT JULY EDDIE'S MOTHER appeared at our door.

We were still living at my Uncle Johnny's on Bellwoods. She knocked at the front door and my mother went down to answer it. I heard Mrs. Skotnicki's voice and I had no idea what she was doing there. She had never visited before. They walked up the stairs to the second floor and both of them walked into the bedroom where I was. Mrs. Skotnicki started first. "Yeah, hi, Cathy, hi," she said to me. She always repeated things when she spoke in English. Geesh, she spoke better than I did. Now that was a phony if I ever saw one. Then she looked at my mother and said, "I hear your daughter's pregnant, yeah, I heard she was pregnant," as though I was no longer in the room.

My mother asked what the hell she was talking about.

"The whole neighbourhood knows about a Cathy who's pregnant, the whole neighbourhood knows," Eddie's mother said as she shook her head and looked at me with disgust. I felt as if I was going to turn to stone. Unfortunately, I didn't, though I wished that I had, because I was feeling pretty terrified.

"Are you this Cathy that's pregnant?" my mother said, turning to me after Eddie's mother left. "Are you this Cathy that's pregnant?" What? Now *she* was talking like Mrs. Skotnicki?

I told her I didn't know. It was true. I hadn't seen a doctor. I hadn't talked about it with anybody. I wasn't even sure if what we had done would make a baby.

My mother stared at me with an expression that I had come to know so well, the one where she clenched her teeth, folded her arms, squeezed her lips together, narrowed her eyes and shook her head. When she began shouting it was almost a relief because I just wanted to get it over with.

"You brought me shame!" she screamed at me. "Nothing but shame and embarrassment by getting pregnant. You disgust me! You've been nothing but trouble your whole life!"

I said again that I didn't know I was pregnant.

"You have sex, you get pregnant. What are you, stupid?" she said.

I tried to explain that I hadn't known I had had sex for the first couple of months. Then I figured it out.

"What?" She shook her head in disbelief. "How can you not know when you've had sex or if you're pregnant?"

We never spoke much about anything let alone sex. I just sat there and listened to her as her curses and screams all morphed into one loud noise that I no longer understood. But I only had to look at her face to know what she was saying; I didn't need the words anyway.

She began to turn away to walk out of the tiny bedroom, leaving me on the single bed where we both slept. I was terrified. She stopped and then looked back at me and said, "If I had known what you were going to be like when you grew up, I would have drowned you when you were born. You son of a bitch!" I wished that she had drowned me too.

"Mommy—" I called after her, crying.

"STOP CALLING ME MOMMY!" she screamed and walked away. She had told me to stop calling her mommy a few years ago, but I just couldn't because I was so used to calling her that. It took everything I had to keep remembering to call her mom or Mary. It took just as much mental work for me trying to figure out if I was pregnant.

It was Mary, Eddie's sister, who told me to see a doctor. I was about six months' pregnant by then. I went alone, to see Dr. Reingold, a nice Jewish doctor who wore thick black-rimmed glasses and a yarmulke. Well, I didn't know he was Jewish, but I soon found out.

"Hey, Dr. Reingold, why are you wearing a beanie on your coconut?"

He laughed and said, "It's a yarmulke, not a beanie."

"A yamaha?" I repeated, and he corrected me, adding that it was part of his religion and that he was Jewish. We talked more about that yarmulke than we did about my bump. Dr. Reingold had me hop onto his stainless steel table and scoot my butt all the way to the end, where I almost thought I would fall off. Because I was very uncomfortable both physically and emotionally, I thought I would make some idle chitchat to take my mind off what he was doing down there.

Being careful to stare only at the ceiling, with my hands folded lightly over my bulging stomach, I said, "Dr. Reingold, my Uncle Johnny said that everyone should have a Jewish doctor, lawyer, accountant and dentist. Uncle Johnny told me that Jewish people charge more, but it was money well spent because Jewish people were fair and honest." I heard my mother's voice inside my head too saying, "I'd rather work for a Jew than a polack any day!"

He ignored me and in no time flat, said, "Yup, you're pregnant all right. Sit up. You'll be due sometime in December." He gave me a prescription for some vitamins and sent me home. I got the prescription filled a few weeks later when I finally mustered up enough courage to ask my mother for the money. The pills were so large and smelly that I could hardly swallow them.

"Those pills won't help much because that baby is going to take everything out of you anyway, like you did to me when I was pregnant," she said as she handed over the cash. It was the hundredth time in two weeks that she'd told me the same thing. That was why every morning when I woke up, I frantically searched my pillow and bed, wondering when I would find every tooth fallen out from my mouth and scattered in the bed. I was already getting depressed. How the hell was I going to not only find a good Jewish dentist, but be able to pay him too?

A short time after that, Eddie started hitting me.

Maybe it was the hormones; maybe it was the fact that I started catching him cheating with different girls. I was pretty excitable without the added hormones and the infidelities, thank you very much, but now I was off the chart with my emotions. Sure, I gave him a hard time, but I don't think reacting to him getting caught cheating warranted my getting punched in the face. But that's exactly what happened. I was at his place, in the basement where his parents had a TV and couch and dehumidifier that never stopped churning in the corner of the room, with a small bathroom and laundry room attached. You could get to the basement from the back door of the house and that's the entrance I used. "Servants through the back" was what it sounded like to me, when Mrs. Skotnicki would see me try to come through the front door of the house and shout something to Eddie in Ukrainian.

I was particularly upset this night, because I'd caught Eddie at the house of a girl that I knew. "Doesn't Erica mean Irene in Ukrainian?" I yelled at him. I was trying to point out that she was a phony-baloney for having the audacity to change her boring name to something nicer because—what? She thought she would be better with a fancy-schmancy name? Please. But deep down, I knew she was better than me in every way, not only in her name. Her looks, her hair, her clothes, her boobs ... she had it all. And I wanted to be sure she didn't have Eddie too.

As always, he denied everything. It was hard to believe Eddie ever told me the truth because I know I would have lied if I were in his place. He told me to shut the fuck up and sit down or else I could leave. It was about midnight and I wanted to stay. But I didn't shut the fuck up. When he'd heard enough about "Erica," he grabbed a conch shell that was on the coffee table and hauled back and punched me in the face with it. I felt excruciating pain as my left eye tooth went right through my lip and sliced it open. Why did I always bring out the worst in him, he wanted to know? I forgave him. But he didn't take me to the hospital for the couple of stitches I clearly needed. Instead he got some tape and said, "Tape it closed." After I put a piece of tape over the cut on my lip, he stared at me. "I meant your mouth, stupid," he said. "Put the tape over your big fuckin' mouth and maybe you'll know when to shut your trap next time!"

Eddie wouldn't hesitate to smack me across the face or push me hard when he felt that I was out of line. He didn't like me to ask a lot of questions and the more I pressed for answers, the more violent he got. He would always tell me after the fight was over that it was basically my fault. I believed him. After all, I was a problem for most everyone else in my life, so why not for him too?

I HAD OFFICIALLY DROPPED OUT of school the summer of 1971.

I was pregnant and had worked a few odd jobs but nothing to make much money and I had no idea what I wanted to do with my life.

Eddie was used to me bitching about how hungry I always was. That's when he taught me how to pull runners—eating in a restaurant and then ditching before the bill came. At first I did this with Eddie, but I often did it by myself when he wasn't around, and then later in life too. You would think that after my own stints with crappy waitressing jobs and lousy tips that I would feel bad about this. But I didn't. Well, maybe a bit at first but it was crazy how quickly I just put that out of my mind. It was like, They have something I want and I'm taking it. After I found out I was pregnant and had no money, I started pulling runners all the time. The truth is, there were times when I realized how fucking hopeless things were and I felt like I was falling down a deep dark hole. But I didn't know what to do or where to go or how the hell I was supposed to climb out. So I just forced my brain to go blank. I stopped thinking about consequences.

Eddie was pissing me off a lot at that time. He was using more and more drugs and I was trying to get him to abstain. I had learned from my mother how to be a perfect co-dependant, spending a lot of time fighting the addict or alcoholic so that the fighting becomes the basis of your relationship. I understood why I wanted him to get clean, but I never understood why he wanted to be around someone who was clean. I convinced myself that it must have been because of his great love for me, and who can control who they fall in love with? I told my mother that I loved Eddie. She said, "What the hell do you know about love? You think because you had sex with a loser you're in love? You don't know how to wipe your god-damn ass and you're in love. You think Eddie is another one of your stray dogs. You're stupid!"

WAS I IN DENIAL ABOUT EDDIE? Hell, I was probably in denial about everything. What I knew is this: I had a boyfriend. A good-looking one too. When I went to Eddie's home, nobody was yelling at me and telling me I was stupid. I could go to the refrigerator and help myself to good food like cold cuts and fruit and real orange juice, not the cheap powdered stuff my mother bought. So the sex was worth it. It made Eddie happy, and Eddie made me happy. Whatever Eddie did was okay if I could spend time at his place, or if I could just be with him anywhere, doing anything.

When my mother told my father I was pregnant, he came around to my Uncle Johnny's house to visit. He stayed for a very short time talking to my mother in the kitchen in our apartment and then announced that he was leaving. I stayed in the bedroom by myself because I knew everyone was disgusted with me and I was sure he would be too. As he was leaving, he passed by the bed-room and walked into the room. He stood with his hands in his pocket, jingling the change in them, and that always irritated the hell out of me when he did that. "Cathy," he said (jingle jingle), "come to the corner store with me." (Jingle jingle.). "Okay," I re-plied and followed him down the stairs and onto the street. We walked in silence until we got to the corner store. He asked if I needed any money, and I told him I did. He handed me a couple of dollars and I spent it on a bag of chips and a Coke.

When my Auntie Nellie found out I was pregnant, she said, "Why the hell didn't you come speak to me? Didn't you know I give abortions? How could you be so dumb as to get knocked up?" Eddie, of course, was his usual sensitive self. After getting me pregnant with Michael, he started using plastic wrap as a condom.

My parents got back together as though they had never been apart, and we moved out of my uncle's place into a building called the Royal Palace on Gladstone just off Dundas Street. It was a one bedroom and I slept on a mattress on the living-room floor. After the baby was born I moved into the bedroom with a second-hand crib. For some reason, my mother started making me breakfast—usually something she called "a bird in a nest." It consisted of a piece of bread she held over a hot stove burner with a knife and toasted, or rather, burned. Then she would tear a hole in the centre of the bread and place a fried egg there. I guess I should have been grateful that she was making any effort at all, but I wasn't. The Shredded Wheat that she also sometimes served up was topped with water, not milk, and I was told not to use sugar. Both breakfasts tasted like crap. And given my feelings about food, that's saying something. After I quit school I spent most of my time with Eddie or with friends or just roaming around. My mother never offered one bit of advice about having a baby or what to expect, but she did inform me that I would be going to a girls' school, run by nuns, for troubled kids, a place where pregnant sixteen-year-olds were sent to learn how to get along without their babies.

"You go to that school, you have the baby, and you leave it there when you come home."

The hell with that, I thought. I knew I was going to keep the baby—that's one thing I was damn sure about. I was convinced I was having a boy and I knew I would call him Jason Michael. Well, I *thought* I would call him Jason but my mother had other plans.

"WHAT? Niggers call their kids Jason. You will NOT call my grandson a nigger's name!" my mother yelled at me. "What are you, fucking stupid? Who ever heard of such a stupid thing, calling a white kid a nigger's name!" I tried to argue my point, but it was no use. Instead, I called my son Michael Jason and she was barely okay with that.

A few months went by at the Royal Palace and my parents' fighting and drinking picked up exactly where it had left off before they separated. Except this time, it got worse. Now the fighting didn't only happen at night, it started in the afternoons. "You're a fucking whore!" my dad would yell. "Yeah, I had a great fucking teacher!" my mom would yell back. Everyone in my family was a whore, I guess. I rarely stayed at home to hear that type of shit. If I couldn't stay at Eddie's place, I was out all hours of the night mostly by myself, hanging out at the Dufferin Mall or riding street-cars or the subway or walking for hours. I was often cold and hungry and I pulled more runners than I can remember. I slept in janitorial closets in various apartment buildings because *anything* was better than being kept up all night by two drunks who fought and argued non-stop. I hated them.

Maybe if my parents had died when I was young, I'd be forever in love with them. But they didn't. And I'm not. I grew to dislike them even more, if that was possible. I couldn't understand how they didn't see how beaten down I was. How I wanted to be at home so badly. What their relationship and the way they lived their lives were doing to me. I was worn out and I was just a kid. I was alone and scared and didn't know what was going to happen to me. Pregnant. Baby. Then what?

When I awakened my mother early one morning and told her the baby was coming, she got dressed, called a cab and we rode in a taxi to the hospital, each of us on opposite sides of the rear seat, Mom staring out the window on her side and me waiting for the next contraction. At the hospital, she gave my information to the admitting nurse, then left. No "Good luck" or telling me what to expect, nothing. Well, that isn't exactly true. She did tell me that she never uttered a word when she went into labour and she seemed very proud of that fact. "All the women were screaming and yelling when I had you, and I didn't say one bloody word. I kept everything inside," she said. "All the nurses asked me how I did it and I told them what's the point in screaming like a crazy person when you're just having a baby!" Then she said goodbye and I didn't see her again for four days.

I found out later that instead of visiting me after I gave birth, my parents had taken my sixteen-year-old cousin, Janice, to the racetrack. I guess they figured it might be their lucky day.

Toronto Western Hospital didn't exactly welcome me with open arms. I was an unmarried teenage mother whose expenses would be paid by welfare.

Rolling down the corridor on the gurney I heard two or three different women screaming, just as my mother had warned, but in Italian. "Mamma mia! Mamma mia!" they yelled, over and over, their voices echoing all through the hospital corridors and probably through the universe, I thought. Their screams frightened me more than the prospect of giving birth and the unknown. "What's wrong with those women?" I asked the nurse. "Why are they screaming?"

The nurse shrugged. "They're Italian," she said. "They're very religious." I thought about the times I'd gone to church and hoped that all the times I hadn't would work out in my favour regarding how much screaming I would be doing, or rather, not doing.

I was wheeled into a room with all the warm atmosphere of one of the broom closets that I sometimes slept in. In fact, I remember a mop standing in a bucket in the corner of the room. It was a large room and just as cold as my home, but quieter. And I was absolutely pooped, eager to flop down on one of the two beds in the room and wake up after my son was born. I took the bed by the window and settled in, ready to pass out. Nurses soon arrived to take my temperature and time my contractions, and groups of students came in with their gynecologist clinician to examine me as though I were a piece of meat. They asked me the same questions over and over again and I got bored with them all pretty quickly. The mop was better company. At least it didn't talk.

I was in labour for two full days, and my plan—that I'd simply fall asleep and get this whole thing over with—never happened. Each time I slept I was wakened within a few minutes and told to roll over and turn this way and stand on my head or do a somersault or something while a nurse or doctor took my pulse and blood pressure or prodded me inside and out and students or the janitor watched. I wanted it to be over, and until it was over I just wanted to sleep because I barely got any sleep when I was at home and I was at home the two nights before I went into labour. It was as if my parents knew I would be giving birth soon so they partied extra hard and were extra loud.

Hoping to be left alone if I gave everyone a hard time, I began to get really annoyed and decided to fight back a bit. So the next time I got woken up and prodded, I pleaded and begged for them to all go away. I told the group of about a hundred standing around my bed that there was nothing to see down there yet but I would let them know when something that might interest them happened, and that I just wanted to get some sleep. Well that was that. The doctor leaped toward me from the foot of the bed and grabbed me hard by my hospital gown,. He pulled me up from where I was lying and I realized I didn't even have enough energy to fight the mop, let alone a grown man. I just hung there from his hand like a rag doll with my head rolling back and my arms limp. "Sit up!" he yelled at me, his face about an inch from mine. "You're here to have a baby, not to get sleep. You should have thought of that before!"

On my second night in the hospital I knew it was happening, or about to. I rang for the nurse and told her I was about to have the baby. She said, "No, not yet," but I insisted so loudly that she brought in a doctor who ordered me to be quiet, and agreed that the baby wasn't arriving yet. They left me alone for a while. When the doctor came back, he took a closer look and the next minute I was flying down the corridor on a gurney, heading for the delivery room.

A new doctor was there, this one a woman talking instructions from a male doctor, and again I felt like a prop, something inanimate that could be used in a play and that didn't really exist. I gave birth at two in the morning on the dot. I was given no meds or painkillers. I heard the baby cry and waited for someone to tell me if it was a boy or a girl. Nobody spoke until I asked. Someone said, "It's a boy," and I had to ask to see him. Stupid fucking doctors, I thought. If I were a doctor, I'd never treat a patient that way, not even a dumb kid who got herself knocked up. I held my son for a minute until they took him away, and I cried tears of joy. I would make sure to tell my mother that I, like her, did not cry during labour. Maybe she would be proud of me and forget the shame and embarrassment that I'd brought to her. But then, she wasn't there for me to tell her. I would tell her later, I thought. If she came to see me.

With the baby it was love at first sight, and I thought if I had to I would die on the spot for him. I named him Michael. He was the most precious thing in my life. I had a baby boy, just as I was sure I was going to have, and I vowed to give him a better life than I had. As I thought about how difficult it was going to be for me to make my promise come true, I let myself cry for what was only the second—and last—time during my ordeal.

My mother visited once, on the fourth day after I gave birth. She didn't bring me anything like a gift for Michael, and she sat across from my bed just staring at me. I felt pretty uncomfortable. Her silence was more shaming than anything she could ever say. We didn't talk about the birth or how I felt. I wanted her to go and thank goodness she didn't stay long.

The nuns stayed longer. Two sisters of St. Joseph arrived after she left, offering to help me put Michael up for adoption. At first they weren't very direct about it; they beat around the bush, talking about what was best for me and what was best for the baby. They stood the whole time and I felt weird sitting when not one, but two, of God's representatives were standing. I told them that the best thing for the baby was to be with his mother, and when they started arguing with me I told them to fuck off and leave.

They edged toward the door, but they refused to leave the room and were still shooting me some crap about giving the baby a better life. I jumped out of bed and immediately felt pain. Blaming those nuns for making me hurt physically and making me hurt emotionally, I picked up the visitor chair that no visitors but my mother had used as yet and threw it as hard as I could at them. That's when they finally left. "That's for making me eat that crappy tapioca pudding when I was a kid!" I yelled.

I don't regret throwing that chair. I only regret that I missed.

My mother denied sending the nuns around to pick up Michael, but I never believed her.

My father dropped by with a gift: a sexy lime-green negligee. I guess it was his way of acknowledging that I was a woman. Well, a mother at least. I was already starting to miss being a kid and I would for some time to come. I walked up and down the hospital hallway, as the nurse advised me to, wearing the negligee and feeling a bit stupid in it. I would have preferred pyjamas.

I'd been there more than a week before Eddie put in an appearance. I called his house every day, and his mother always gave me the same answer: Eddju was sleeping. He's *tired*. He's *whatever*. When he finally showed up at the hospital I told him I had given birth to his son. Eddie came to the hospital about five minutes before visiting hours were over, saw his son through the glass nursery and said he had to leave.

"Don't you want to hold your son?" I asked.

"Not now. I've got some business to do." And with that, he left. I stood in the hospital hallway staring at Michael, who'd been born with jaundice, wondering what he and I were going to do with our lives.

Mrs. Skotnicki called for two reasons: one, she grilled me like a prisoner under hot lights about whether or not Eddie was actually the father. I assured her he was. I had been a virgin and he had been the one and only. Next, she wanted to know if I was going to have Michael circumcised. I said I would.

She went nuts.

"You can't do that!" she shrieked. Then she started yelling for her husband. "Stanley, Stanley, come here. Cathy … !" The rest was in Ukrainian, but I knew what she was saying. You'd think I'd suggested having the kid beheaded. She went back to English. "You can't circumcise him! You just can't! Only Jews circumcise their kids and he's not a Jew. If you circumcise that baby, you'll have a scar on your soul, don't you understand that?" This was too depressing. First my son would have a nigger's name. Then he would have a Jewish private part. Was everyone crazy? No one wanted to be a part of my pregnancy, but they sure had a lot of things to offer once I gave birth. As for any more scars on my soul? I'd given up on trying to grow my soul or to get God to accept me. I figured he wouldn't miss my trying at all.

I left the hospital with Michael about two weeks after giving birth. The doctors told me I could leave a lot earlier, but Michael would have to stay because of his jaundice. I insisted on staying with my son for however long was necessary. Plus, they fed me three squares a day and both Michael and I didn't have to listen to the fighting and yelling going on at home.

A nurse showed me how to bathe myself and Michael and then I had a quick chat with the doctor before being released. One of the last things she advised me was to stay away from Eddie. It was too risky, she said, for me to have sex for six weeks because I had stitches and the delicate vaginal tissues were strained, bruised and torn. "No sex. Understand? No intercourse, no oral sex performed on you," she said sternly.

Like I needed a doctor to tell me that. I said, "Look, I feel like I just had a small explosion go off inside me. I hear what you're saying." The last thing I wanted was to have a jackhammer poking through all the rubble.

The day after I got home, Eddie came to visit me. He spent a few minutes looking at Michael and then pushed me onto my bed.

"Eddie, no. I've got stitches and I'm sore and torn up inside and the doctor said it could be really bad for me."

I lay there in excruciating pain, praying he would get it over with quickly. I spent the next two weeks being treated for the infection he gave me.

CHAPTER FOURTEEN

Now what?

MY PARENTS WERE pressuring me to marry Eddie.

Let's say I've made my own share of stupid mistakes in my life. Marrying Eddie was not one of them. Thank God.

I guess I had enough smarts to know a bad idea when I heard it, and marrying Eddie was a really bad one. But like my mother, I had to start thinking about the lesser of two evils: living at home or moving in with a loser—exactly what she used to tell me her only two choices were. Eddie's addiction got so bad he would do anything he could find that would get him high. He would steal his mother's nail polish remover, soak Kleenex in the fluid, and walk around holding the Kleenex to his mouth and inhaling the fumes. I still had a little girl's romantic idea of marriage as a permanent thing. Spend my life with Eddie Skotnicki? I wasn't dumb enough to fall for that, so that's why I considered living with him instead.

As a mother, I've let my son down in various ways but I was June Cleaver a a mother compared with Eddie as a father. Eddie didn't know how to be a parent, even with his dad as a pretty good model. The fact is, Eddie didn't know how the hell to do anything except steal and score drugs and manipulate people, so why should he have known how to be a good father?

It didn't help that Eddie's family refused to accept Michael. Eddie's mother continued to believe that I had corrupted her son. She was ashamed of Michael and me—but not of her drug-addicted son.

From time to time, when Michael got older, Eddie would show up demanding to take him somewhere, and I usually agreed because Michael loved seeing him. Whatever else Eddie might have been, he was Michael's father, and Michael knew it. As Michael grew older, he would ask when his daddy was coming to see him again, and I would have to say that I didn't know but it might be soon. Eventually Eddie would show up, often with a car he had stolen, and I would watch with my heart in my throat as he drove away drinking a beer with Michael seated on his lap. On other days, he would promise to take Michael for a ride or to the park. I would dress him up for a day with his dad and Michael would sit by the door, asking when Daddy was coming. He would sit there for an hour, two hours, three hours or more until I would tell him Daddy wasn't coming today after all, and Michael would often blame me.

I couldn't bear remaining at home surrounded by all the tension between my parents, yet I felt a lot of pain and guilt whenever I left to get away for a time, sometimes with Eddie, sometimes by myself, and later with whoever showed they gave a damn about me. Someday Michael and I would find ourselves a new family, a *real* family. Meanwhile, I had Eddie.

There have been more successful thieves in history than Eddie Skotnicki, but none more brazen. To Eddie, every honest job he managed to get was another opportunity to steal something. He drove a truck for a furrier company and, of course, had no idea what happened after he left the warehouse with forty fur coats and arrived at the store with just thirty-five. He especially loved getting work as a valet, parking cars for hotels and restaurants. The job would last long enough for Eddie to get his hands on a fast, hot car and pick me up.

We'd head for a wealthy neighbourhood where Eddie would choose a place with open windows or a door he could open with a single kick in the right place. Sometimes he'd steal disability or welfare cheques out of the neighbourhood mailboxes and cash them. He was good at spotting houses where the people were away on vacation or doing honest work somewhere. Once he got inside the house he would steal jewellery, stereos, whatever wasn't nailed down that he could sell for a few bucks. I always refused to go inside with Eddie. I knew what he was up to and I was grateful for any money he might give me later to feed Michael and me, but I never broke into somebody's house or followed Eddie in.

In some ways, Eddie was a recycler. He managed to make something out of everything he stole. Almost nothing was wasted. If he didn't find money, jewellery or something to sell, he would take the person's identification. Bank and credit card statements were good; a driver's licence was even better. He would use the information to open a bank account and immediately write bad cheques on it, using the stolen ID. If the ID had the owner's picture on it, Eddie knew how to insert his own picture. The phony ID scam was one of Eddie's favourites because nothing connected him with the deal. By the time the cheques came back NSF, Eddie had gone through the money, leaving nothing behind.

Eddie once promised to take me to Nassau, telling me we could have a ball there scoring big with phony cheques. He must have scored enough cash to cover the airline tickets at least, because he showed them to me. We were booked on an early flight, but Eddie picked up some dope the night before and got so stoned that I couldn't wake him up the next morning and we missed the plane. This was no big deal to Eddie. He stole his father's credit card, took off for the airport and bought two one-way tickets on his dad's card.

In Nassau, Eddie had booked the penthouse in one of the most expensive hotels on the island, and this alerted the hotel manager. He looked us up and down, two shabbily dressed kids, and called us into his office where he played detective for nearly two hours, interrogating us individually. We had enough answers to convince him that we were for real, so he let us stay for a week, and during that time Eddie loaded his dad's credit card to the limit. Eddie's father reacted the way he always did when he realized what his son had done. He called Eddie a good-for-nothing bum. That was it. That's all the punishment Eddie got. The next month, Mr. Skotnicki bought Eddie a bright purple mini-bike because Eddie got what Eddie wanted.

Eddie never looked beyond making the next score. To him there wasn't a time when he might get caught and have to pay for things one way or another. There was only now. Now he could steal something, and now he could sell it so that now he could get high. Tomorrow they would catch him but tomorrow never came for Eddie. Everything was now.

When the police would trace the stolen cheques he cashed or the items he pawned back to him, Eddie's first reaction would be to call his lawyer, whom I knew as Mr. Hoolihan. This guy could have gotten Adolf Hitler sprung on a technicality. He was so good at getting Eddie out of jail or getting him a suspended sentence that I called him Mr. Houdini. Whenever Eddie faced a "breaking and entering" charge I'd say, "Mr. Houdini'll get him out," and he always did.

Eddie was plain bad news. Everything he touched somehow got marred or ruined or totally fucked up. Like my very first car. My dad's friend Certainly was over one day and my dad told me that he had arranged for Certainly to give me a car. I was around eighteen and I didn't have a driver's licence. I only had Eddie giving me driving lessons in all the cars he stole. Certainly gave me the keys; he told me that the car was in front of the building and it was a beige-and-white 1956 Chevy. "Oh, my God!" I yelled. "That's the same age as me!"

"Three hundred bucks and she's yours," said Certainly.

"I thought you were giving it to me?"

"Well, certainly, certainly, I'm giving the car to you, but certainly, certainly, I have to get paid."

How was I going to get three hundred dollars? It was more money than I had ever had at one time. There was no way. But Certainly and my dad were plastered so I saw this as my chance to take the car for a test ride. I coaxed the keys from Certainly, who made me promise to be careful, and I ran down to see the car. It wasn't the best-looking car I had ever seen, but it was mine—well, sort of mine—and it was my age. It was fate. It was meant to be.

I ran back up into the apartment and called Eddie. I told him that I had a new car and he needed to come over right away. I hung up the phone, grabbed my coat and went back down to the car to take a better look.

Walking around the car in the January snow, I inspected every inch. It was really old, but it was perfect. It was a two-door, beige in the front and three-quarters down the body, with a white hardtop roof, white fins and whitewall tires. Its chrome sparkled and I wondered if it had even ever been driven. The interior was leather with a large steering wheel and when I turned on the ignition, it fired up strong even though it was freezing outside.

It wasn't long before Eddie showed up and as soon as he got off the bus, I flagged him down from the driver's side window. He was wearing jeans and running shoes and a jean jacket over a sweater. He stood by the driver's side door, hands in his pockets and his jean-jacket collar turned up. "Wow, what have you got here?" he said, all smiles. I could see that he was cold because his cheeks were red. At least he was sober and happy. Before I could say that I wanted to take him for a drive, he opened the driver's door.

"Move over, Cathy."

"But I just got it and I want to be the first to drive it. Please?"

"Look, I'm fucking freezing and you called me here, so now let me drive the goddamn car. Move over!" I slid over to the passenger side as he climbed in. "Besides, you can't even drive good." He put the car into drive mode and left the curb. I couldn't believe I had a car. I was thinking about where I would take Michael in it and how Eddie would now want to be with us both more often, and that was my last thought because just then Eddie clipped the left side of three parked cars and crunched and sheared off the whole front right quarter of my new car. Eddie didn't stop. "Oh, fuck, sorry," he laughed. He quickly glanced my way, the way he might have if he'd just forgotten to do something for me, and he sounded anything but apologetic. I yelled at him that this was my first car and he'd gone and fucked it up in less than five minutes. I called him a loser and an asshole and he just kept laughing. I started punching his right shoulder and Eddie, ducking to miss my punches, pretended he was scared. Basically he thought it was all a big joke. I cried and cried until eventually the whole front of the car started steaming and it rolled to a dead stop. Eddie turned off the ignition and we got out to assess the damage. Eddie shook his head and said he had to leave. As he walked away he called back to me over his shoulder,

"Just let it cool down and it will start up again. It'll overheat again though." I stood there in the middle of the road, cars veering to the left to pass. It was snowing again and I was freezing. I stood at the front of the car, my beautiful car, my first car that was now useless, then I got behind the wheel and waited for who knows how long, head on the steering wheel, crying.

After some time, I started the ignition again and just as Eddie said, the engine did turn over. However, smoke soon began coming out of the engine and I had to stop the car, let it cool down and then start it up again. It took me hours to get back home.

Back in our apartment, my dad and Certainly were even more drunk than when I'd left them. Michael was playing on the kitchen floor. I gave Certainly the keys and said, "Eddie crashed up the car." I felt terrible about it.

"Why certainly, certainly," he stammered. He looked like Mr. Magoo in the cartoons I sometimes saw on Saturday morning, with his bald head and short stature and eyelids that were permanently shut. Except Mr. Magoo could never see where he was going because he was nearsighted, and Certainly couldn't see because he was always drunk.

"Cathy," my dad slurred, waking me out of my Mr. Magoo daze. "What did you do to Eddie to make him smash up the car? You need to get married and give Michael a father!" His voice grew angry. "You whore around and now you need to get your shit and take your kid and go live with Eddie!"

I picked up my son and tried to figure out where we were going to sleep that night.

CHAPTER FIFTEEN

Out of the frying pan...

I GOT A FEW THINGS TOGETHER and bundled Michael into a brand new baby-blue coat that I'd recently bought him and as my dad cursed and shouted in the background, I ran down the stairs crying, not knowing where I was going to go. I ended up taking a bus and then the subway, waiting for there to be no people on the subway so I could change Michael.

I rode the subway all night. I had no job and no money and soon enough I ran out of options and returned to my parents' place. I knew I was making a mistake. But I figured I had no choice. There was so much I didn't know.

Oh, I loved that baby of mine, and in my own awkward and hopelessly ill-informed fashion I tried to give him a happy life. All I wanted was for him to escape all the crap I had put up with. Soon I would learn that that was not enough. Not by a long shot.

We had laughs and warm times, but there weren't enough of them. I never felt I did a good enough job of being a mother. In fact, I know that I failed Michael miserably. Why else wouldn't he want me in his life in his later years? If I could have gone back and met the sixteen-year-old mother that I was, things might have turned out very differently. They say that kids don't come with a handbook but neither do teenage mothers. In fact, I think my teen years made me stupid.

I tried to be a "regular" mother. I always made sure my baby ate and had diapers and his own bed. From the time Michael was two, I would sing that Helen Reddy song to him many nights before he fell asleep: "You and me against the world."

My Auntie Sophie knitted Michael a beautiful blue blanket with satin trim around it and Michael loved it. I used to watch him running the satin trim back and forth between two fingers of one hand until he fell asleep, his pacifier in his mouth. He was so cute! Then my mother said Michael was too old for a pacifier and forbade me to let him have it. When Michael cried for it, she told him that the rats had taken it; I don't know if he stopped crying because he was confused or because he felt it was okay because an animal took it. Regardless, he would stop crying. My mother told me that Michael would get buck teeth if I let him keep the pacifier and I believed her. She said I knew nothing about being a mother and that I acted as though Michael was a toy doll.

Maybe I didn't have a clue how to be a mother, but when I stared into his beautiful blue eyes, I thought that we would always connect just like that, so fully, so easily, no matter what life had in store for us.

MICHAEL WAS SUCH A GOOD BABY. He rarely cried or was fussy.

I took him everywhere I could. I would carry him to nearby Dufferin Mall and sit on a bench watching other kids my age, still in school without a baby to care for, hanging out and having fun. The two of us would fall asleep, me on a bench and Michael in his stroller, and there we'd stay until security told me we had to leave. I did the same things that I'd done before I had Michael, but now I took him along with me. Some nights we slept in schoolyards or anywhere I could find a bench or a dark, quiet corner. The worst was finding shelter from the wind and snow in winter. So many times I prayed for a warm house for us both.

I loved feeding him and spending as much time with him as I could. I remember teaching him the words "eyes," "nose" and "mouth" and pointing to each part of my face so he would start learning how to speak. He had a round, green walker that he could sit in and he'd propel himself around the apartment on his tippy toes in it. Once when I had dozed off he rolled right up to my face and yelled "EYES!" and poked my eyes hard with his fingers. It hurt like hell but he laughed so hard and I couldn't help but laugh right along with him.

By the time he was two he wasn't talking yet except for the odd rare word. I used to panic, thinking that I'd done something wrong when I was pregnant to make him slow; my dad told me that he might be a bit retarded. Around the age of three he started speaking just fine, but it was stressful waiting to see if he had any mental challenges. (When Michael got glasses years later as a teenager, again I convinced myself that I had done something to cause him to have to wear glasses. I believed that all the bad that happened to Michael was my doing.)

At about the same time my mom told me that my dad did things to Michael that she didn't want to tell me about. "What kinds of things?" I demanded to know. "What difference does it make, I don't want to say!" I pressed and she got angry but all she would tell me is that my dad, in drunken stupors, would pick Michael up by his arm and he used to make Michael cry. I felt so horrible about that. I remembered how my dad used to be rough with me and the last thing I wanted was for Michael to get that same treatment. The only difference was that my mother was sticking up for Michael.

At first I supported Michael and me with welfare payments and later by working at various jobs. I got work as a receptionist for a clothing company, sitting at a desk and telephone switchboard, greeting people and connecting callers for $67 a week. I loved the job while it lasted, but after a few months I was unemployed again. I was fired after leaving without permission when I got a call that Michael got hurt at the daycare he attended.

I had enrolled him in daycare so he would be around my dad as little as possible. Michael had to get stitches on his forehead and I blamed the worker for letting my son get hurt. I guess I figured that yelling at her would absolve me of my responsibility or make me feel better as a mother. It didn't. I took Michael out of daycare and got another job. My parents decided to charge me room and board—babysitting included—and since I made only about seventy dollars a month I didn't have much of a choice. They took almost my whole pay, but at least Michael was eating. I was obsessed with making sure he always had food from the time he was born and guilt played a part in my neurosis. I didn't breastfeed because I couldn't stand the process. I tried, but I just couldn't. Plus, the doctor told me that since I would probably be going back to school after I had my son, he would give me medication to dry my milk up. I didn't go back to school. And I ended up with breasts that looked like pancakes, which only added to how ugly and insecure I felt I was. Regardless, he was always well fed.

I WENT TO EDDIE'S PLACE as much as I could in the cold months but that was a hassle too. Mrs. Skotnicki would not let me come through the front door for fear the neighbours would see that I was bringing in a baby. So, even in the winter, she used to make me walk up the alley and wait outside at the back door until it was either dark enough or she was satisfactorily convinced that the neighbours would not see Michael and me. Sometimes she never let me in the house and Michael and I slept in the garage behind the house. The garage had an old couch in it and Eddie would bring me a blanket and something to eat in the middle of the night when his parents were sleeping. Sometimes he wouldn't be home and I would still sleep there. I started to sleep in apartment buildings that had warm hallways or apartment janitorial closets or with strangers I met on the street.

When Michael began walking and responding to his name, my mother's attitude toward him changed. She began calling him her son, which upset me. "I have two children," I would hear her tell somebody, "a son and a daughter." I didn't want to take away potential love that my mother might now be giving my son, so I didn't say much. If she couldn't be loving toward me, then I was happy that she loved my son. Inside, though, and over the years, it broke my heart to learn that my son felt closer to my mother than he did to me. One time when we moved to a place far away from my mother's house, Michael cried and cried because he was so upset to be away from her. That ripped me apart. To know that he loved my mother more than me was too much for me. I knew Michael never cried for me like that. Michael called my mother "Baba" at first and then "Ma." He called my father "Pa." I think because of my mother's intervening with Michael, he saw me as more of a sister than a mother.

From the time Michael was about one year old until I moved in with Eddie when Michael was about four, my mother became a different person because of Michael. I used to think that she did this because she'd blown it with me and now she had a second chance. She used to feed Michael and make sure that he always had food and milk, and then she stopped letting me take him out with me when I wanted to. "You're not taking that goddamn kid with you while you go whore around!" is what she always told me. It would even get physical. I would insist, saying that Michael wasn't going to stay there with them drunk and fighting. She would stand right in front of me and push me hard, challenging me to take him. I felt helpless. I thought at least I would have one person in my life that I could be with and who would love me and my mother stopped that from happening. The only way I could have Michael back was to either move in with Eddie or marry him. If I didn't marry him, my father said, then my kid would be a bastard.

Soon after, I left my parents to live with Eddie. Jumping out of the frying pan into the fire best describes that move.

CHAPTER SIXTEEN

My hero

EDDIE PICKED ME UP one day in a stolen white van and we checked into a motel near the Toronto airport. I knew he was up to something because he was always up to something. Eddie didn't take me to a motel just for sex. Not that day anyway.

You had to hand it to Eddie. He thought big in a really small way. All night long when he wasn't in bed with me, Eddie was out in the hall looking for rooms he could enter. He'd walk into a room bold as brass and walk out with the television set. He'd load it in the van and come back to our room for a while, wait for a few minutes, then go out looking for another room and another television set.

After all that hard work he finally fell asleep. In the morning we woke up to find the van blocked so it couldn't be driven off the parking lot, along with a note from the manager on the windshield advising that the police would soon be arriving. I thought, Who leaves a note on the windshield of a stolen van full of hot TVs?

When Eddie was identified as the van's driver, he used a brilliant tactic to have the charges against him dropped. He said I did it. While he had been sleeping in the motel room, Eddie claimed, I had scooped the TV sets into the van, which, by the way, I had stolen as well. Eddie was just an innocent guy with a larcenous girlfriend.

The police saw this as a crock of lies but Eddie, whom Mr. Houdini arranged to get released on bail, begged me to tell the police it was true. "You're a girl and you're young, without a criminal record," he said. "They'll do nothing to you with a kid, but I'll get a three-spot in the can this time. Do you want me to go to the big house for three years, away from you and the kid?"

No, I didn't want that. So I told the police Eddie was innocent. Somehow the charge for stealing the van was dropped but I confessed to stealing the TV sets out of the rooms. To the cops it was either laughable or tragic and they didn't believe for a second that I pulled off a classic Eddie Skotnicki scam. But they had a detailed confession from me that they couldn't ignore. And the cops got me to carry the TVs one by one all they way down the long cop shop hallway to prove that I could carry them all by myself. So I did and that took all the physical strength my five-foot-eight, 110-pound frame could muster. I was fingerprinted and charged and sent to the Don Jail, a place where people from hundreds of years ago would feel right at home, if home was a dungeon. The walls were stone, the cells were cold, the food was awful. I spent an entire week there, just me and the rats and every tough female in the city.

After the female prison guard thoroughly checked me over inside and out, if you get my drift, I was taken to a cell where another female prisoner was lying on the bottom bunk bed. "That's yours," she said, pointing up toward the top bunk. She did not take her eyes off of the magazine she was reading. Eddie told me that jail was a criminal college, so I was interested to see who I would meet there. He also said that cops were stupid to think that putting people in jail rehabilitated them. Instead, they organized their next score and made even more contacts for more and more criminal success once they got out. He said it was like the government was paying you to become a better thief. And you didn't have to pay bills or cook food and how fucking great was that?

I wasn't interested in meeting future accomplices; I just wanted to be accepted. During the day, I did hundreds of sit-ups during our free time, showing the other inmates that I felt right at home. A few women asked me what I was in for and, although there was idle chit-chat here and there, I didn't make any new friends, or rather not any that I wanted to keep on the outside. One day I saw a bunch of women in the general socializing area all sitting down doing something. I was curious to find out what was going on so I walked over and asked one of them what they were doing. "We're making tampons. You need any?" she asked. "Ah, no, I won't be here that long, I'm hoping. But thanks anyways," I replied. She went on to explain that the prison didn't provide tampons, only sanitary pads, so the inmates had a bit of an assembly line every Wednesday at two o'clock, taking sanitary pads apart and refashioning them into tampons. People can sure be creative if they need something.

At night in prison, especially the first night, I felt claustrophobic when the cell door closed for lockdown. I had to talk to myself to keep from freaking out. Only when the rats came into my cell did I calm down a bit, because they gave me something else to focus on.

The rats owned the jail, not the prisoners. They were the only things that were free inside the place. The guards had to work and the inmates had to wait, but the rats went wherever they chose, especially at night. I felt a bit special that a few came to see me. It was almost as if they were sent from my parents' place to welcome me.

The other inmates in the women's wing of the jail freaked out over the rats, but they didn't scare me. I didn't make pets out of them, which I'd wanted to when I was a kid; I just watched them the way I used to when I'd crawl around under the kitchen table and feed them cheese.

Seeing rats was far less upsetting than not seeing Michael. He was with my parents, and I hated being away from him, hated leaving him in the middle of the same disgusting mess I had experienced as a kid. I didn't have to wonder if he was being fed now that my mother had taken on that responsibility, but I did wonder if he was crying as my parents threw punches at each other and he watched. I felt sick to my stomach and if I didn't get out of that hole soon, I knew I'd start thinking about breaking out.

Aside from feeling guilty about Michael, I slept okay in jail once I got over feeling claustrophobic. Compared with the years I spent with my parents fighting and yelling, jail was a breeze. If I could have been with Michael in jail, I would have been just fine.

Although I was only in jail a week, no one was being proactive about getting me out. I called my mother and "pestered her"—her words—to get me out on bail. "What the hell do you want me to do about you being in jail?" she'd say. "It's your goddamn fault. You're no good and you're trouble for me all the time. Stay there and rot!" And she'd hang up the phone. I'd hear Michael crying or gurgling in the background when I called and that made it all the worse. I thought, Well, she's got Michael and she's much happier with him, so I'd better forget about her finding a way to help me out. The next day, I would call her again. "I told you, I don't have any bloody money, so stop asking me!" she would answer.

Finally I told her to call Uncle Johnny, explained what she should say to him and insisted she call him as soon as she'd hung up the phone with me. A few days later my mom and Uncle Johnny showed up to the prison. I was advised by a guard that I was getting bailed out and a judge appeared to sign some papers. I was put on probation for two years. As I walked by him, now out of prison garb and in my street clothes, he said to me, "Well, now that I see you all dressed, maybe you really don't belong in prison after all." I said, "I probably do," and left.

I didn't blame Eddie for telling the police I had stolen the sets. You do what you have to do to survive. Besides, I sort of liked that I was helping him out. Maybe he would eventually see that it was better to keep to the straight and narrow instead of living the life he was living. I imagined Eddie giving up drugs and drinking and becoming the person his family and I thought that he could be. But that never happened. Eddie knew how to sweet-talk almost anybody into doing whatever was needed to save his ass.

My parents' wedding, the saddest day of my mom's life, she would always say.

My dad just after he married my mom.

My dad with me when I was born.

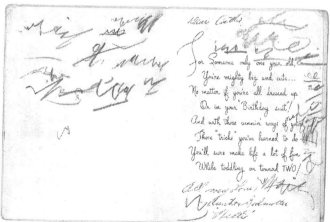

My mom and me in our backyard on Niagara Street.

The kind of scribbling I did because my mom wouldn't give me paper. Card was from Auntie Nellie, the abortionist in the family.

The only real birthday party I ever had as a child. I was nine.

My ill-fated birthday tricycle Sally, on Cameron Street.

My Uncle Johnny and one of his disposal trucks.

My dad after his ankle surgery from falling off a scaffold at work.

The picture on the table at my Auntie Nellie's place. She's in
a nurse's uniform that she bought from a second-hand store.

With two of my cousins in front of Bellwoods just before
Mrs. Skotnicki confronted me and my mom about my pregnancy.

In front of the apartment on Brock Road just before I was
molested under the bridge.

With my cousin Janice when I was fifteen years old.

First year at Central
Commerce and
already pregnant.

Me at ages fifteen
and sixteen and
holding Michael.
Taken at Dufferin
Mall where
I sometimes
slept all night.

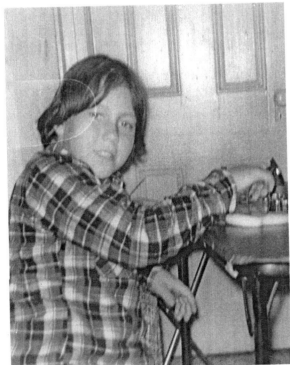

When I was living with Eddie and Michael in Scarborough.

Michael at my parents' place.

Picture taken
when I lived with Louise.

In Florida, when I
went with Louise.

The infamous wedding
cake with the daisies
patching up the crack
on the bottom layer.

Dancing with Michael
at my wedding to Henry.
I am wearing the dress
my mother picked out
for me. I hated it.

The cruise I took Michael on.

At my dad's funeral.

My student cards from the University of Guelph
and University of Saskatchewan Medical School.

In Saskatoon, weighing in at 260 pounds.

The basement room Michael and I lived in just before I met Marc.

With Marc, my best friend and love of my life.

CHAPTER SEVENTEEN

You can always depend on family

EVERYONE IN OUR FAMILY respected my rich Uncle Johnny.

He was a hustler and a con man and a swindler. The truth is, he was a sick bastard with a demanding nature whose idea of a good time was humiliating people. No one liked him. When he told you to come visit him, you ran. In exchange for his humiliating you to no end, or berating you for being stupid or fat, or not letting you get a word in edgewise while he preached what was right and wrong about you, you could expect to eat or get a few bucks or maybe both. He would take you to restaurants and let you order things that you wouldn't otherwise be able to afford on your own, like seafood or hundreds of dollars worth of Chinese food, or he might take you on a trip to see a famous comedian perform in New York, or take you grocery shopping. But let me explain what you might have to put up with if you visited Uncle Johnny:

If you were at his place, he'd offer you a drink. He'd serve it up and then ask you to taste it and let him know what you thought. When you said it was fine, he would then laugh his head off and tell you that he had just shoved his finger up his ass before putting it in your drink and giving it a good stir. It was as if he'd just told the world's funniest joke. That was Uncle Johnny's sense of humour. Sometimes he would pour half a glass of hot sauce into your drink. He was crazy, but everyone still kept coming around. Me? I was a squirrel trying to get a nut.

Uncle Johnny looked like the actor Alec Baldwin on a bad day and twenty years from now. He had Baldwin's knife-edge, piercing blue eyes. He smoked cigars, and when he looked at you with those strange, mad eyes, a look that practically pinned you to the wall, you waited for him to tell you what he was going to do or more precisely what *you* were going to do. "Now, you gonna go to the grocery store. Right? Then you gonna buy two lemons. Right? Not three lemons. Two lemons. Okay? Then you're gonna git in the car and drive to the next store. There you gonna buy muzzels. Right? Make sure da muzzels are fresh, goddamn it!" He was a control freak extraordinaire. I would have to drive to three or four different stores miles apart, just to save a few cents on sale items at each. I'm sure that it cost him more for the gas it took me to drive to these places in his car than if he'd just had me buy everything at one store, but there was no telling him.

He couldn't read and couldn't write and he could barely form a sentence that you could understand. Potato was podadoe. Bounced cheque was bouncie cheque. Across was acrossed. Ask was axe. Barbwire was bobby wired. And his company, Wellington Disposal, which my father helped him start after his own construction company closed, was his bidness. You get the point.

Once he bought two beautiful Doberman puppies named Casey and Judo. They were amazing. He abused them terribly before literally kicking them out the back gate into an alley, telling them to fuck off. The dogs never returned and I always wondered what became of them. Uncle Johnny never cared. He said it was a "doggy dog world." "Dog EAT dog world, idiot," I said under my breath so he wouldn't hear.

My mother tried to explain that Johnny had been terribly abused by his own father, as they all were, and that's why he enjoyed dominating and humiliating others—his employees, his friends, his own family. All the crap he took from his father he passed along to everyone else in his life, almost every day of his life. It's as if he multiplied the pain and spread it around to other people like some virus, some epidemic of misery and degradation.

Johnny made a lot of money from his company and, I suspect, from other things he did as well. For example, he told me that he would bring his dump truck to the dump and pay off the worker if he said that he was bringing in more copper scrap than he really was. Whatever money he made, he spent a lot of it on gold and silver bars hidden in his house and his office, and on flashy cars like the Corvette and the Mercedes that he rarely drove. He collected property and houses like some people collect stamps. In our family at that time, the money gave him power over everyone, including me.

But it was more than money. He had charisma, an ability to draw people to him and make them do things they would never do, or never imagine doing, for anyone else, even though they knew Johnny was evil. I always believed that evil existed, but I didn't know that it also attracts a lot of normally intelligent people. In later years he asked me to bring some women that I knew to his place— a friend of mine and Eddie's sister, Mary—and he slept with both of them. Hookers were his dates of choice, though, but he developed such bad business relationships with all the escort agencies in Toronto that eventually they wouldn't send him any girls because he was too much trouble and he was too warped. Now, if a hooker says you're too warped, you've got problems.

Just after I had Michael, I went to Uncle Johnny for the same reason others went to him: I was desperate and I needed money. I was out of a job and starving—there was even less food in the house than before because over time, my parents' drinking, smoking and gambling increased. So I raided restaurant dumpsters or wrote bad cheques or pulled runners. But pulling runners with a stroller and baby was ridiculous. I didn't dare try to pull that stunt in the same restaurant twice, and considering that I had to have flat pavement to escape with a stroller, the pickins' were getting slim. I was on welfare for a while, but my dad made me give him the money for rent, and since he always borrowed in advance, I never saw a penny. Finally I visited Uncle Johnny, looking for help, money, a job, a shit sandwich—anything. I mean, I was desperate.

He listened to me, leaning back in his chair, looking me up and down and grimacing. Then he took his cigar out of his mouth and pointed it at me as he spoke. "Let's face it," he said, "you got dished a lousy life with drunks for parents and no chance at nothin', so you gotta' accept it an' make the most of it, right? Take whatever you can get and be happy about it. There's lots a' guys out there, right?"

He was setting me up for his advice. He had a nervous twitch in his shoulders and every so often he would jerk one or both shoulders. It was very distracting.

"You got yourself knocked up, right?" he said, blowing cigar smoke at the ceiling, "and you got no education to speak of. No skills, no work experience, so you're not a hell of a lot of use to anybody, right? You're big like a baby pony too with a fat ass, right? No one likes a fat baby pony in a girl. Am I right?" Then he started to laugh like crazy. "Buddha said you should have called her when you got knocked up, but you ain't smart like that, right?" He called my Aunt Nellie Buddha because she was overweight.

I nodded, wondering where the hell he was going with all this and when I would get to eat. When he talked, he often talked just for the sake of talking. Like my mother, he expected you to nod and listen, no matter what shit he was dishing out. He leaned forward and lowered his voice a little. "Once in a while, I hire some girls," he said. "Nice girls. They just got a lousy start in life, like you. They make a lot a money. Right? Ya' understand? You'd be surprised how much fucking money these girls make, and it ain't hard work. It ain't work at all, you come right down ta it. Mind you, they're not fat baby ponies like you are." He then went over to his fridge and opened the door. From the back of the fridge, he pulled out a huge bag of pot. "Most of them like this stuff," he said, "so I make sure I always have whatever drugs they want on hand. Stupid bitches. I never touch the stuff," he added, as he pounded back a huge glass of straight vodka. Yeah, that was better, I thought.

I didn't have to ask him what these girls did. I already knew.

For a few months after that, I slept with guys who worked for Uncle Johnny and guys who hired his company, and he would pay me. The pay was more than I could expect to earn from a regular job, assuming I could have found one. And most of the guys treated me all right. Will was the first set-up. I came to Uncle Johnny's apartment one day, without Michael, as he requested. When I walked into the kitchen, he was sitting at the kitchen table with Will.

"Ya' wanna' drink?" Uncle Johnny asked. I declined. He laughed. He told me to come with him and he walked me into his bedroom and shut the door. "Look. Will's here," he said, stating the obvious. "He wants to show you a good time, right? You go to the Executive Inn with him. You have a good time, right? Don't leave the hodell. And here." And with that he presented me with five twenty-dollar bills. My eyes lit up. He laughed and said, "See. Pretty good, right?" He walked me back into the kitchen. Will had obviously been given the pitch before I got there.

"Okay, let's go," Will said. Will was about a foot shorter than me, he had false teeth and he wore a gold wedding band on his ring finger.

Later on when I called Uncle Johnny when I was broke, he told me to show up at whatever hotel to meet whomever and I did. The money always went toward toys or clothes or food for Michael and me and I didn't feel one bit guilty for what I did. I hated my uncle, but I didn't feel guilt.

When he wasn't playing the role of pimp, Johnny would get his jollies in strange, cruel ways. Once he called me at home and told me to take a cab to his house. "I got a lot a Chinese food comin'," he said. "Are you hungry?" Dumb question, I thought. I was already salivating. "Come on over and have some. Call a cab an' tell 'em I'm payin' for it, right? Okay?"

So I rode to Uncle Johnny's place and told the cabbie to wait while I went to the door and got money for the fare. But when I rang the bell and pounded on the door Johnny didn't answer. I could hear him laughing inside. He wasn't going to open the door no matter how hard I banged on it or for how long.

I realized what he was doing. He was having fun making me feel and look like a jerk, and when the cabbie looked away for a moment I ran like hell down the street into an alley. Let the cab driver bang on Johnny's door all night. I walked as long as I could and then decided to hitchhike, because not only was it freezing but it had also started to snow.

Another time, he said he was taking me to the Bahamas for a few days along with Will and Will's wife. He got the tickets, made the airline reservations, drove us to the airport and when we arrived he claimed he'd forgotten his passport. He told us to get checked in while he went back home to get it.

He never returned. I flew to the Bahamas with Will and his wife, who kept looking at me suspiciously as though she must have known something was going on between Will and me, even if it was strictly a business deal. Uncle Johnny had made no arrangements for me to stay in the Bahamas. He never intended to come.

Will and his wife had money and hotel reservations, and he made sure they avoided me because he didn't want his wife to learn about the two of us and the deal Uncle Johnny had made. I had nothing. No money, no hotel room, nothing.

I thought about sleeping on the beach but after two nights of staying up with five days left to go, I figured that I needed to do something else. So I did the only thing I knew how to do, the only thing that worked for me. I slept with guys who would let me share their bed and would buy me food. One of them was a football player with the Miami Dolphins. He was huge, the biggest guy I had ever seen in my whole life. I stayed with him for a few nights until he left for home.

Then I hooked up with another man from New Orleans who was a big-time gambler and very wealthy, or so he said. We spent one whole night drinking champagne on the beach and we watched the sun rise and although it was as beautiful as a picture postcard, I could only think about the goddamn hard, cold sand and how a nice warm bed would have been preferable. I thought to myself, geesh, if I knew earlier that I'd be sleeping on the beach all night anyway, why the hell did I spend it with this idiot? But I only called him an idiot in retrospect, because he gave me his contact number to call him when I got back home. He was from New Orleans and wealthy like I was an heiress. In reality, I was hoping that maybe he really did like me, and if that meant that my life would be just a little bit better, then great.

When I returned to Canada, Uncle Johnny asked, "Did Will's wife 'n' you have fun? That was pretty good, right? Never take your ol' uncle for granite again, okay?" And he laughed his stupid head off.

Uncle Johnny never tried to have sex with me. I guess screwing his own niece was too much even for his lousy standards. But he did the next best thing. He had a videotape machine and a library of porno movies, and he would invite me into his bedroom to view them, telling me to sit on the foot of his bed and watch the TV screen while he lay in bed behind me. "Keep your eyes on the screen," he would say, "and watch what happens with this really volumptuous broad, okay?" If I started to turn around he'd tell me to keep my goddamned eyes on the TV, and I realized he was masturbating while watching the dirty movies with me sitting between him and the television set.

Later at my Uncle Johnny's funeral, one of his employees would tell me that my uncle did things that a man should be put in prison for. What my uncle did with me was only a drop in the bucket next to what he did to other people.

CHAPTER EIGHTEEN

Learning from my mistakes?

ABOUT A YEAR AFTER I had Michael, I got pregnant again.

I had just turned seventeen. I had no idea who the father was. Between Eddie and guys I slept with when Eddie threw his fooling around with other girls in my face, plus the guys Uncle Johnny set me up with, the father could have been anyone of them.

This time, I called Auntie Nellie. All I said was, "I need to talk to you," and right off the bat she asked how far along I was. I guessed two months but I didn't know for sure. "Come over and see me tomorrow morning," she said, "and bring sixty bucks with you. If you don't have the sixty bucks, don't bother coming over. Understand?" I did understand. But I didn't have sixty bucks.

At the time I was living with a girlfriend, Alice. The place was cold and dirty; my room was in the basement and I slept on a used mattress on the cold concrete floor beside a drain that gurgled endlessly. The mattress was squished between double washing basins on one side and the hot water tank on the other. From the mattress you had a great view of the furnace, which was never on. I brought Michael there to live with me and after a few weeks, I brought him back to my mother's house and I stayed at Alice's alone.

Alice was married to a Yugoslavian man who beat her up nightly while calling her a fat pig and other obscenities in Yugoslavian. It was just as bad as what happened at my house. And also like at my house, they had a baby who had to listen to all that crap while crying in the background. I used to wonder the same thing about Alice as I did my mother: Why didn't she just leave the jerk?

Alice had this ring that had been her mother's. I don't know why but she gave it to me. It was a big diamond in a pyramid setting of eighteen-carat white gold. It was ugly, but I knew it was very valuable.

I had to think fast so I called my Auntie Olga and told her that I needed money for Auntie Nellie. Olga knew exactly what I was talking about because she herself was a client of Auntie Nellie's. When we all lived together at Johnny's house, Olga came home one morning after being out all night and when I looked at her, I knew what was going on. As she walked by me she said, "It was twins."

Anyway, that night I took the ring to Olga. "Can you please hold this for me," I said, "until I can afford to pay you back the sixty dollars?" Auntie Olga looked at the ring and was instantly interested in helping me out. She gave me the money. However, when I eventually had the money to buy the ring back a few months later, Auntie Olga told me the ring was hers and that I had in fact sold it to her. Besides, she said, I had taken longer to pay the money back than I had promised. "But I'm your niece," I was about to cry. I'd never seen that side of her before. I know years later she had the ring redesigned and she proudly showed it to me. "Look what I did with your ring. Remember this?" Adding, "I had it appraised and you were right, it's worth a lot!" Great. I told her that the ring sure looked better now, but to myself I thought, That ring has bad blood all over it. I think she passed the ring down to her daughter when she died, although I never saw Janice wearing it.

Auntie Nellie kept budgie birds and she used to breed them too. She let them fly around her apartment as if it was some tropical rain forest. They crapped all over the place; I guess the upside was she actually trained them to talk. I was pretty impressed. I thought only parrots talked. She gave them all names and her favourite was Georgie Porgie. That bird said his name over and over again non-stop. At first, it was cute. But when you're in the situation I was in, lying on your aunt's bed naked from the waist down at 7:00 a.m. and having turned over all the money you own in your life, well, it got a bit much.

When I arrived, she told me to come in and as soon as she shut the door behind me, she held out her hand and said, "Where's the sixty dollars?" Maybe she thought I didn't have it with me or something. I handed her three twenty-dollar bills and she relaxed.

She told me to go into the bedroom and take my pants off and lie on the bed, ass as close to the bottom edge of the bed as I could get. She walked into the room with a brown paper bag and a stool, which she sat down on; then I could hear her rummaging through the bag. I let my mind watch Georgie Porgie fly around the bedroom, trying to guess where he was going to crap next and lost. Just like I was losing on that bed right then and there. Eddie's words rang in my head. "You can't have another fucking kid! I'm a kid and you're a kid and when that kid asks me for something, I'm gonna have to go to my fucking dad and ask him for shit for my kid!" I had told Eddie it was his baby because I wanted to believe that it was and that I would have a brother or sister for Michael. I really didn't see the difference between having one kid or two. I knew it would be tougher, but I simply dealt with whatever life dished out to me unless someone said something otherwise. Eddie, however, said a lot otherwise about this pregnancy.

My aunt never told me what she did down there as I lay on her bed, and I didn't ask. While she was doing what she was doing to me, I kept wanting to yell out, "NO, STOP!" and run out of her apartment. It took everything in me to not do exactly that. I kept thinking about what kind of life I would give this baby and I was torn between believing that it wouldn't be much more work and that it might grow up hating me for letting it come into my messed-up life.

I just wanted to get it over with already so I could get the hell of out there, away from her yappy birds and her phony-baloney pictures of long ago showing her in a nurse's uniform—even I knew she never was a nurse; no one had to tell me that. She also had pictures of her in an army outfit and she told everyone that she'd been a WAC. However, the army outfit was purchased at a second-hand store, as was the nurse's outfit; everyone in the family knew that. But few knew she had performed literally hundreds of abortions that kept her sisters eating and partying it up. My mother says she ate lots of times because of Auntie Nellie. I wondered which sisters would be invited to splurge on my sixty bucks.

When she'd finished she told me that it was done and it would now "happen." That's all she said. She was as gentle down there with me as an auto mechanic. I was glad it was finally over so I no longer had to decide one way or the other. As the day went on, though, I felt regret, remorse and guilt. I hated myself for not standing up to Eddie and for being too confused to be able to think the whole thing through properly. I wanted there to be someone I felt I could have gone to about this, but there wasn't. Eddie controlled what I did with little effort and, his kid or not, he wanted me to have an abortion.

When the intolerably painful cramps finally came, a few hours after I left Auntie Nellie's place, I was happy and thought of nothing except letting in the pain. I believed I deserved to feel as though I was dying and maybe I would, because I didn't know what to expect. I knew I couldn't go home. Last thing I needed was to hear my girlfriend Alice and her loser husband fighting. And I couldn't go to my parents either because they'd be drinking and fighting too. So I went to the Grace schoolyard alone and huddled in the corner against a cold brick wall, where I stayed in a fetal position for who knows how long. The pain became so intense that I started moaning and rolling around on the ground. I had to go somewhere, but I didn't know where. As I thought about my limited options I remembered a friend I met at school lived really close by. I somehow pulled myself up and eventually made it to her front door. By this time, it was around 11:00 p.m.

When Gail answered the door, I was in a heap on her porch. I couldn't stand and I was moaning, unable to speak. Immediately she helped me to my feet and took me up the stairs to her bedroom. Through my pain and in short gasps, I told her what had happened and I asked if I could just please be alone. She went to bed and I stayed on her bedroom floor. A few hours later, I ran to her bathroom, waking her in the process. As I sat on the toilet, something dropped out of me and into the toilet bowl. But it just hung there and I started freaking out. "Gail, Gail," I sobbed, "please help me." There was blood all over the place. Handing me a straight razor, she told me to cut the umbilical cord and I reached into the toilet and did just that. Then she told me to stay there because the placenta would come out next. I was covered in blood. I didn't look into the toilet; I wanted to, but I couldn't.

I prayed, almost begged, for God to strike me dead. Later, when I had time to think things over, I told myself that I really didn't want the abortion and that I had no right to take a life. I wanted a refund and it was too late.

At 6:00 a.m. I left Gail's house. I hung my head down and walked back to the schoolyard and stayed there until the kids started showing up for school. I hated myself. I hated my life. No one gave a shit about me and I felt as alone as when you're dead, except that I had Michael. That was the only reason I could justify not being dead. I heard my mother's voice in my head saying, "You're born alone and you die alone and no one gives a shit about anyone!" I agreed. I thought of Michael, who was at my parents' apartment right now, probably screaming at the top of his lungs from all the fighting and yelling and drunkard craziness going on. No one was on my side and now I'd just killed the chances of having a second person in the whole world who would maybe really love and care about me some day.

I went to my parents' place, still bleeding profusely. With no money for sanitary pads, I did what my mother did and packed a wad of her rags into my pants. Then I bundled Michael up, put him in a stroller and walked the streets for hours. We didn't go back home for days. I found an apartment building with a dead-end area on the main floor, and Michael and I slept there. I begged for money and took care of Michael. I didn't eat. Then we stayed in the little janitor's closet outside my parents' apartment. Although I could hear the yelling and fighting through the walls, I figured I had no choice: I had to move back home. It was no better living at Alice's place. But I would wait one more night so that at least they'd be sober and quiet in the morning. By that time my parents had stopped carousing at night. I think having Michael around had something to do with it.

When I walked in looking a mess my mother said, "You goddamn no-good slut. Where have you been?" My dad chimed in,

"You're nothing but a whore!" My mother picked Michael up and told me I was to never take him out of the house ever again without her permission. Once more she was acting as if he was her kid. Michael said "Ma" when he saw her and I corrected him: "That's Baba, not Ma!" She never corrected him. She said, "So what's the big problem with what he calls me?"

While in my mother's arms, Michael turned his head to look at me. He was smiling with that cute chubby face and those beautiful, bright blue eyes and my heart melted. I knew that I would probably only ever be able to give him love because I had nothing else to give. But even showing love to Michael was getting more and more difficult for me. Just surviving took up a lot of my energy and focus. Every time I moved out of my parents' place, I'd try to take Michael with me to get him out of the craziness, and then I'd realize we'd have to move back in.

It was mentally and physically exhausting. I wanted nothing more than to be with my son in a quiet, safe environment and I never could do that for him. I started withdrawing emotionally and feeling defeated. Life seemed to hold nothing in its big hands for me and I wondered if I'd ever live on my own with Michael and be happy. Though I still found joy in my son when I spent time with him, often I was depressed, miserable and sad.

I had to find a way to get out of my parents' place once and for all.

CHAPTER NINETEEN

I fly into the cuckoo's nest

IT SEEMED MY RESOLVE to create a better and more stable life for Michael and me was just a dream.

I met this guy—I'll call him Steve—on the street and it didn't take me long to tell him that I needed a place to stay. I didn't tell him about Michael until I just showed up with him one day. He wasn't thrilled. He never said one word to Michael the entire time we were there. I slept with Michael on a cot out in the hallway. After a few weeks Steve started pressuring me to have sex in exchange for a place to stay.

I couldn't stand living there. I wanted to move out so badly, but I stayed anyway for about three months, keeping my eyes and ears open to find another place to live. I began to realize that Steve was really mean and might become violent. He would make loud noises around the apartment, dropping and banging things, and this was just as bad as being at my parents' place, except this guy didn't drink. But he did smoke a lot of weed. He started giving me dirty looks and the looks turned into threats. "Look, either you start fucking me," he'd say, "or you're out on the streets. It's your call. But I'm not going to have you here for fucking nothing!" So, I did what I always did: I went somewhere else in my mind while he did what he wanted to do with me. It was best if I took Michael over to my parents' place to live again. But every time one of Steve's friends came over to visit I would size him up as a potential new guy to live with.

I was on and off welfare for years. If I wanted a place of my own it would have to be dirt cheap. One day I found a one-room dump on the third floor of an old house in the College and Spadina area of Toronto. The place was furnished but with the oldest furniture in the whole world. It had a pull-out couch and a small table with one chair. It was dark and cold and musty. I had a blanket and a pillow that the landlord provided and they must have been in use since the early 1900s because the pillow was so yellow it was almost brown, and the extremely rough blanket had more holes in it than Swiss cheese. The landlord said that I could use his phone, but only for emergencies. That was fine. No one called me and I rarely had an emergency that I couldn't fix on my own.

I wasn't doing any better than my parents had done, I thought, as I stood in the middle of my new one-room shack trying to figure out what to do about getting Michael again. Then all of a sudden, I started getting really bad pains in my stomach. That whole night, I was in excruciating pain and I didn't sleep. The next morning I made my way down to the landlord's place and asked him if I could use his phone to call the doctor. He said, "I thought you never had emergencies, eh?" and laughed. I was unable to laugh because I was in agony, but I managed to look up Dr. Reingold, the doctor I had been seeing for years, and he told me that the gynecologist, Dr. Valtchev, was in and could see me. Dr. Valtchev had put an IUD in me a few months earlier. I hitch-hiked to his office, which was reasonably close.

Dr. Valtchev examined me and told me that my IUD, called a Lippes loop, had somehow gotten imbedded in my uterus muscle wall and that wasn't good. I told him that I thought something with such a stupid name would only cause problems and he laughed and said that maybe I was right. He then told me that he was going to have to tear it out of me, which would be very painful, but there was no other choice. He did what he had to do and the pain was horrible. It felt as though he were ripping my insides right out of me, and I could hardly walk afterwards. Then he told me I would now have to use an alternative method of birth control. Later I would find out that I was sterile and could not have any more children even if I wanted to, and I felt this was God's way of punishing me for having that abortion.

Dr. Valtchev gave me a prescription for Percocet (acetaminophen and oxycodone) and told me to be careful because the drug was highly addictive, but for the level of pain that I was in, I needed to take it. I was in so much pain that I gobbled up the meds as soon as I got the prescription filled at the pharmacy below the medical clinic. Trying to hitchhike while standing hunched over, holding my stomach and moaning out in pain every few seconds made it really tough to get a ride and I was pretty sure no one would pick me up. Well, no one except some sick fuck.

A car pulled over; the male driver was about forty years old and that's all I noticed because I just wanted to get inside the car and get home and I was focused on getting into the car carefully and slowly. He asked where I was going and I gave him the intersection. He said, "Give me your address and I'll take you right home, no problem." I run on instinct and I didn't think giving him my address was a good idea. "My boyfriend is picking me up there and I'm already late, so that's okay," I replied.

He started driving and there I am, obviously something wrong with me, and this guy starts undoing his pants and playing with himself. Half of my moan is now from total disbelief and the other half is real pain. I glance over at him and say, "Oh, no, please ... " And then I just put my head down, unable to do what I wanted to do, which was jump out of the car. There was a lot of traffic and the drive was slow but he did end up taking me where I wanted to go. He pulled over and as I got out, the sick fuck still kept playing with himself, watching me hobble away like a wounded animal. Cars are honking at him to start driving because he's blocking them from turning right so finally he drives off. I still had quite a slow walk ahead of me, and with all the stops to lean on trees and fences, it was hours before I got back home.

When I finally did, I was pretty drowsy and I was still feeling some pain. I got the med bottle out of my purse and opened it up to take another pill. I then heard the doctor's voice in my head, telling me to be careful. As I sat there on the couch, I thought that maybe these thirty little pills were enough to end both my physical and emotional pain once and for all. Who would miss me anyway?

The apartment had one small window, so small that one ray of light wouldn't have been able to penetrate it, so it was always dark and gloomy inside and that matched my disposition quite well. I had a bathroom that I shared and nowhere to cook and no fridge. I used to buy cheap baloney and keep the package on the window-sill, hoping it wouldn't rot. When it did rot, I just tossed the rotten looking edges away, which was nothing new for me. Neither was not having any money. I had no friends and not much hope. I didn't even have Michael. During those hours of loneliness, of black un-ending despair, I would cut myself with a knife or razor, slicing into my own flesh and watching the blood flow out. For a long time I believed it might be a preliminary act to suicide. I hadn't the nerve to kill myself with pills, but I figured maybe a big slit up my arm would do it. I had built a shell around me to prevent others from hurting me, and I needed the pain and maybe the horror of self-mutilation to restore my ability to feel anything.

Even after all the Percocet was gone, I remained in the room for days, not eating or sleeping, feeling crazy changes happen inside me that made me feel less and less human. I had conversations with myself. I would cry and then be happy and then cry all over again. I paced the small room back and forth, back and forth, trying to think of the reasons that I should live. I wrote a list: reasons to live, reasons to die, and I had a longer list under the reasons to die. I sat on the big, old, overstuffed couch that came with the room and I don't know what smelled the worst, the ancient couch or me. I didn't shower and the darker the room was, the better. But then I started seeing shadows and was convinced that either the house was haunted or my mind was. My mother always said that she saw ghosts because we were all gypsies and now I was beginning to think maybe that was it. Regardless of what it was, I kept the lights on around the clock and felt panic at the thought of the power being turned off. I didn't know what the changes I was experiencing were or what they meant, but when I began having out-of-body experiences, when I started to feel that my soul or something like it was floating away from my body, I grew frightened. I'm finally there, I thought. I have finally become totally, certifiably insane.

No matter how hard I tried to think about anything else, my mind always took me back to gloom and doom thoughts. I tried to think instead of Michael. But that just made me feel all the guilt again over being a crappy mother and human being, and the torment became unbearable. I also thought, what if when Michael got older he missed me or was hurt by his mother killing herself? And I didn't want to fuck him up more than he would already be as it was.

Then I did something that I hadn't done for years. I got down on my knees on that old smelly carpet in that freezing cold room and I blessed myself and I prayed. I prayed and cried. And then I prayed and cried some more. I told God that I knew He wasn't going to answer me back, and that was okay, but that I just needed Him to listen and then maybe after that, He might realize how much I really needed some help. I told Him that I wanted to die. I asked Him to forgive me for being a rotten daughter and a rotten mother. I wanted to do better and become better but I said that I didn't know how to do that. Nothing else mattered except my prayers, and for quite some time I even forgot where I was because I was so sincerely wrapped up in praying.

When I was all cried and prayed out, I slowly got back on the couch, feeling emotionally drained. My knees hurt from being on them for so long and my insides still felt raw too; slowly, little by little, all the pain started coming back. Yet I no longer wanted to kill myself. I wanted to get some help. I thought about my body and what I was doing to it and what I had been thinking about doing to it and realized that it was the only place I had to live. So I took the meds the way they were prescribed to be taken and I told myself that I had to get help, not tomorrow, not next week, but now! Looking back, I think that God put a comma in my life that day when I was just about to make it a period.

I DIDN'T MAGICALLY get my life or my emotions sorted out overnight. There would be other times in my life, every couple of years, when I would go to a doctor, mentally exhausted, stressed out and haunted either by things in my past that I'd done or things that were done to me, or aspects of my upbringing, or whatever. I was given Valium and any number of prescriptions for depression. But I never took the pills because I was scared. Each of the ten or so doctors I saw was convinced I should be on medication. Sometimes I would simply start crying in front of the doctor, unable to say even one word, but every time I'd get the prescription filled, I just couldn't take the pills.

I put everything I owned into the one suitcase I had and hitch-hiked to the Clarke Institute, a facility in Toronto that treated people with mental problems.

My first experience at the Clarke might have driven me crazy, if you know what I mean. I didn't think that I already was. I told the receptionist that I had to see a psychiatrist. She asked why and I replied, "Because I think I'm crazy." She said that thinking you are in need of treatment for a mental condition didn't mean you needed therapy. I screamed that I was a frickin' mental case and rolled up my sleeves to show her my sliced-up arms, now with dried up blood all over them. I went on to say that the whole world was really hell and I was thinking that I had to kill myself to escape it. This seemed to convince her that I might have a point, so she asked me to sit down while she found someone to examine me.

It took nearly three hours for a psychiatrist to arrive. During that time, I really had to fight the feeling of wanting to run out the front doors right into traffic but I couldn't be positive that I would get smucked by a bus, so I stayed put. I don't remember exactly how I acted or what I said, but it was convincing enough for the psychiatrist to agree that I needed help and to set up a series of sessions starting the following week. Just knowing that somebody had agreed to help me lifted my spirits a little, and with that, I told myself that I should hold on just a bit longer in case killing myself wasn't my only option.

I began weekly therapy with a psychiatrist I'll call Dr. Jekyll, who matched all the clichés about psychiatrists that you or I have ever heard about. He was bearded, wore tortoiseshell glasses and tweed jackets, and was so soft-spoken I had to often ask him to repeat himself. I trusted him right away, trusted him so much that I opened up my soul and my past to him. I told him about everything: the sexual abuse from my father's friends and the smelly neighbour who made me masturbate him along with all the other perverts that had forced themselves on me; about Eddie, becoming pregnant and giving birth to Michael; my week in jail with the rats; my abortion at Auntie Nellie's; my own uncle pimping me; my mother's rages and how she hated me; all of it. Every bit of it. I held nothing back.

It felt so good to purge. I was flattered when Dr. Jekyll told me how my sense of humour, which developed as my depression lifted, lightened the room. I had problems, he agreed, but I was responding well and he would help me work through them.

Every week of therapy made me stronger. I had no more out-of-body experiences, no sense of being smothered by a heavy black weight descending on me. Somebody at last understood what had happened to me and why I felt and acted the way I did. A man—an educated, cultured man—liked me in spite of everything he knew about me. He was warm and friendly to me without wanting anything in return. He understood, he sympathized, he supported and he didn't judge. The impact he made on my ego, my sense of self-worth and, most of all, my mental health was enormous and all of it was positive.

One day I entered his office to find files and boxes piled everywhere. I asked him what was going on.

"Oh, you're early. Come in. I was going to discuss that with you today. I'm going to a different hospital," he explained. "It's a good move for me. Too good to pass up."

I asked him what the hell he had just said, because I'd heard him all right, but I was in shock. He was about to repeat himself, as he often did. "I heard you just fine," I said. "I meant what about me. What's going to happen to me and our sessions and my fucked-up head?"

"Oh, don't you worry about that," he smiled. "I'm transferring your files to another therapist. You can keep seeing him just like you see me. So, where do you want to start today?" he continued,

still smiling. I was still in shock and wondering if somehow Dr.
Jekyll—with or without his potion—had somehow awakened in the
body of his darker self, Mr. Hyde. Did he honestly believe that this
meant as little to me as it did to him? In that instant, I lost my mind.
Again.

"Who do think you are?" I screamed. "You think I'm a fucking
file? I tell you everything that's gone on in my life, all the pain and
abuse and bullshit I've had to put up with and you have the nerve to
treat me like a *file*? Maybe you're just the janitor here and not a real
doctor at all!"

I grabbed the nearest stack of paper and threw it across the
room, then began turning over everything within reach while Dr.
Hyde kept repeating, "Cathy, Cathy, Cathy ... please ... please ... "

He was still saying my name when I left his office and
slammed the door behind me. I wanted out of there. I wanted to
get home before anybody could see me cry or whatever the hell
I was going to do, but I couldn't. I kept getting lost in the damn
place. I used to get lost when I arrived for my sessions, getting off
the elevator on the wrong floor or turning down the wrong
corridor, and Dr. Jekyll said that was because my subconscious
was trying to stop me from getting the help I so desperately
needed. Yeah, well, who the hell was it now stopping me from
getting that much-needed help? I started panicking and became
claustrophobic not being able to find my way out of the building.
I cried all the way home, back to my room on the top floor of the
haunted house. I had thought, finally, that I had someone to listen
to me and someone who truly cared about me, and it turned out
that wasn't the case at all.

I sat very still for an hour, unable to believe what had happened
to me. This betrayal, by someone whom I thought incapable of
doing anything like that, was shocking. Nothing, not even my
father's friend abusing me, going to jail to save Eddie's ass, staying
with strangers and stealing from them, my mother accusing me of
being a sexual deviant for supposedly drawing the picture of a penis
on my wall, none of it was as upsetting as Dr. Hyde passing my file
on to someone else and assuming I would understand.

I didn't understand. I couldn't understand. And I would never understand.

Talking to some new shrink wasn't going to help me. How could it? Whatever they read in my file would never be enough for them to fully understand what and who I was without talking to me about it in detail. And I was too depressed to think about having to go through all that shit over again. No one would be Dr. Jekyll. Period. I felt betrayed by the one person I had trusted totally.

I'd given the landlord's phone number to the hospital as a contact number, and about an hour after I had been sitting in that vegetative state there was a knock on my door and the landlord told me that I had a call. I walked down the two flights of stairs to the kitchen and picked up the receiver. I heard Dr. Jekyll's voice and I cringed. "Cathy, I didn't realize how sick you really were," he said after apologizing. "Please come back. You can see me any time at the new hospital." The fucker calls me sick because I flip out in his office but he isn't able to diagnose me before that? He was a quack, I decided.

I didn't want to hear it and I didn't want the landlord to hear me tell him this either. I whispered loudly into the phone that he was the sick fuck for not knowing how much I needed to keep seeing him, and that I couldn't stand going through all of that crap again with somebody else. Then I hung up the telephone and swore I would never see another psychiatrist ever again. Next time around, I would just run the razor as deep across my arm as I could and end it. Then I went back to my room and, for another few months or so, just existed as best as I could.

CHAPTER TWENTY

My ball and chain

I DON'T KNOW HOW MANY PLACES I spent a night or a week with a different man, or how many men there were, but if I had to guess, I'd say maybe a hundred. Sometimes it was a package deal and I'd bring Michael with me, other times it was a solo one-night stand. Sometimes I would wait around for breakfast, other times I would leave before the guy woke up. Some men would give me money to buy food. Others let me stay two or three nights or even a week before growing tired of having me around, and I would leave at the first hint. I never needed to be told to go; I went on my own. I kept that much control, at least. Sometimes when I left, I took cash or jewellery or other belongings they'd left lying around. I learned that pawnshops were my friend and they helped me meet my many immediate cash-flow crunches.

THE MEN WERE VARIED AND DIFFERENT. A few brutes. A lot of losers. Now and then a nice guy. But very few were long-term relationships. And of course, all through this time there was Eddie— the proverbial bad penny I just could not get rid of.

My mother always told me that I was boy crazy. I didn't see it like that. I was looking-for-love crazy. Besides, I don't know how she ever came to that conclusion, because she never met even a handful of the men in my life. Maybe because most of them were one-night stands or one-week stands or I stayed with them to get away from her and my dad when it was crazy at home. I wish a lot of things could have been different in my life, but they weren't. If I hadn't been that lost kid growing up, I probably wouldn't have been that lost teenager and lost young woman. But I was.

It had been four years since I'd been in school—I was nineteen—and I promised myself that one day I would get a degree and prove to myself and the rest of the world that I really was smart. But for now, I had to work to do my best to support myself and my son.

I worked on and off at menial jobs that never lasted very long. The fact is I got fired a lot. Maybe my attitude was not the best; certainly it wasn't like I had a sparkling résumé or the kinds of skills that would dazzle an employer. No high school degree. A kid. And sometimes not even a permanent address or a phone. Real CEO material. One time I got a job in a small office working for the vice president. He had a big meeting to go to and I was supposed to type out the meeting agenda and content for him. I had one whole day to do this. But when I still needed more time, the boss became visibly antsy, pacing in front of my desk while I typed away, making me more nervous than I already was. I hit the foot pedal of the Dictaphone machine over and over again so many times that he finally stopped pacing and shouted, "How long is it going to take you to type that damn thing for me?"

I was used to being yelled at. I just kept typing. When I finally finished typing his report he said, "Now I don't have the time to check it, so make twenty copies and distribute it for the morning's directors meeting!" And I did just that. The next morning, another assistant working in the company handed me a letter. It read, "You're FIERD!" and regardless of how it was spelled, I got the message loud and clear.

I also worked for a magazine subscription company as a clerk. This job didn't require me to type or spell. I just had to process the new magazine subscriptions manually, copying down people's names and addresses and contact information from mailed-in coupons. Although my typing wasn't an issue here, my tardiness was. I was late most mornings, as I was in every job. My mother was always late for everything and although it annoyed me greatly as a kid, I became exactly like her in ways that I was not happy about. But if it bothered me so much, then why did I do it? I didn't have the answer. I would come in five or ten minutes late maybe half of every work week in every job I had. I also started realizing that I had some problems. For example, I couldn't remember things that were said to me if they contained more than one question or thought at a time. So, if I was given a directive by my boss and he told me to do two or more things, I only remembered the first thing I was asked to do. My writing was so messy that no one could read it, not even me. When I was asked something, I couldn't repeat what I had just been told, and when I read something, it wouldn't stick in my brain. I would listen to every third word or so that someone spoke to me and only get the general idea of the conversation without listening to everything that people said. And I often reversed letters or words that I copied from the subscription forms onto a master sheet. For example, if a person's name was Fred Smith, I would copy in pen to the master list Fred Smiht.

A few weeks after I was hired the boss called me into his office. "So, Cathy, how are you liking the job?"

"I love it," I eagerly replied. I actually thought I was going to get a raise, so I was beaming.

"Well, that's interesting that you feel that way because, in reality, you are doing a very poor job. Look, don't you know you can't copy names down correctly and that you're really slow? You take a lot of time and you still don't do the job right." He went on to tell me that I was also late more than anyone else who worked there and that, unfortunately, he was going to have to fire me.

I stood up and shouted, "Well, you don't have to fire me because I fucking quit. Stick your job up your ass!" I stormed out of his office. On the way out, I yelled to the other girls working there that I liked, "Oh, and don't make any mistakes because Mr. fucking Perfect in there will fire your ass before you know it!" Outside at the streetcar stop I cried and cried because yet again I had to kibosh my plans to move out of my parents' place with my son.

My big break—that's what I thought it was—came when I got a job as a teller at a new bank located in downtown Toronto. I was so happy because now I could really finally move out of my parents' home with Michael for good. This was the best job I'd ever gotten and I just knew it would work out for me for a very long time.

I called up Eddie. He was still living at home and for some reason I had not given up completely on the dream that we might actually be able to make it as a family. I told him that we needed to start looking for an apartment because I now I had a great job and we would now be able to fend for ourselves. Just the three of us. I told him that he could find a job too, and together we would be okay.

We found an apartment in a suburb of Toronto a huge two-bedroom spread with a great balcony and was the best place I'd ever lived. Eddie's father co-signed a loan for us at a local furniture store and we bought a TV, a couch and chair, a coffee table, two end tables, a queen-sized bed and a kitchen table with four chairs, all on credit. I also needed money to get to and from work and to give to Eddie for his daily spending money, or else he would freak out and get violent with me. A while back I had decided to dye my hair platinum. I still had platinum blonde hair and with all the expenses, I didn't have enough money to even buy bleach for my hair, so I had about two-inch-long roots that really bothered me. That may sound trivial, but looking like hell reminded me too much of how much I was turning out like my mother. Then I bought Michael books and some new clothes—I was still buying second-hand for me, but never for Michael—and I was pretty happy overall.

Eddie still didn't have a job, but I figured I would give him some time to look. This was the first time he'd moved out of his parents' place and I didn't want him to go running back because of my pressuring him. Plus, I was making enough at the bank to support us all.

The first sign that things might not work out according to plan was when Eddie started staying out every night. He was doing a lot of drugs. He was selfish and he fooled around. Things I had known about since the beginning but just didn't want to take into account. Once while Michael sat waiting for his father to come home Eddie was next door with a neighbour's girlfriend. I forgave him every time. Like I would always forgive him when he beat me. Just like my mother forgave my dad.

My father told me that I had to stay with Eddie since I had his baby. So that's what I did. Since I had to work and Eddie was never home I had to take care of Michael every night by myself without any help from him, I became increasingly angry. I also had to arrange for babysitting because I never knew when Eddie would be home in the morning to watch Michael and I didn't want to miss work. I took my frustrations out on Michael. For example, Michael wasn't reading as well as I thought he should have. He would try reading to me from a book and I would get frustrated and yell at him: "God, why can't you learn this shit! Are you stupid?"

His face would crumple to tears and I could feel a stab in my heart like a knife but I had no one to blame but myself. I kept hearing in my head what my mother had said to me the day I moved out with Michael. Angry that I was taking him, she said, "You know shit about being a mother!" and she was exactly right.

AT LEAST MY JOB at the bank was going well. It wasn't a giant operation but it was a good one, with beautiful modern offices, comfortable sofas and chairs for customers, reasonable pay for employees and a policy that gave newcomers like me a chance to show off their skills. The bank was bright and big and I loved the smell of all the new exposed wood.

I also loved the job. I earned enough money to buy decent clothes and makeup and something most women are crazy about, shoes. I especially loved dealing with customers. Many became friends, or at least familiar faces, people who would greet me with a smile when they came to make a deposit or withdrawal or cash a cheque.

Eddie was doing the best he could, I guess. He would find work for a week as a valet and then for a week as a courier or a driver somewhere else but nothing that ever lasted and all for minimum wage. I rode the bus and then a subway to work each day and night, and in total I travelled for three hours a day. The bank was in the middle of the financial district of Toronto, where people scurried here and there, busily doing things and living out their lives without worrying about where that night's dinner was going to come from or where they would sleep. And I felt that I too was one of those people, finally fitting in and relying on myself.

I might have been happy staying at the bank for years, but I'll never know.

Eddie loved the bank almost as much as I did. Why wouldn't he? It provided steady work for me, a good income for us and a place for Eddie to kill time during the day, sprawling on the comfortable sofa, helping himself to the free coffee and cookies and watching me work. I didn't mind it, but Eddie's presence began to bug other people at the bank, especially Assistant Manager Marge. She would mention that it wasn't good to have Eddie hanging around the branch as much as he did. I would tell Eddie, he would avoid coming in for a couple of days and then return to hang out until Marge would insist that he disappear again. This went on for a few months.

One Friday, the bank had just closed and I was tidying up my workspace when Marge asked me to step into the boardroom with her and the manager. I sat down. She asked me how I liked my job at the bank. As soon as I heard those words I thought, Shit, I'm being fired. I had heard exactly that too many times before.

I loved my job, I said, and I thought I was pretty good at it. They started asking some frankly odd questions. How well I thought the bank was doing, how well I thought it was being run, how good I thought the security was. I answered everything truthfully. Finally, they got around to the real subject: Eddie.

Eddie had been in the bank every day that week, but since Marge hadn't said a word to me about telling him to stay away I thought they were finally okay with him coming in and hanging out. Now they were asking me about him. How long had I known him? Did I know about his criminal record? Why was he in the bank every day? Did he and I ever talk about the bank's operations?

I had no idea what they were getting at and eventually, after maybe half an hour of interrogation, they realized this. Marge sat back with her arms folded, staring at me. "We think Eddie comes in here because he's planning to rob the bank."

I burst out laughing. Were they kidding? I suppose—once again—I was protecting Eddie. I tried telling them that it was impossible.

That's when they fired me.

Maybe I could have saved my job. But I didn't try. I didn't scream or yell the way I had in the past when I got fired. I said nothing. I just shrugged, walked out of the bank for the last time, and rode the bus and then subway back home to our apartment where I found Eddie unconscious on the sofa, his belt still tightened around his arm and Michael on the kitchen floor playing with the used syringe and spoon.

I gathered up as many clothes as I could carry. Then—once again—Michael and I went back to my parents' place, back to all the violence and drunkenness and chaos that I had vowed my child would never experience and that I felt I had no way of stopping.

CHAPTER TWENTY-ONE

Livin' the high life

I BASICALLY SAID TO HELL WITH IT.

The best way to live, I decided, was day to day. I no longer thought about having a husband and a family, and I believed that I would never trust another man in my entire life. The only thing I knew was that I had to be with my son and figure out a way to do that.

One day I happened to meet a young woman behind a cosmetics counter at a pharmacy. Her name was Louise and we knew right away we would be great friends. Louise had a French surname, Doucet, and claimed when I first met her that she was from Paris, but after a week or so when we became friends, she admitted that she was actually from a small town in northern New Brunswick. We had the same goal because she too had a son, a year older than Michael, Pierre, who lived with her parents in St. John.

She knew I need a place to stay. Louise hated the place she was living in but a room was available cheap and she lent me a month's rent and I moved in. It was what used to be the living room on the main floor. A guy who dressed as if he came from Africa, except he was white, lived in the basement apartment, I lived on the main floor with a guy in the room next to mine, another guy lived on the second floor with his girlfriend and Louise lived in the one-room attic. My room came equipped with an old carpet, ratty old drapes that covered the huge window and a big overstuffed couch that pulled out into a bed, which I slept on.

The guy living downstairs in the basement, I'll call him Sam, was involved in a lot of things; one of them was acting as a middle-man for male immigrants who wanted to stay in Canada, which they could do if they married a Canadian woman. Sam provided the women for a healthy fee.

Sam quickly spotted Louise and me as potential wives for his clients, and after befriending us, he outlined the deal. He would pay us $5,000 each to get hitched. All we had to do was stay married to the guy until our "husband's" immigration status became permanent, and then have the marriage annulled. Sam would be taking a cut of the immigrant's fee, of course, but hey, that's business. That $5,000 had more zeros than I knew what to do with, and there was almost nothing I wouldn't do to have that much cash in my hand. I figured that would be enough money for Louise and me to get a place together and get our kids with us faster.

I thought about it. The truth is, one of the things I wouldn't do was marry a man I didn't love. Despite everything, I was holding out for true love. Marrying a man I did not love was as outrageous an idea as giving up my baby for adoption. It just wouldn't happen. I wanted to be married, and I was determined to do a better job of being married than anybody I ever knew and do it better than anything else I had done in my life. I kept the idea of marriage as something sacred.

When I told Sam why I couldn't go through with the deal, he thought I was negotiating, and he raised the offer to $10,000 cash. I took a minute to figure out in my head how many zeros that would now be, but I still said no. He didn't believe me, not until I stood my ground over several weeks of pressure. When he realized we were not going to budge, he told us to find some other place to live, and even though he wasn't the landlord, he said he would make our lives unbearable. I was used to unbearable, but Louise thought we should probably look for another place to live, somewhere we could least be on the same floor. So we started searching for an apartment to share.

Louise knew all the feminine tricks: how to dress and apply makeup, how to do your hair, how to walk into a room and get all the men's eyes on you, how to smile at a guy as though you're promising him everything but planning to give him nothing. I hadn't picked this up yet. I was just me, nobody else, but Louise was whoever she wanted to be or, more correctly, whoever the guy she wanted to hit on wanted her to be. I learned that we become who we pretend to be. I pretended to be a lot of different people in the years that followed, but with Louise I learned to be more confident—on the outside at least. I also discovered the value of a sense of humour and grew confident using it. If I could make people laugh, they felt better about a lot of things, including me. I could make myself and others laugh. When they did, the pain faded, and when they liked me in return for making them laugh, the pain vanished.

I was twenty-two and I was just happy to use whoever I needed to get whatever I wanted, which happened to be what most single women my age wanted: fun, attention, nice clothes, cute guys. Scoring nice clothes with bad cheques made the other three things easier to get, so that's what we did. I was never charged with writing so many bad cheques that I lost count, but I came close to paying for them in different ways.

Like the time that we were all packed and ready to move away from Sam and our rooming house. We thought, What the hell, we need to get another place to live pronto, but first let's buy some amazing clothes because by the time the shop owner realizes that we paid with a bounced cheque, we'll be long gone. So, in a glitzy designer store downtown I found the most fabulous black jumpsuit I had ever seen. It fit me perfectly. It also cost a couple of hundred dollars, which was more money than I'd ever had in my purse in my life. But Louise agreed that I just had to buy it. She bought a lot of stuff as well, and we covered it all with a bad cheque, as we always did. We used to take our real ID and open up bank accounts at different banks. We had cheques printed up by the various banks and we wrote cheques to our hearts' content for most anything we wanted. I made a mistake this time, however. I used our real address instead of an older one that I no longer lived at, because I figured we'd be moved out in a couple of days and they'd never trace us.

Maybe it was the size of the cheque we wrote, maybe it was

the way we acted, but something made the store suspicious. They must have checked the account shortly after we left with our purchases and discovered the truth, because that night Louise and I were going to go out and hit the bars, me in the jumpsuit and her in the outfit she'd just bought. Louise was downstairs in my room and I was finishing my makeup when there was a knock on the front door. I was usually the one who answered the rooming-house door, because my room was right there. So I pranced out, leaving the door to my room wide open, and swung the front door open. There stood three of the meanest looking bastards you can imagine, glaring at me. Louise didn't hear me saying anything after I opened the door, so she came out of my room to see where I was.

One of the men pointed at the pantsuit and said, "That's gotta come off. It's going back with us."

I could tell there was no sense pleading with them. I mean, they weren't exactly from the store's accounting department. I assumed they had parked their Harley Davidsons at the curb. So I shrugged and said, "Okay, give me a minute to change ..."

"No," the guy said. "Here and now. And you"—he pointed at Louise—"come here too."

So with the front door wide open and three hoodlums watching, Louise and I took off our new clothes and stepped aside wearing only our bras and panties and high heels. One meathead scooped up the clothes while another pulled out the cheque and handed it to Louise. "Consider this your refund," he said, and then they left.

Eddie and Louise were alike in their rejection of the straight life, but different in the ways they got their hands on whatever they wanted. Before we left the rooming house for good, Louise asked me to go with her to New Brunswick to get her son. We would then look for a three-bedroom apartment upon our return. I agreed. We packed a few items and made our way to the Toronto airport and boarded an Air Canada flight to St. John. We paid with an NSF cheque.

When we got to St. John I was not impressed. There were pigeons everywhere and it reminded me of my Auntie Nellie's house except there were more birds and they were bigger than the budgies, but they crapped all over me just the same. (My Auntie Nellie told me once that it was good luck if you got bird crap on you. And I replied, Yeah, sure, for the birds!) And there were too many hills for me to walk in my five-inch platform shoes and it was rainy and cold.

When we got to Louise's parents' house, Pierre, her son, was playing in the front yard. I was getting ready to get out of the cab, anxious to get Pierre and get the first flight the hell out of there, but Louise grabbed my sleeve and told me to wait. She said she was scared to see her son because it had been a couple of years since she'd seen him last. I wondered then if the story she'd told me about recently getting divorced and moving to Toronto was true. A couple of years just didn't fit. But I didn't ask her anything more. I just waited with her until she was ready to roll. We waited in that cab for a full ten extra dollars on the fare.

When we got out of the cab, we walked to the front yard where Pierre was playing. He stopped what he was doing and looked at her and smiled. I thought he would go running over to her or she would go running over to him, the way I did when I saw Michael, but she didn't. Neither did he. Then he did something that shocked me. He went back to playing. Louise's face dropped and I am sure mine did too. He didn't recognize her! I wondered how long it had to be before your kid didn't recognize you, and I got really scared for me. What if Michael didn't recognize me one day? I'd better get him with me as soon as possible, I thought.

Louise walked up to Pierre and said, "Hi, Pierre. Do you know who I am?" and he said "no." Louise started crying and Pierre got scared so he ran into the house and called his grandmother, who came outside. Louise's mother was really happy to see her daughter, and over the course of the that day, Louise talked to her parents and her son and made plans to take Pierre home with us. We left the next morning and it wasn't soon enough.

Pierre was a very quiet kid. He had big brown eyes like his mother and he had a nervous twitch: he tapped the tip of his thumb against every finger over and over again. I felt sorry for him, but I was glad that he was reunited with his mother. At our rooming house he spent a few days getting to know his mother all over again, and before you knew it, we found a huge three-bedroom apartment, in Scarborough. I, on the other hand, got Michael from my parents' house for the gazillionth time, promising again that this would be the last time I would be apart from my son. Michael was happy as usual to see me, but he had become much more attached to my mother. So I made my departure short and sweet and we were on our way with Louise and Pierre in her car, all set to move into our new place.

Pierre and Michael became just as fast friends as Louise and I had. They had separate beds in one big bedroom and Louise and I had our own bedrooms too. Louise had a bathroom to herself and I shared one with Michael and Pierre. One night while the boys were getting ready for bed and Pierre was changing, I noticed that the skin on his legs looked different from regular skin. I asked him what had happened to him but before he could answer, Louise stormed into his bedroom and said, "I left him in the tub when he was a baby and he turned on the hot water and scalded himself," adding, "And it was an accident, okay? I feel horrible about that, but I didn't mean to leave him!" She got all defensive and I could relate. I never mentioned it again.

Louise kept her job at the cosmetics counter and I worked at various clerical and secretarial jobs, but never for more than a few months at a time. Michael and Pierre went to school together and came home together every weekday. On the weekends, both boys started playing hockey in a league and Louise and I used to get up early on Saturday morning to see their games. I used to sit in the stands and laugh at Michael because he paid little attention to the hockey coaches. One time when he was supposed to be facing off, he decided to pretend he was in the Ice Capades instead, and right there in the middle of the game, he began skating backwards, oblivious to the referee who was madly blowing his whistle to get his attention. He looked so cute all decked out in his hockey equipment doing his own thing on the ice.

Okay, so some Saturday mornings I went to Michael's games. Others, I didn't. You see, Louise and I went out every Friday night or even more often and the younger the boys were, the earlier their hockey games. After Louise and I went to the clubs all night and then entertained back at our apartment as we often did, we just couldn't get up to go to their games all the time. So, Michael and Pierre used to take the bus and find their own way to the arena. This didn't seem to bother Pierre, but it did bother Michael and I knew it. He used to get mad at me when he would wake me up at 6:00 a.m. on Saturday morning and I would say that I just couldn't get out of bed to take him to his game. He would then say, "Fine, I'll go all by myself … again!" and leave. When Michael became an adult, he told me how much this bothered him. My perspective was that we were together, it was quiet and peaceful, we always had food and beds, he had new hockey equipment and a good friend to play and live with and I couldn't understand why this wasn't all better than it had been for Michael in the past. Later on I also learned that Michael resented the fact I'd left his father and that I was with so many men. He felt that I put him second and often he was right. Going out to party usually came first. Michael and Pierre were left alone in the apartment, supposedly and hopefully safely tucked in bed for the night, while Louise and I then went to the bars.

If I could do it all again, I would do things very differently, but it was what it was. And what it was, I see now, is that I was wrong so often that I lost track. I guess my mistakes weren't impactful enough to make only once because I kept making the same ones over and over again. My mother always said that I was thick in the head and obstinate and maybe that had something to do with it. Now in my fifties I look back and think that experience is the worst teacher; as they say, it gives the test before the lesson. I read somewhere that you should never have regrets in life. Well, I have a dump-truck load of regrets and most of them centre around what a horrible mother I was. I could only hope that there would come a point in my life when my present would be more important than my past.

About six months after moving in together Louise announced she wanted to visit New York City. Since school was out for the summer holidays and I was between jobs—again—I also thought that New York would be a good idea. We needed a break. A week earlier Michael had just gotten into a bit of trouble with the police. I was at home when there was a knock at my front door. Louise and Pierre were out shopping and I was watching TV while getting ready to go out that night. When I opened the door, there stood a police officer. Michael was standing beside the officer, his head hanging down. The officer told me that Michael had gotten a can of red spray paint and proceeded to paint a few of the local cars with "FUCK YOU" and "FUCK OFF." I invited the cop into the house to find out what would happen next. After spending about an hour in my living room, he told me that he wouldn't press charges if I went out with him. Jesus Christ, I thought. I certainly didn't have enough money to pay the fine. I dated him for about two months until he started pressuring me so much to have sex that I told him someone his age with kids really should be with his wife and not me. It isn't always the most pleasant thing coming to terms with how the world really works.

Anyway, my mother was looking to spend more time with Michael now that I never took him to her place. She kept visiting us without asking first if she could come over and Louise was getting pissed off because my mother kept telling her how to feed her son and how to clean and how to do laundry. I asked my mom if she would mind taking care of Michael at our place for a while and she was thrilled. Funny, me she couldn't get rid of fast enough. But for my son Michael, she walks across a scorching desert in bare feet to be with him.

HAVING NO MONEY to go to New York was not a problem. Louise was convinced we could write a bad cheque for the fare and by the time they figured it out we would be in New York already. When it came time to clear US customs, the officer asked Louise and me where we were going. New York. Why? To dance at Studio 54 and the Saturday Night Fever Club. How long are you planning on staying? Who knows. Maybe a few weeks—it depends. On what? Who we meet, of course. How much money do you both have? None.

Access denied! It was no loss for us, given the bad cheque for the airfare. So we hitchhiked to Buffalo and crossed the border with a trucker who covered for us and it was smooth sailing from there all the way to New York.

When we got to New York, I was in love. What a fabulous city! The people were great and the energy was amazing. We went to Studio 54 first, at its peak, and once again Louise knew all the tricks: how to dress so we would get inside, how to schmooze with celebrities, how to act as though we belonged there. If there was a wilder place on earth than Studio 54 back then, or any time in history, I can't imagine it. You couldn't go to Studio 54 back then without meeting somebody famous, and of course when you did you had to act totally cool about it. We mixed with the cast and crew of a hit TV show. Men went into the ladies' restroom; everyone, it seemed, snorted coke in the open; and people made out all over the place on the second floor. This club didn't take credit cards, it only took cash, but Louise and I didn't have a problem finding guys with wads of money who were more than happy to get rid of it. I met a guy who said he was with the Rolling Stones. He asked me to meet him for breakfast, but I told him to forget about it, which really seemed to surprise him. He handed me his business card, which had the Stones' red-tongue logo on it, along with his telephone number. I never called him. He was way too ugly for me, even though, as Louise's sidekick, I was used to her always getting the best-looking guys.

Without any cash of our own, we continued to resort to other means of survival. We would hook up with anybody who would take us home for the night and buy us breakfast in the morning. Then other people would pay for our drinks each night. If we saw jewellery or cash lying around anywhere we stayed and we figured we could get away with it, we helped ourselves on our way out. That happened more often than not. We stayed in some of the most amazing apartments I had ever seen.

There wasn't a thing I didn't like about New York. We were two wild girls in a wilder city and it was fabulous.

It was at the 2001 Odyssey that Louise and I met two guys, one of whom was a cop and who drove a big new Cadillac with his initials on the driver's door: LAD. Larry A. Demann, whom I ended up staying with for over a week.

When Larry and his friend saw us sitting at a table at the Odyssey, they walked up to us and asked if they could join us. Their accents were straight out of a movie and both of them were very attractive. Larry started talking to me and his friend started talking to Louise. As soon as a guy would talk to her, she became a different person. She pretended to be shy and coy, yet she had an appendectomy scar that she showed everyone who would look. She'd say it was a gunshot wound, then she would laugh in this phony voice and say, "Oh, I'm just kidding, I wasn't really shot!" And some stupid guy would think that was the funniest thing in the world. At the end of a great night of drinking and dancing on that fabulous dance floor, Larry told me, after I explained to him that we had nowhere to stay and no money, that Louise and I each had to go home with one of them; we couldn't stay together. I didn't like that idea, but, then Larry was a cop, so I trusted him. Louise left with her guy and I went home with Larry.

His apartment was in a low-rise complex in Brooklyn. As soon as I walked in, I was in his kitchen. I took a look around and saw that he used old pieces of bars of soap to wash his dishes with. I commented on that and he said his mother did that too, and I told him that my mother washed her hair with a bar of soap and wasn't it interesting all the things you could use soap for. I was making stupid conversation because I was a bit nervous away from Louise. Larry seemed politely interested and then said he had to get to bed because he had to be up early for work. He slept with his handgun under his pillow. "Don't you think that's strange?" I asked him, but he didn't think it was strange at all. "If I need to blow somebody's head off in the middle of the night because they're breaking in, then I can." I prayed he would remember that he'd brought me home of his own free will if he happened to get up in the middle of the night while I was there.

During the day Larry would leave me to go to work as one of New York's finest. Louise's guy would drop her off at Larry's place during the day; then she had to go back home with him when he picked her up after work. I never stole anything from Larry. I actually really liked him. Every night for dinner we would go get pizza or calzone or something else to eat, and he left me money to go to the store each day to buy what I wanted. We even got ice cream cones together. We talked and laughed and told each other about our lives. Well, he told me about his. I did tell him that I had a son, and since now I lived with Michael and was doing better than I had in the past, I shared a few stories about my life with him.

One day when Larry was at work, I phoned my mother to see how Michael was and to tell her that I'd met a great guy. I told her all about Larry since she liked cops or men in uniforms. I added that this time, unlike that gross older married cop who tried to date me, Larry was young and good looking and funny and, more importantly, single. And he liked me too. Just as I was telling her what precinct he worked at, she freaked out on me.

"Well, aren't you just a phony fucking liar!"

"What?" I said.

"Do you think I'm goddamn stupid or something? Precincts are only on TV shows." She refused to believe me. She said I was full of shit and when I tried to tell her that, no, Larry really did exist, she got more and more adamant about what a liar I was and how I always was and always would be. I tried to tell her when I was coming home and she slammed the phone in my ear. I didn't even get a chance to ask about Michael or speak to him. I felt totally deflated. My mother always thought I was a liar. There would be no way that I could ever get her approval or get her to love me, I thought. For now, I would put that out of my head and try to enjoy our last week in New York.

We stayed in New York for about three weeks. I didn't want to leave. I daydreamed about how great it would be to be single and rich in New York and have the world at my fingertips. Larry and I could get married and he would love Michael and it would be perfect. And it actually seemed like we might have a chance. Larry even gave me money to buy Louise and me tickets back home. We told each other that we would see each other again. I think I was in love.

When I got back home, we picked up where we left off. School had started again, and I got another job as a clerk. Louise decided that she was going to be a model. In fact, when we went out on Saturday night to clubs now, she told all the guys that she met that she *was* a model. I wanted to say I was a model too, but I knew no one would believe me if I did.

I tried to keep in touch with Larry. I called him often and wrote letters. But all he wanted to do when I called him was tell me about this girl in Brooklyn whom he'd met after I left and how he'd fallen in love with her, and he wanted me to provide a compassionate ear. Fuck that. I was heartbroken. I would never go to New York again, I told myself.

When my mother dropped in on us about a month later, she asked me, "So, what happened to your Larry?"

I replied, "Larry who?"

OVER THE WINTER, Louise decided that what she wanted was a Florida vacation during spring break. Of course, we faced the usual small problem of not having any money, but who cared. We would hitchhike. Louise made arrangements for Pierre and my mother agreed to watch Michael and basically that was it: we were gone.

We worked out a strategy. We would hit the truck stops, asking who was heading south and would appreciate our company. This was good planning, but we both knew there were few saints in the cabs of long-distance trucks. We'd seen the signs on lots of eighteen-wheelers on the road: *Gas, grass or ass— nobody rides free.* We'd be expected to sleep with some of those guys, or at least one of us would, and I actually convinced Louise that she should be the bait and the prize. She portrayed herself as both beautiful and smart and I agreed, saying that's why she should be the one to sleep with the drivers. I still had my seahorse nose and flat chest; Louise had the perfect face and big boobs. If we were really going to get our butts to Florida together and at all, it would be her butt that did most of the driving, so to speak.

She went along with it. She was actually flattered that I thought she could get us to Florida faster than I could. Louise would bat her eyes and stick out her chest to get us a truck-stop meal and a lift for a few hundred miles, and I'd be the one who stepped outside the cab and smoked a cigarette while the truck cab rocked a little bit after they crawled into the bunk space. Later, the driver would be grinning like a hyena as he got on his CB and announce to anybody listening that he had two beavers going to the bikini state, which usually got us an offer of another free meal and ride from the next truck stop. Those truckers never left us on the highway alone either. Quite frankly, they were all pretty nice guys. A few even offered us a few bucks as they saw us off.

We wound up in Hollywood, Florida, a classic resort town with a good beach and lots of motels that would accept personal cheques from a couple of sweet Canadian girls who were there to soak up the sun. Louise and I loved to sunbathe. We met a lot of guys who bought us a lot of meals, mostly local men who would then take one of us back to their apartment or home or office.

We never stayed more than a single night at each motel in case the owner pulled the same stunt as the shopkeeper back in Toronto who demanded his clothes back. This went on for a week until the wife of one motel owner cornered us in a hallway. "I know what you girls are up to," she said, glaring at me, "coming and going all hours of the night."

"You know nothing," I replied, adding, "You're not my mother." I suggested that she mind her own business, but I was scared.

Her answer was that the people in Hollywood didn't need girls like us in their town. I started getting angry more than scared and I muttered something about the Wicked Witch of the South who was probably going to stir up a real modern-day witch hunt where we would be sacrificed. And sure enough, that's exactly what happened.

A couple of hours later someone knocked on our door, and I opened it to find her standing there, looking very determined. "I've talked to other people in town," she said, "people you've given cheques to, and they want two things. They want money to cover all the cheques you wrote, and they want you both gone. Now." She tapped her foot and Louise walked over and slammed the door shut in her face. She started to bang on the door and said she was giving us five minutes to be down in the motel's front office.

She sounded like the sheriff from cowboy movies, the one who tells the bad guys to get out of Dodge City by sundown or something like that. There was no sense arguing with her and I started to get scared again. Louise was as cool as a cucumber, as she always was, and she even giggled about the situation. As long as Louise was in control, I would follow her lead.

We trekked down to her office and she stood behind the front desk, arms folded, looking very pissed. Louise explained that we had no money, which is why we wrote the cheques. This didn't impress her at all. If we couldn't cover the cheques, she would call the police and we could explain things from jail. Oh, no, jail. Been there, done that. No thank you.

So I started negotiating. I offered to leave all our jewellery with her as security, and promised to send her money when we returned to Canada. She thought that was fine as long as we wired the money to make sure they received it. Once the money was in their hands she would mail me the jewellery. Little did she know that most of the jewellery she sent me was stolen from her fellow townies.

We trucked our way back north again, the same way we had gone south. Within a few weeks I had enough money to pay for the cheques we had written in Florida by writing more bad cheques in Canada. I sent her the cash and she sent the jewellery. Boy, I liked the rules that sherriff played by.

Back in Toronto after spring break, we again picked up where we'd left off, looking for parties and, if we couldn't find one, starting a party of our own. Although if you peeled back the eternal party-girl attitude you would uncover a couple of women who honestly wanted the usual middle-class dream of a loving, faithful husband, a comfortable house and maybe a couple of kids. The problem was getting them in that order, and the first goal—snaring a guy whom you could trust to stick to his promises—was the least likely to be achievable.

It didn't really matter if the guys we partied with were married or not. And it sure didn't matter to the guys either. The idea of married men behaving badly was hardly new, but we saw them behaving at their worst.

Like the time Louise and I hooked up with a couple of well-known Toronto Maple Leafs hockey players who got a suite for the four of us, in a downtown hotel just off Yonge Street. The guy I was with was too drunk to do anything except fall asleep, so I curled up on the sofa and watched TV, while Louise and her date, a really cute curly-haired guy, spent the night in the other room.

The next morning Louise's date came out of the room in a bath robe, looked at his watch, and said, "Holy shit, I gotta go. My wife had a baby last night, and I gotta get to the hospital," and he ran back into the room and got dressed. What a classy guy. Shit-head, I thought. When he came out of the room looking like a million dollars, he pulled a hundred-dollar bill from his wallet and set it on the table. Louise picked it up and acted all insulted that he was paying her. I was watching, trying to shake my head "No" to tell her to take the bloody cash already. She batted her eyelashes and stuffed it into the pocket of his shirt and said "Goodbye, Daddy." What a couple of idiots.

For years, whenever I watched this guy play the hockey hero for hometown fans who went nuts over the mention of his name, I remembered the guy who spent the night his wife gave birth with Louise and me in a hotel, maybe six blocks from the hospital where his wife and new baby were sleeping.

Maybe my mother was finally right about something. How could I ever really trust any man?

I DON'T RECALL WHEN or how the idea entered my head but somewhere along the line I connected Louise with Uncle Johnny, first in my head and then in person, and almost overnight they were together like Bonny and Clyde, Anthony and Cleopatra, Sonny and Cher. Talk about perfect couples. Louise was an opportunist and Uncle Johnny was lovestruck: a leech and an endless blood supply. Soon Louise was roaring around town in Uncle Johnny's Corvette with a fistful of his credit cards, off on a clothes-buying spree with

Johnny's permission and me at her side. They took vacations together, flying here and there whenever the urge struck them and staying in the best hotels. Forget the family-run motels two blocks from the beach when Johnny was buying. It was all Hiltons, Westins, Hyatts and Ritzes on his tab, and I was around enough to sop up any spilled gravy. I was also around to babysit not only Michael, but Pierre as well.

One night, I was invited to go to dinner with them both and we ended up driving to a seafood restaurant, Captain John's. My uncle ordered ribs and Louise and I ordered shrimp and lobster. After Johnny had slurped every rib dry, he nonchalantly tossed the bones behind his back, where they landed on the floor and even on other people's tables. One even landed in the live lobster tank. Louise and I were laughing hysterically while my uncle stayed poker faced—as if this was the norm, something everyone did. When he noticed that Louise was choking from laughing so much, he said, "It's okay, I can save ya because I know the Heineken remover."

It had to end eventually, and when it did I didn't need or want to know the details. But years later, when Uncle Johnny was lying on his death bed, one of the last things he whispered to me was, "I should have married Louise. I always regretted never marrying her." The romantic regrets of a pimp. My mother also heard him say this, and when she knew we were out of his hearing range she turned to me and said, "He's full of shit!"

FOR YEARS, I had the same recurring dream: I wake up in a jail cell, locked away in solitary confinement with no idea when I will be released, if ever. Strangely enough, the dream wasn't frightening. It was almost reassuring, as though somebody somewhere was telling me to prepare myself because this would be my life. And I could see me ending up that way. When I was diagnosed with colitis and irritable bowel syndrome, a condition that affects me to this day, I almost welcomed the pain and embarrassment because I felt I deserved it and because I was feeling something. I had cut myself off from so many of my feelings for so long that it was a relief to feel anything at all, even knife-edged pain. I felt that cutting my arms up or cutting my insides up was what I deserved.

I was living my life in every wrong way possible. It was not what I wanted to do. It was what I did while waiting for something else to happen, although I was never sure what this would be and whether it would cure me, imprison me or kill me. All I could do was survive long enough to find out which. It was until much later in life that I realized *I* was the one who had to make that "something else" happen.

Eventually, things grew strained between Louise and me. I was no domestic goddess but she lived like a pig and I told her so. We began to get on each other's nerves like some old married couple, and then it all blew up over a modelling assignment.

Louise and I listed ourselves as models with an agency and got a call for a "go-see," where the client could meet us and decide if we were right for the job. Sometimes they needed just a pretty face, sometimes a spectacular body, sometimes a girl who could string two sentences together and talk to customers about a product. We didn't get many jobs, just enough to make it worth our while to answer every go-see invitation that came our way.

One summer day in 1979, we heard about a hot-air balloon promotion that would tie in with major companies like Coca-Cola. Louise really wanted this job, and when we went to the go-see she overdid it, coming on as though she were a princess instead of a single mother looking for work. Her attitude convinced everybody she was a major phony. I wanted the job as well but I was pretty laid back. Plus, I had only my personality to rely on. If they wanted tits and ass, Louise would be the winner, so why fight it? I just tried to be myself, making a few jokes here and there and staying relaxed.

The next day the marketing firm called us, and I answered the phone. Louise could hardly contain herself when I silently mouthed to her who was on the other end. "We have good news and bad news," the marketing guy said when he learned he was speaking to me. "Which do you want to hear first?"

I told him to give me the good news.

"Congratulations," he said. "We want you to be part of our

team on this project. Please come in Wednesday morning at eight and we'll get started."

I think I laughed and said something like, "Wow, terrific!" Louise was jumping up and down with excitement. Then I asked what the bad news was.

"We're taking a pass on your friend Louise," he said. "Sorry."

After I hung up she couldn't wait to know what had happened. I knew in advance how she would react, so I really didn't want to break the news, but I finally told her.

"Wow, Louise. I don't know what to say. I got the job and you didn't. How can that even be possible?" I was trying to appeal to her on any level I could, berating myself as I often did to appease her.

Right before my eyes Louise, gorgeous seductive Louise, turned into Medusa. I almost expected her hair to start hissing like snakes. Her face turned first red, then purple. She sent a lamp flying across the room and screamed, "You ugly fucking bitch! I didn't get that job and you did, with your big nose and your flat chest and your huge ass? How could that happen? Why don't you and your nose that's about as big as another person tell me!" And on and on.

I couldn't tell her she'd probably turned the people off because she was such a phony bitch. I couldn't say anything. I actually cried because of all the terrible things she was saying about me. But I also knew that I was seeing the true Louise, and that our friendship was over.

CHAPTER TWENTY-TWO

Looking in the mirror ... and who do I see?

I FOUND A SMALL TWO-BEDROOM apartment for Michael and me, where I nursed a crazy plan of starting over.

I had a great job as a receptionist at a legal firm located in one of the highest skyscrapers in the city. Some of the furniture cost more than I would make in a year, and the walls were covered in original art by painters whose names I didn't recognize, but was told that they cost a fortune. The women receptionists looked as if they had just stepped out of *Vogue* magazine, and the men were either cool grey-haired types who acted as though they had bought and sold Manitoba that morning, or slim young guys who paraded through the offices as though they were taking some movie star to dinner after they'd worked out at the gym that night. Meanwhile, I was working on wills and contracts and correspondence in the word-processing department.

Gradually, I saw the reality peeking from behind all the image bullshit, and after a couple of months I realized that the guys who were so intimidating and impressive in their executive suites were basically the same as the guys I had been meeting in bars and on the street except that they dressed better and had law degrees.

I was building on the confidence I'd acquired from Louise, and the good pay and classy office environment added to it. I was dressing better, eating better and living better, and it all showed in my ability to charm the lawyers and their staff with my sense of humour and my typing skills. Despite my history with spelling mistakes, I discovered I had a real knack for typing and because of all my other previous jobs, I had my typing up to over one hundred accurate words a minute without breaking a sweat.

Soon I was partying with the lawyers, the clerks, the interns and eventually the partners, raising hell and telling them I never realized that the law could be so much fun. My dad *did* say I should have become a lawyer. The parties happened a couple of times a week, more often when some big deal was closed or it was a holiday of some kind. There were too many to count, but they can be summed up in one image and one event.

Here's the image: I have two of the partners and a bunch of secretaries back at my place for drinks and these guys, these heavyweight masters of the law, get so smashed they go into my bedroom, get undressed, put on my clothes and start dancing and jumping on my bed while the radio pumps out the latest tunes. I don't know how I expected Michael to sleep through that, but I used to shut his door and tell him that I was right outside in the other room if he needed me. Crazy.

Here's the event: One of the senior lawyers, a guy who really wanted to become a partner, made it obvious that he liked me. He liked me a lot. I'll call him Brian. Brian was very sweet, maybe ten years older than me, and a rare exception to my description earlier of the lawyers in the firm. He lacked both the hot physical presence of the younger men and the cool powerful look of the older ones. Short, balding, soft-spoken, his head a bit too large for his body, he was just Mr. Nice Guy, still unmarried at age thirty-five, making lots of money as a lawyer and desperately looking for a woman. We had a few lunches together but that was it.

Meanwhile, I had made friends with a neighbour in my apartment building, a pretty woman named Diane who liked men but didn't like or want commitments, which is why she preferred married men. I told her to find a man with the money and the ability to give her the stuff she wanted in her life. She just shrugged and said she was happy with the way things were going, so I dropped the idea.

I also learned about a fortune teller who lived down and across the street from my apartment, and for a laugh one day I went to visit her and have my fortune told for twenty bucks. She sat in this dimly lit room, looked at my palm and did all the usual stuff, then told me that I had a curse on me, to which I replied, "So tell me something I don't already know."

For five hundred dollars, the fortune teller said, she could have the curse lifted.

I leaned across the table toward her and said, "Are you serious? You've got two chances of me giving you five hundred bucks: slim and none." I was about to leave when I realized I was on the edge of a business deal but she just didn't know it yet, so I calmed down and made her an offer.

"What if I send you people," I said, "and they mention my name, and you give them the same bullshit about a curse and how you can lift it for a few hundred bucks. Will you give me some of the money you're charging?"

For somebody who supposedly could read the future she didn't see this one coming. She thought it was a fabulous idea. So for several months whenever somebody started bitching about their troubles, I would send them to my neighbourhood fortune teller, who would kick back part of her fee. One of the people I sent was Diane, who not only had her curse lifted but played a part in changing my life forever.

I had changed in many ways since I was a kid, and I expected to change in others as well. My confidence and my determination to achieve something with my life and put all the poverty and abuse behind me were a beginning, but I was still painfully self-conscious of my nose. As long as I could not walk past a mirror without trying to catch my profile in the reflection and convincing myself that I had the biggest, ugliest nose in the history of the human race, I would never do everything I secretly believed I could do.

My nose haunted me. Really. It was like constantly being with someone who insulted and embarrassed me in public, someone I never wanted to be seen with but whom I could never get rid of. I became obsessed with the ugliness of my nose and began comparing it with noses on other women my age. Most women compare their figures with those of other women, maybe wishing they had a bigger bust, slimmer waist, longer legs or nicer hair. I did too, but this came later. At the time it was all about my nose, and I kept comparing mine with every nose I saw.

I became a self-taught expert on the shapes of noses, straight or turned-up, large or small, and even on nostril shapes. I would pass a beautiful woman and think, Not a bad nose but the bridge is a little wide or the nostrils are a little too open.

One day I saw a woman about my age with a nose that measured up to everything I thought constituted the ideal nose shape and size. I was so impressed by it that I congratulated her. "I just had to tell you that you have the most beautiful nose I have ever seen," I said. "I love it! It's perfect!"

She was naturally a little surprised but got over it quickly. "Really?" she said.

"Yes," I answered. "Look at my nose. I hate it. I'd love to have a nose like yours."

"Oh, in that case," she said, and she mentioned some doctor's name. "Go and see him. That's how I got mine."

It was a revelation. My salary at the law firm and the few bucks I picked up from the fortune-teller commissions couldn't begin to cover the cost of a nose job by a first-rate cosmetic surgeon, and I sure wasn't going to trust it to some bargain basement butcher. I wanted it done by one of those specialists with clinics that looked like a Beverley Hills health spa, and I knew the person who could afford to pay for it. I just needed him to owe me a favour.

So I introduced Diane to Brian. First I began raving about Diane to him, how pretty she was, how much she admired successful men, all of that. Then I told Diane about this really nice lawyer at the office, a great, smart guy who would treat her like a queen and expect nothing back in return.

They hooked up. I went to see Diane one morning and guess who answered her door? Brian! And he was beaming. I was just about as happy as he was. He owed me and he knew it, and a week later when I told him how much I needed cosmetic surgery to change my nose, and how I had been teased and rejected because of it all my life, he agreed to cover the cost. What a guy.

The procedure itself was a breeze, and the surgeon was an artist. What an effect it had on my life! I changed my hairstyle, I changed my walk, I changed my expression, and suddenly there was a new Cathrine in town. Yes, I used to be "Cathy" but now I was "Cathrine." A few days after the operation, when the swelling had gone down, I walked into a bar and wow, did I get attention! For years I had been working on improving my personality and self-esteem, trying to overcome the pain from all the jeers I'd received as a kid. Now, with my perfect new nose I honestly blossomed. I carried myself with assurance, not in a snobby way, but in a way that said I knew exactly who I was, even if I didn't, and it added a whole new dimension to my attitude.

It also added a sense of power. With the feature that I resented most corrected, I lost any remaining inhibitions I had about my looks and about my appeal to men. Looking at myself in the mirror now I could see beyond my ugly nose and admire my eyes, my hair, my smile and all my other features. More than admire them, I could pay attention to them and enhance them, and I did.

Now I felt I could walk into any bar any place in the world, choose any man who appealed to me and walk out with him on my arm, and I spent a very long time proving myself right. I was no longer going to put up with whatever I could get in a man or take sloppy seconds as I did with Louise. If somebody who didn't measure up to my standards approached me in a club or bar to ask for a dance or buy me a drink, I told them to get lost and leave me alone. Okay, maybe I did get a bit snobby. I had spent too much time getting the prettier girls' leftovers and now I wanted a proper main course.

If guys that I met were gorgeous and good in bed, I was theirs. I didn't give a damn about their personality, their charm or anything else. I wanted good looks and great sex. That's all I needed men for. I was blossoming from a scared little girl who let a whole lotta men do whatever they wanted to her because that's what she thought she had to do to keep them happy and make them like her, into a woman who believed she wasn't bad looking at all, someone with a great personality who made people laugh and was smart enough to hold down the job at a prestigious law firm. Where did all this come from?

In essential ways, however, nothing had changed. I was still the angry nut job who threw the chair at the nuns in the maternity ward and wanted to destroy Dr. Jekyll's office when I thought he was treating me like a file instead of a real person. I sure demonstrated it at my favourite bar, Brandy's, one night when a guy I was dating said something to upset me. We were outside on the sidewalk, where tables were set up in the summer, and I had just bought a bottle of Oscar de la Renta perfume, which is not the stuff the Avon lady peddles. I don't recall what he said that made me lose it, but I reached into my purse, grabbed the perfume bottle and hurled it at him. My aim was a little high, and the bottle smashed against the brick wall just above the Brandy's sign, and for the next week anybody who walked past Brandy's entered a cloud of Oscar de la Renta's best scent.

At this time, Brandy's was the ultimate singles bar in Toronto. On the Esplanade, just off Yonge Street, Brandy's was crowded elbow to elbow every night of the week, and many elbows belonged to out-of-town celebrities. I didn't care if they were famous or not. I just wanted to be there to party every night I could make it, and I managed to do it without spending a cent. Somebody, or more correctly, some guy, would always be there willing to buy me a drink and maybe buy one for my girlfriends hanging out there with me as well.

For a very long time Brandy's was my life and almost my home. I would go straight to Brandy's after work on Friday; Michael would be at home being watched by Diane my neighbour or another neighbour named Alison. Sometimes when I went out on Saturday nights, Michael would be by himself after I put him to bed. This was not a regular thing, but it did happen. And when I brought men home from Brandy's, Michael stayed in his room, and at the time, I didn't believe he knew what was going on even if they were there in the morning when he woke up. Looking back, I realize I was wrong. But I was caught between having a fun-filled life and the responsibility of being a single mother. Having become pregnant so young I never had a "carefree" period where I felt I could just do whatever I wanted and with whoever. Again looking back, I realize how selfish I could be. How much I was hurting Michael. I felt so angry and hurt all my life about how my parents treated me, and I could not even see that I had been hardly much better to Michael.

It was my time to be free. The shy, big-nosed girl was long gone, or at least out of sight. She was still there inside me, of course, and always will be. But during those years at Brandy's, I don't believe anyone would have used my name and "shy" in the same sentence. We were something of a gang, my girlfriends and I, and I became the ringleader or at least the mother hen. We developed our own ritual: get together at Brandy's, meet some nice guys who'd buy us drinks, party with them for a few hours, then gather at Mother's restaurant for veal sandwiches before heading home or wherever. When we were leaving for Mother's, if one of the girls got into a car with a guy I didn't know, I would write the licence number on a piece of paper and hold onto it until I saw her at Mother's. Otherwise I threatened to call the cops. I really cared about the people I considered my friends, since most of my life growing up I didn't have any. And if I had some past experience or lesson in my life that I thought could help them, I would offer it up to spare them a potentially bad experience, especially where guys were concerned.

Whenever I went into Brandy's I was on a mission. I would scan the room for the best-looking guy in the place and set my sights on him. I was a predator, not just in the way I hunted for young, attractive men, but also in the way I reacted if anybody got in my way, including the girls who hung out with me. I dominated them, in the same way my mother dominated me, and I suppose you could argue that I chose younger men for the same reason. I could figure out a younger guy's actions before he knew them himself, and I would intimidate him.

I liked dancing with good-looking men because it gave both of us, especially me, a chance to show off our stuff. I wanted to move, I wanted to communicate with my body, not with words. Besides, the music was so loud that you couldn't talk anyway, you would end up shouting at each other, never saying what you wanted to say the way you wanted to say it, which ruined the dancing. I mean, how can you concentrate on dancing when you're both yelling "What? What'd you say?" to each other? So if the guy kept trying to say something while we were dancing I would stop right there on the floor and say, "Look, do you want to dance or do you want to talk? Make up your mind because I only want to dance!"

If he was exceptionally good looking I might put up with his talking, but only if he said something funny or interesting. If he just jabbered away with dull small talk, he became less attractive to me. I wanted them young and handsome. If they were smart, hey, that was a bonus.

And I made the decisions. All of them. Just dancing with me, for example, did not give the guy a right to sit at the table with the other girls and me. I had to invite him over. If he came on his own I told him to get lost.

I never hesitated in approaching anyone I saw at Brandy's who looked attractive, which made me popular with passive men. I found it interesting that the guys who swaggered up to women and delivered all the corny, bullshit lines you could imagine ("If I could rewrite the alphabet, I'd put U and I together," or "Do you believe in love at first sight, or do I have to walk by again?") didn't know what to do if the woman was just as aggressive.

It was fun. It was frivolous. No commitment and no strings attached. Eventually, of course, I would get serious about a guy and start thinking about the future. And eventually the wonderful dream would blow up in my face.

I HAD BEEN GOING OUT LOTS and basically ignoring Michael. I wanted to reconnect with him.

Looking back I realize we did a lot of laughing together over the years, but there were a lot of bad times too. I think what I could never do is find a happy medium between who I wanted to be as a successful independent woman and who I should have been as a mother. As I result, I think I was more an older sister to Michael than a mother.

I had had lots of experiences with men: lots of one-night stands and a few relationships that might even have been trial marriages. But I didn't have a trial child. Even though having Michael was like having my heart walk around outside my body, I never felt that I was able to ever really make him understand this and I don't think he ever believed me when I told him. I never quite understood how giving birth didn't automatically make me a mother.

Michael had turned eight and I was becoming increasingly impatient with him—and with everyone else in my life, frankly. I was like pure uninhibited ego, always expressing my feelings or acting out first and only thinking much later about the consequences, about what I'd said and how I'd behaved.

I could tell Michael was getting angry. He was growing up and he was doing that typical kid thing, not listening to me. I should have known that and dealt with it maturely. Instead, I would get pissed off. I would say mean or hurtful things. Just lashing out like a wounded animal. That only made him listen even less and get even angrier.

I thought I could make up for my mothering skills by giving Michael material things. Like nice stuff might make him love me more. I thought that being Michael's friend would be better than being his mother. I was wrong about most things. If only I'd known back then that Michael needed my presence more than my presents, I might have done a better job.

No, I wouldn't have won any mother-of-the-year awards.

I had one week of holiday time owing to me and it was spring break 1980. I asked Michael if he would like to go to Florida for a week's vacation, just him and me, and play on the beach and have some fun. I think I still felt guilty for going there with Louise and leaving him behind. He got all excited and before we knew it, we were on a plane to Clearwater. We got off the plane and picked up our rental car, making our way to our little hotel right on the beach. I promised that this vacation would be just about me and Michael and he would have all my time. Well, that was my plan, until I met Janice Berger.

It was our third day enjoying the beach and the sun and the

food, and I told Michael that I was going to go into the ocean for a swim. I happened to wade in beside two women, a daughter, Janice—around my age—and her mother. Striking up conversations with strangers was something I did easily and often; I have a natural curiosity about everyone and everything. Anyway, the family was originally from Montreal but lived in a suburb of Toronto. Our little group spent the next few days together eating and going sightseeing; we were having a great time. Michael seemed to be enjoying himself and I so did I. But—like usual—I started feeling restless. I asked Janice if she wanted to check out some local bars and the nightlife. She seemed up for it and I felt that familiar thrill I always felt before a wild night on the town. Her mother offered to watch Michael. I didn't give him a second thought. I wanted to party.

Janice and I got all done up and hopped into my car, letting the wind take us wherever it wanted. We went to a couple of different clubs and had a blast. And when it was time to go home, we got into my rental car and I drove back to our hotel. We were laughing and had the radio blaring with the windows rolled down, and we were singing when I decided to go blast through all the red lights and stop signs. Before I knew it, I saw brightly coloured lights flashing in my rear-view mirror. I pulled over and turned off the radio.

I watched the officer walk toward my car from the driver-side mirror, and thought, This is it. I am so fucked. It's back to jail for me. Janice looked like she had just discovered she was sitting next to Charles Manson. Then I wondered what silver-tongued Louise would say. It's all I needed to know. "Well, good evening, officer!" I said in my most seductive voice, all the while taking a long and appreciative look at him. I smiled.

"Ma'am, do you know you were going through red lights and stop signs?"

"Oh, officer, those are just suggestions," I replied, and Janice and I started to laugh. "Officer, we're Canadian and we're lost, and I guess I panicked a bit, not realizing I was doing that." I kind of pouted and smiled, then asked, "Do all the officers in Florida look like you?"

He shook his head, but I could tell he was amused. He didn't ask for my driver's licence or ID or anything else. He only asked us where we were staying, and then he told us to be careful and go right home. It had been a gorgeous evening.

ON THE PLANE BACK TO TORONTO, Janice and I exchanged phone numbers and addresses and promised to stay in touch. At Customs, the officer asked Michael who he was travelling with. "Her," he replied, pointing at me. "Is that your mother?" the officer asked Michael. Michael paused for a few seconds. "No," he said. I looked at him to see if he was joking, but he was serious. I must have looked shocked; my immediate reaction was to do what I always did: yell. "Michael! What the hell are you talking about? Tell this man right now who I am or else you're in big trouble!"

Michael started getting angry, and I was wondering if he really thought that my mother was his real mother and I was an imposter. I didn't have any identification for Michael with me so when the officer asked for some, I couldn't produce any.

I said, "Look, officer, I'm twenty-four years old and I have an eight-year-old kid. Do you really think I would steal him?" The officer looked at us and was obviously thinking. I added, "Look at our faces and tell me this isn't my son. We're carbon copies of each other." Janice and her mother broke out laughing, and the officer finally said, "Go ahead, ma'am." Things that other people might think should be a given, like travelling with your kid's identification, were often things that I just didn't understand.

When Michael and I visited Janice it gave me a chance—my first real chance—to observe another family and how they behaved with each other. I never really spent time with other girls and their mothers, so I had nothing with which to compare my own relationship with mine. I realized that Janice's parents would do absolutely anything for her. I mean anything. They made sure Janice had everything she needed. The family apartment was always peaceful and quiet, they had regular meals and Janice's laundry was done for her. Her parents let her keep the money she earned for things that she herself needed. They took regular holidays. And the way that

Janice's mother talked to her, well, to say that I was envious—in a good way—is an understatement. Janice's mother was concerned about how Janice felt not only in general, but about herself. I was in awe. And they kissed and hugged and said "I love you" to each other.

This may seem like an odd story, but it's relevant and I have to tell it: When I went into Janice's bathroom, I looked under the sink. Don't ask me why, because I don't know. I saw a box of tampons that was ever so neatly trimmed around the top of the box for easy access. I took Janice aside and asked her to come with me into the bathroom. I opened the cupboard and said, "What's that?" She replied, "Tampons!" I said I knew that they were tampons, but who bought the tampons? She said her mother did and I think, from the look she gave me, she was wondering if I'd lost my marbles.

I reached down and got the box and said, "Did your mother buy the tampons and then put them there for you to use and open the box like that so you'd be able to get to them easily?" Of course, she said, like it was the most normal thing in the world.

I was stunned. My mother *never* bought me tampons. I started to cry. Janice asked me what was wrong.

What could I say? Where would I begin?

CHAPTER TWENTY-THREE

The jackpot

I WANTED MORE OUT OF LIFE.

I was sick and tired of sharing a room or apartment with any-one except people I loved and wanted to be with. I didn't want to have to sleep with strangers in exchange for a place to lay my head. I'd been poor and I didn't like it. I hated not having money for food and bills, and even with my good job at the law firm, I was still struggling to pay my rent and the bills. I wanted to either find a way to make money myself or team up with someone so we could become a success together.

One day passed into another. I worked at the law firm and spent my nights dancing and drinking at Brandy's. I was twenty-five. Jesus, I thought, there had to be more out there for me than this.

One evening I noticed a man sitting at a table with three other young guys. He was wearing an expensive suit, mirror-polished shoes and a watch that wasn't cheap. Packaged up perfectly, he was all ready to be bought and taken home. He was slim and tall, over six feet, I guessed, and everything about him said "class," not in a shout but in a kind of elegant whisper. He had thick and wavy brown hair and deep blue eyes. I suppose I was staring as I left the dance floor, because he smiled across at me and said, in the same English accent you might hear in Buckingham Palace, "Would you like to dance, darling?" except he pronounced it "dawnce."

We danced, and as I watched him moving in that gorgeous suit with those blue eyes on me, I told myself that I would marry this guy. It wasn't a promise so much as a prediction, one that I wanted to see come true the more I learned about him.

His name was Henry. He told me he was twenty-five years old. He had recently arrived from Bahrain and he was a foreign exchange trader, making mountains of money by buying even bigger mountains of money and selling them for a profit. He was brilliant at it. In fact, he had been handling foreign currency since he was just eighteen. Born in England, he had been educated at the best schools in Britain. He was truly brilliant, and one of the most appealing men you could imagine meeting. At least, I thought so. He asked me how old I was and I replied, "Unless you're cheddar, who cares about age, anyway?" and he smiled.

When we weren't dancing, we were laughing. He enjoyed my sense of humour and I adored his. All his buddies were money traders like him, an occupation I was very interested in learning more about. We closed Brandy's that night and Henry and I stepped outside into a waiting limousine, which we took to my apartment.

The apartment I had at the time was always cold. I used to complain to the landlady, and she simply said that the radiators were very old and didn't work well. So I had to constantly keep the oven on with the oven door opened and all four electrical burners running on high. My electrical bill was often higher than I could afford, and every now and again it would be shut off.

Michael was in bed when I got back with Henry.

"Bloody hell, it's fit for brass monkeys in here!" Henry said.

I had no idea what that meant at the time, but I agreed that it was damn cold. I got a couple of blankets from the closet, and joined him on the couch. It seemed time to not pay the rent again and keep the stove and burners going full time instead.

The next morning we were awakened by a cabbie, who sat waiting at the curb while Henry got showered and dressed. Before leaving he scribbled a $2,000 cheque for me to cover both my heating bill and my rent since I'd casually mentioned the situation with my landlady and our game of heat/no heat to explain to him why it was so cold in the apartment. I was more impressed by the fact that he'd had the foresight to order a taxi pickup in the morning and that the cab was actually waiting than by the two grand. I accepted it. And that very evening we agreed to live together.

The thought of being in love with someone as fabulous as Henry and settling down meant more to me than anything. Of course, something had to go wrong.

A WEEK OR SO EARLIER I had visited a doctor for a regular pap test and examination and the sample came back with some abnormal cells. The doctor called me into his office. "Cathy, you have severe cervical dysplasia and we have to do something about it right away."

What? What the hell was that? He explained that this was a progressive step to cervical cancer and it was a good thing that we'd caught it in time. He said that awhile ago, he would have had to cut out the tip of the cervix, but there was a new procedure now called dysplasia laser ablation and he wanted to set me up for a couple of consecutive appointments to get this done. I didn't ask how I might have gotten this, but he volunteered.

"Cathy, we think you got this from having too many sexual partners."

I winced. The fact is, I wish they had been "partners." Faceless strangers and complete losers and fuck-ups was more like it. I was devastated. I had just met the most perfect man in the world and it felt like my past had just come roaring back to life.

The procedure was painful as hell but it was a kind of wake-up call. I realized I had to get my life together. I needed to be with one person. One person who would love me and be faithful to me and show his love by wanting to marry me and accepting my son as his own. I loved Henry and I thought—I determined—that I would be with him for the rest of my life.

My two-bedroom apartment wasn't suitable for Henry, Michael and me, since Henry wanted much better, so he found a new apartment for the three of us, larger and a lot more luxurious. It was a remodelled older home with a fireplace and exposed wood everywhere and the nicest place I had ever lived in my life.

My emotional life kicked into warp speed. Within a few weeks we were planning marriage. It was unreal. It all seemed just too good to be true. Henry said we would have to meet his family in England. I left Michael with my mother and off we went.

You can measure distance in a lot of different ways, but the distance I had gone from living in ratty apartments to marrying Henry is just about as far, culturally and economically, as anybody can travel. Before leaving, Henry told me about his family, how his parents were divorced and how his Uncle Peter was a little eccentric. I figured I had a PhD in eccentric, so how tough could this crowd be?

It was one of the biggest thrills in my life landing in London. But best of all was shopping at Harrods. I could have spent all week in that store just wandering the aisles. I thought back to my days as a child snipping buttons from pretty dresses so I could make my own paper dresses and dream about having my own real dresses ... one day.

My one day had arrived. Beautiful dresses—as many as I wanted—and beautiful buttons too.

IT TURNED OUT the uncle lived in a castle, a real brick and stone fortress-like palace, dark and cool, with a suit of armour waiting around every corner. Uncle Peter had founded the first British chapter of a UFO society, and he and the other members spent their time and money tracking flying saucers and little green men. Although Henry had a great job and earned a fat salary, his family didn't have a lot of money. Uncle Peter tied up the family treasure, so everybody tolerated the old guy's eccentricities, believing they would be in line for an inheritance when he died. Eventually they realized that he had other ideas for his cash and it didn't include people, not on Earth, anyway. When he died, Uncle Peter left everything to the flying saucer people.

Henry's father, Bob, and Bob's wife, Mavis, were pleasant and wished us well. They lived in an average English home in Derby. I loved the English countryside.

Then I met Henry's mother.

TALL, SLIM AND ELEGANTLY DRESSED, Henry's mother looked like a female version of her son. When Henry introduced me to her, she looked me over slowly from my head down to my toes and back again, before turning to Henry and shaking her head.

"This ... won't ... do."

She acted like somebody who had gone shopping for a Mercedes-Benz and had been shown a bicycle. Or who ordered steak and got a hot dog. I had an engagement ring on my finger and a date to marry her son, so I held on to my temper and avoided tossing a bottle of perfume at her or even a nasty word in her direction. With a little work, I told myself, I could win her over.

This woman had her eye on royalty, literally. Over tea she bragged about watching Prince Charles play polo the previous weekend. I kept thinking that maybe one day she would get to like me and then I would get to meet the prince and all those important and famous people that she knew too.

I particularly liked Henry's sister, Sarah. He had another sister too, Penny, who had a couple of kids. We returned home and made plans for the wedding. I was so excited. We would invite Henry's mother and sisters and pay for their airfare, and they would stay with us. We decided on a big church wedding with a flamboyant reception. Henry chose the Royal Canadian Military Institute. It was a beautiful choice.

I hired a choir of a dozen singers to celebrate our marriage. Of course, I wanted the perfect dress.

FOR OVER FIFTEEN YEARS I had carried around my disappointment and anger at not having the princess-style Communion dress with crinolines and black patent leather shoes I'd wanted. It was like a scar that I never thought about until I happened to glance at it in the mirror. Now it was my time to complete that picture, in a lovely white dress with crinolines a yard thick and new patent leather shoes, but in white this time, and with high heels.

Facing my First Communion I had had to deal with poverty, hunger, my nose, and my mother's dominance. Now I was twenty-five years old, on the brink of marrying a man whom I loved and with whom I thought my son and I could have a fabulous life. Poverty, hunger and my embarrassing nose were all behind me.

By this time my mother and father were living apart and though they would never divorce would never live together again. My mom had gotten to hate my dad even more after they split up for good. I would think that she would have been happier without him, but she only became more verbal, expressing how she had wasted her life away. "I don't know why I stayed with that bastard. He was rotten just like my father," she would say.

My dad, now living in a run-down, two-bedroom apartment near High Park in Toronto, said that if they divorced, my mom wouldn't get his army pension or something like that. My mom moved into a welfare building on the east side of Toronto, where my Auntie Nellie was already living: their mother also lived nearby. I wondered why it took my leaving home before she split up with him. She did tell me that kids needed their parents and I used to think that was funny and a lot of crap too. Kids didn't need their parents fighting like idiots if not being together meant food and sleep and quiet nights for everyone.

Anyway, for reasons that would take me a lifetime—and then some—to completely figure out, my mother was still controlling me.

"You can't wear that!" she responded when I described the wedding ensemble I wanted. "Don't be stupid. You'll look like a goddamn bloody idiot."

I told her I wanted to look like a princess.

"You can't look like a goddamn princess," she sneered. "Grow up. Princess my ass. I'll pick you out a proper gown."

I had an eleven-year-old child and a lifetime of experiences, I was about to marry a man who I was convinced was destined to become a heavyweight player in life and I was still terrified of my mother. Somewhere, in my genes or maybe as a programmed part of my personality, something told me not to argue with her. She had the same hold on me as when I pleaded for a proper First Communion dress and she dismissed me as a spoiled little brat for wanting something special. So I gave in. I wore a wedding gown I hated, one my mother chose and approved of for me. I also agreed that my dad would not be invited to the wedding. She said he would get drunk and ruin things.

"Uncle Frank should give you away," she told me.

"Are you kidding me, Mom?" My mind went back to what he'd told me years earlier about girls who deserved to get raped. But more important, yeah, maybe it *was* true that my dad might get drunk and ruin things. Then again, maybe not. He was my dad, though, and this was supposed to be *my* perfect day. The fact is, it felt like the wedding had been ruined already. Once again I went along with everything my mother wanted, just as I had when I was eight years old at my First Communion.

HENRY'S MOTHER and his sister Sarah arrived a few days before the wedding and did stay with us at our condo, although Penny was a no-show, as was Henry's father and his wife. I was so excited that the day was almost here and I would be surrounded by people who were coming to our wedding because they were happy for us. But by the time my future in-laws had been in our condo for a day I knew it was a mistake putting them up.

It was impossible to please Henry's mother. She didn't like the food I cooked, so we had to eat out; she didn't like the suits I'd chosen for the men to wear, so we had to scramble at the last minute to find proper English morning suits (or was it mourning?); and she demanded Henry give her money—that's when I found out that he was regularly sending her and his family money—and on and on. Do you know how stressful planning a wedding is? However, she did give me a beautiful lace hanky, and maybe that was because she knew I would need it later on when I ended up crying—and I'm not talking about tears of joy either.

Then, I was informed that Henry's mother would be wearing a yellow dress, after I had let her know that the colour theme of the wedding was pink. She said she didn't like the colour pink. I called the bakery that was making my cake and told them to hurry up and make a cake in yellow instead of pink to match her dress and honour her. My bridesmaids would be wearing pink, the décor would all be pink, but this didn't appear to matter. The cake would be yellow. And one bridesmaid, my best friend Janice, would be wearing a hat. Nobody else would be wearing a hat except me and I didn't want any other girl in the wedding party to wear a hat, but Janice insisted, so I gave in. I wanted my hair to be long and my mother told me that I needed to get it cut. Big mistake. I hated it. Originally I didn't want to wear a hat, but my mother liked the idea so now that I had this crappy haircut, I gladly wore a hat to cover up the mess.

The whole damn wedding was about everybody but me. Henry chose the location, my mother chose the dress, my future mother-in-law dictated the colour of the cake and my best friend Janice insisted on wearing a frickin' hat.

Well, all right. I gave in on this stuff but everything appeared to be in place until the man delivering the wedding cake dropped it and it split right across the middle. I saw it happening and it was just like in the movies when some tragedy happens in slow motion. I tried to dive under the cake before it hit the ground, hoping to save it, but I couldn't. Splat! I looked down and saw that one of the three layers of this rectangular cake, which was not even half as beautiful as the one I'd ordered and paid for in pink, landed right side up, with a huge crack diagonally through the rectangle. It looked like what you would draw on a heart shape if you were showing the heart was broken. Great. Was this some sort of sign? I pulled out that hanky and I used it to dry my tears.

The deliveryman and I lifted the cake and put it onto the main table where the wedding party would be sitting. I had to stop crying and think fast. I ran outside and didn't stop until I found some daisies. I took a handful of the yellow and white flowers and laid them across the crack as though it had been planned that way. It simply wouldn't do, to quote Henry's mother, to have anything less than a perfect wedding cake.

We hired limousines for the family and Michael rode in one with my mother and my aunties to the venue. Michael insisted on wearing a brand new suit with a tie and he looked like a mini Henry.

I was so proud. Henry, I thought, was having a positive influence on Michael. Henry and I rode in a baby-blue Rolls Royce equipped with a black leather-gloved chauffeur who also wore a cap. As everyone was entering the church, I peeked up the aisle to watch everyone arrive. The church looked beautiful. I saw Henry's mother arrive and at the same time, so did Henry's best man, Robbie, along with Henry.

As Robbie and Henry walked up the aisle to their place at the front of the church, Robbie saw Henry's mother and said, "Bloody hell, who invited Mary Poppins?" and he laughed out loud. I had to admit, she did look like Mary Poppins—only a lot more regally uptight and "la dee da." It was pretty funny.

Icily, Henry said to Robbie, "That's my mother."

Robbie immediately stopped laughing. With a sinking heart I noticed then that Henry's mother had brought her suitcase to the church. Later, she could be heard whispering loud enough for everyone to hear, "And just how long do you think *this* is going to last?"

She skipped the reception and went directly back to the airport to catch the next flight home to London.

WE HONEYMOONED IN PUERTO VALLARTA. I had chosen it after watching an episode of a TV show. Hey, if it was good enough for *The Love Boat* it was good enough for me, proving that I had difficulty separating life on television from reality. Puerto Vallarta was a disappointment that became worse when I caught an intestinal bug and had to pay $100 to a hairy Mexican doctor with about a hundred gold chains around his neck openly displayed on his "fur" because his shirt was totally unbuttoned. After the painful shot he gave me in the ass, as if he was throwing a dart or something, I swore the hotel accidentally called a veterinarian and not a people doctor.

The disasters just kept on coming. Shortly after we returned from our honeymoon, Henry's company declared bankruptcy. But things quickly began turning around.

One of the world's largest foreign exchange companies was looking for someone to manage its Toronto office, a position I told

Henry he could fill perfectly. He disagreed, claiming he was too young and lacked managerial experience. I convinced him he had the skills to do the job, and when it came management expertise I would help him out. And I did. When he got the job, as I knew he would, he relied on my opinion of the traders he hired. I used my instincts and understanding of men to spot winners and losers, and they were always correct. Playing the perfect young executive's wife and doing, in my opinion, a damn fine job of it, I also helped him entertain clients and their families and made pretend friends with people I couldn't stand. I put up with all the entertaining and with Henry being away so much because my whole life was about helping him become a success.

Having learned so much from my working career, as scattered and unfocused as it had been, I began believing that I had been born with natural business skills the same way some people are born with an ability to sing and play music better than the rest of us. I saw opportunities clearly and knew how to manage people. Don't get me wrong. I love people. But I knew that you could never become a success dealing with and choosing to be around only the ones you liked best.

Henry's success and his substantial rise in salary brought all kinds of rewards for us. I got new boobs, I had my big butt and thighs chiselled down by the finest surgeon in Toronto, I had a husband, I had money, I had a life. I started showing the two dogs and Tara and Baron were often in the local newspapers. We all celebrated two fabulous Christmases and our birthdays, and Michael and I both got fantastic gifts. The best part was that Michael started calling Henry "Dad." The story should have ended right there, but of course it doesn't.

I started my own business, Wordstream. It was a word-processing service targeting large, prestigious law firms needing a reliable service to prepare documents accurately whenever their own word-processing staff became overloaded. I bought office equipment second-hand—saving me a fortune—and my freelance employees were contracted by the hour and as I needed them. Soon we were working nights and weekends producing material for lawyers, taking a load off their own staff and making ourselves a bundle.

I soon ran out of qualified word-processing people familiar with preparing legal documents perfectly, and when I realized nobody was training word-processing operators, I began training my own. When I had enough qualified people in my files, I launched a placement agency to connect them with law firms and others who needed their talents. I hired an assistant, whom I recruited myself from a company that I had worked with in the past. Michelle was like a mini-me, I thought. She was smart and just about as fast as me at typing on our word processors. I then hired other staff, including my mother as our receptionist, and my business grew to a substantial size.

I got backlogged with work one day and asked Michelle if she could stay late and maybe work on the weekend to help me out, because I already wasn't getting any sleep. She said that she couldn't, because she had a date with her boyfriend, or something like that. Well, I flipped. I told her that if she didn't stay and help me, she was fired. She said she wouldn't and so I fired her. I was so feisty back then and almost on a mission to sort out my life. I was as close as ever to becoming a personal and business success and I worried that if I stopped, I would tumble much like Humpty Dumpty did. I didn't want to ever fall off that brick wall that I had climbed so hard to get on top of.

As inflexible and uncompromising as I could be sometimes, I knew a lot of things about life and was proving I had a knack for business, but Henry taught me about class. He had good taste when it came to clothes and decorating, and I absorbed as much of it as I could. The little girl who had scuttled with rats on the floor for pieces of cheese knew enough table etiquette to dine at Buckingham Palace—if she were ever invited. Henry taught me which fork to use, how to spot a real Rolex among a pile of rip-off copies, the way to speak to waiters and household servants, the whole upper-class attitude.

Either he was one hell of a teacher or I was one responsive student, because almost everything about me changed—the way I dressed, the way I spoke, the way I entered a room, and the way I saw myself. The world was divided into winners and losers, and I moved from one side to the other in a matter of months.

There is something else, though. It's about confidence. I know this now but I didn't then: confidence isn't something you are born with like blue eyes or curly hair. It's something that is always there but you have to take hold of it and nurture it. You can't let people take it away from you. I wasted too many years believing I couldn't do something but it was because I believed I couldn't do it. Why? Because people I trusted told me I couldn't do it. And I believed them. There is really only one person in the world you really need to believe in: *yourself.* Having someone in your life who believes in you is a joy. But you have to believe in yourself first.

SOMETHING WAS STILL BOTHERING ME.

A few months after the wedding I invited my dad to stay at our condo. I thought maybe we could discuss a few things. I felt so horrible for not inviting him to the wedding. He arrived late and he was sober. I didn't have any liquor in the house, which visibly upset him. I made dinner and Michael and I ate with him—Henry had to work late.

We talked. Well, I tried to.

"Dad, I'm sorry I didn't invite you to my wedding."

"It doesn't matter."

I remember how much that hurt. Of course he couldn't have meant it, I thought. He was just hurt. But what if it was true? What if it *hadn't* really mattered?

My dad stayed up all night seated at the kitchen table playing with a toy of Michael's—a silly plastic container with little silver metal balls in it that you moved every which way to try to get the balls into grooves. He sat there for hours playing. All night I could hear it: ting, ting, ting, ting. I got up out of bed and watched him from the kitchen doorway without his knowing. He was mesmerized, staring intently at that stupid little toy. I felt so sorry for him. I went back to bed and lay on my back, staring at the ceiling while the traffic dimly lit the bedroom.

A few nights later, Henry was working late again and I fell fast asleep. When he came home finally he stood in the doorway of the bedroom, loosening his tie. I woke up instantly, startled by the honking of some cars. I didn't see Henry, I saw my father. I blinked my eyes a few times and I still saw my father. I was terrified. I knew it was Henry, but somehow it was my father's image. It took a few minutes until I saw Henry in the flesh. I will never forget that.

Henry's company kept an apartment in New York and we travelled there frequently, on business or just for a getaway to catch a show or visit one of his friends in the music business.

For a time I was in a totally different social whirl, one I could never have dreamt of a year or two earlier. We dined and hung out with the guys from Dire Straits and Simon Le Bon from Duran Duran, who brought his new girlfriend, Yasmin.

On another occasion, Julian Lennon and his girlfriend joined us for dinner; Julian was one of many contacts Henry had made growing up in England. Through all of this I was never knocked over by the fame or the power of these people. I enjoyed them and I loved being among them, but I never had an "Oh, wow!" response. For the most part I just felt I belonged there. I was right at home.

One weekend I took Donna and Debbie, two girlfriends from my years at the law firm, to New York for the weekend. We stayed in the company apartment and planned to hit clubs like the Palladium. As soon as I saw the clothes they'd brought, I knew we'd never get past the club bouncers, so we grabbed a cab to Saks Fifth Avenue, where I outfitted them in entire new wardrobes suited for doing the town on a Manhattan Saturday night.

I was experiencing a lifestyle and meeting people I had only seen in magazines and movies. It seemed like the best of everything. Having lots of money was never enough to become part of that life. You had to possess an instinct for style, for attitude, for a range of things that some people are born with and most people never learn.

This doesn't make you a better person, by any means. I'm not sure it even makes you happier. In my case, it gave me confidence to achieve the level of success I had always wanted, and I eventually did. It just took me a long time and cost me a lot of heartache.

AFTER A YEAR I convinced Henry to move to the suburbs.

Through a deal I arranged, we flipped our condo, meeting our commitment to the builder and pocketing an $80,000 profit in the bargain, and purchased a custom-built home next to the Glen Abbey Golf Club, site of the Canadian Open.

I didn't give a damn about golf, but living next to a place where Arnold Palmer and his buddies showed up now and then appealed to me. We spent the $80,000 profit from the sale of the condo on upgrades to the house.

At that point, it was clear the kid had made it.

That house was everything I could have dreamt of. Henry—*my husband*—was everything I ever wanted. Michael adored Henry. Money was never a problem. Nothing was a problem.

Okay, there were still a few problems. No matter how fast you run, the past is never that far behind.

Henry and I went on a weeklong cruise while my mother stayed with Michael. Returning home I noticed an empty bottle of expensive cognac in the garbage; it had been almost full when we left.

"What happened to all the cognac in here?" I asked my mother, who confessed that she drank it in our absence. "Do you know this stuff costs over two thousand dollars a bottle?" I said.

My mother just shrugged. "So what? You can afford it."

After she left, we found empty beer cans under the couch and stashed away in the corners of our backyard. It wasn't the dollar value of the booze that she polished off that upset me, it was that she was still drinking like a fish. I was hoping that she too had changed her life, especially since she and my dad had separated. I think my mother thought she was showing great strength by staying with my dad all those miserable years. But to me, leaving him would have proved she had even greater strength. But neither one of them got better at anything. They both continued to live their lives as poor as ever.

HENRY BOUGHT ME A HORSE, a beautiful thoroughbred gelding named Top Hat, but I called him Harry. Harry was a lovely animal. I enjoyed riding and caring for him. I stabled him at an upper-class riding academy near Oakville, visiting him as often as possible, nearly every day in the summer, just to ride him, brush him down, feed him apples and carrots and nuzzle him.

Harry had the best tack, the best blankets and the best food I could afford. I tried to get Michael interested in riding, even bribing him with news about all the girls at the stable, but he just wasn't interested. I kept Harry for almost twenty years, which is a hell of a lot longer than I kept any man around, trucking him literally across the country with me because I couldn't stand the idea of anyone else owning and caring for him. In later years, when I was as down and out as I had ever felt in my life and Michael was living on his own, I actually paid Harry's stable fees before I paid for my own rent. I even considered sleeping in his stall with him on more than one occasion when I didn't have anywhere to live, but I always ended up leaving in the wee hours because stable hands started work pretty early and I didn't want to get caught.

Harry was a luxury I never dreamt I could afford, but then so was my whole life at the time. One day while grocery shopping I decided I would prefer to carry the groceries home in a new car, preferably from the BMW dealer across the street, so I bought one. Nice car. Loved it. Loved my life with Henry. My wildest dreams had come true. What could go wrong?

HENRY'S BUSINESS WAS COMPLEX, and because he dealt in global currencies he was often on the telephone or fax machine with Hong Kong, Tokyo, Singapore and other locations where currency traders were starting their day around the time we were ending ours. So I didn't become too concerned when he worked evenings and arrived home late, or when he didn't come home until morning, spending the night in a downtown hotel and doing deals from midnight to dawn, if necessary.

Like any wife, I grew annoyed at his absence from time to time. If I asked why he wasn't home most nights, which went way beyond what an understanding wife should have to deal with, I thought, he told me I didn't really understand his business and how much of his life it occupied. I would reply that I did understand, but spending so much time away from me was really starting to bother me. He responded to a comment like this once by waving his arm at the house and the furnishings and the BMW in the driveway and saying, "I pay you to be my wife!" That really hurt.

My mother was the first to express suspicion of Henry. She wondered if he really needed to stay downtown overnight all those evenings, and claimed he often received telephone calls from women we didn't know.

"He thinks he's so smart, but he's not smarter than me! I know what he's doing coming home and getting clean clothes and staying out all night. Yeah, thinks he can fool me, eh? You're so stupid you don't see anything."

I thought she was judging Henry by my father's actions; she didn't trust him so she wouldn't trust Henry. I ignored her.

Anyway, my mother kept saying Henry had to be fooling around on me until one night, a day before he was to fly to Tokyo on business, I decided to drive downtown and check out the bars he favoured, hoping to surprise him. The first bar I walked into, I saw him right away.

He was standing at the bar, buying a girl a drink, looking as smooth as ever. Perhaps what shocked me most was I couldn't see Henry's wedding ring.

I lost it. I walked across the room and slapped his face, right there in the bar. I called him a son of a bitch and other names, screaming at him to humiliate him and told him I wanted a divorce. Then I left him standing there, giving all the other people in that bar something to talk about for the rest of the night and the next day at their office water coolers. ("Then this tall broad comes in, screams at the poor guy, hauls off and slaps him right across the face and yells, 'I want a divorce, you prick!'")

I made it home that night. Henry didn't. I assume he stayed overnight downtown or near the airport and caught his flight to Tokyo in the morning. He phoned home a few times, and eventually announced that he was coming home and he wanted to patch things up. I forgave him, until the next, and last, time.

It was a similar scenario: he hadn't been home in days; he was busy working and entertaining. Couldn't be helped. I told him I was going out with girlfriends that night but maybe we could meet at our favourite bar later. Great, he said. I took a cab to the bar. As I pulled up in the cab I saw a limousine at the curb. Out climbed a gorgeous girl with long legs, and right after her emerged Henry. He dashed into the bar alone. I fucking couldn't believe my eyes. I marched up to the woman, grabbed her by the shoulder and spun her around. "What the fuck are you doing with my husband?" I shouted.

I yanked off my engagement and wedding rings and flung them into the street. Then I walked into the bar, went up to Henry, and I hauled back and punched him in the face. He fell and got back up and just stood there, not speaking. I was so mad I couldn't think of anything to say. Finally he walked out.

I thought the owner was going to call the police, but instead, he bought the bar a round on him and then asked everyone to please leave. I sat at the bar with him all night long, drinking champagne while he told me how his wife had left him for his best friend.

I WAS ANGRY, angrier than I could ever imagine myself becoming again.

Basically, I ran away from it. I didn't stick around to work things out in a logical manner. I made it impossible to return to anything like the life I was leaving.

The next night, with Henry away again, and me trying to sort out in my head how I would leave, I put on my black taffeta Wayne Clark dress, made sure Michael was all set to spend the night at a friend's house and then climbed into the BMW and went cruising the downtown bars, checking out the action not from inside the bar but from inside my car. At one bar, I noticed a long line of people waiting to be admitted, and in the middle of the line was the prettiest man I had ever seen. Not just handsome—pretty. Pretty in the sense of a young Robert Redford, with thick, wavy blond hair, blue eyes, a great physique and perfect features. In fact, he was so pretty that my first thought was, He must be gay. Well, what the hell, I told myself as I parked the BMW, let's find out.

CHAPTER TWENTY-FOUR

Picking up the pieces

HE WASN'T GAY.

I confirmed it that night when we went for a walk and found an abandoned house not far from the bar, where the dust on the floor made a hell of a mess of my Wayne Clark dress and turned it from black to black and white.

Shane was from Edmonton, Alberta, and he was in construction. It was outrageous—the guy should have been working as a male model. He was so good looking that he didn't need a personality to hit it off with women, so he didn't have much of one. I didn't care. I didn't want Mr. Congeniality. I wanted Mr. Beautiful, and Shane was just about as beautiful as they come. He was also younger than me, which was the norm. Older guys always seemed to live in basement apartments while their ex-wives lived in a big house on a hill. I wanted nothing to do with basement apartments or men who were spending their money on alimony and child support. If they were going to spend money on anybody, I wanted it to be me.

I took Shane home with me the next night, just in time for a friend of Henry's to drop by, see Shane, figure out what was going on and alert Henry, which I guess is what drove him to be openly seen with his girlfriend, his hairdresser. Shane needed to start earning money and I was damned if he would make it in construction. He was natural model material, and despite his protests I hustled him off first to Holt Renfrew, where I chose an entire new wardrobe for him and charged it on Henry's credit card, then to one of the largest male model agencies in Canada, where I insisted the president of the agency check Shane out and sign him up.

"He's going to be huge," he agreed.

Well, he wasn't huge. He scored a few jobs, including one that put him on the cover of a Harlequin romance novel, but that was about it. He lacked drive. He was quiet, sweet, laid-back. Okay, fine, I guess. But he made me restless. I wanted to shake him, like my mother used to shake me. *Why are you so stupid?* Only with Shane it was, *Why are you so lazy?* I guess I had spent so much time as a kid feeling horrible because people kept telling me I *couldn't* do anything I just couldn't deal with people who didn't *want to* do anything. I had ambition to the point of being driven—maybe in the wrong direction sometimes—but Shane had no drive at all.

LIFE GOES ON, as they say. Henry launched divorce proceedings. I could have hired a lawyer and fought him for every cent. But I just wanted it to be over. It was like waking up from a glorious dream and being back in a life you thought you had left forever. Once again I figured that I was to blame. I was being punished for something. Best to just accept it.

I had already sold my word processing business. Against my lawyer's advice, I sold most of the contents of the house. Henry could do whatever he wanted with it. To hell with it. To hell with *him*.

Shane and I moved out of my dream house and into a tiny apartment that could barely accommodate the two of us plus Michael.

I needed a change. I needed a new life ... again. The problem was, who to have it with? Shane's only passion was smoking pot every night. But he looked so good doing it and I really was crazy about him.

I probably should have seen it coming. Probably should have seen the signs. This was not a relationship that could last. But I chose not to see anything except my life with Shane in it. Plus, he and Michael got along great together. So I decided to do something really crazy: I followed my heart.

With my son Michael and my horse Harry and my boyfriend Shane, we moved the sixty kilometres from Oakville to the small city of Guelph, Ontario. So there I was, the mother of a teenager, and about to become a divorcee. I had a relationship with a nice guy who had the looks of a movie star and the ambition of a tree stump. I had no education, an acquired taste for the good life, some success as an independent businesswoman, a really good nose job, some cosmetic surgery and not much else. I know, it doesn't sound like much. So I became a cocktail waitress, student and a part-time veterinary assistant. Go figure.

SOMEWHERE AMID THE CONFUSION of my life, I began to take stock of things.

Turning thirty probably had something to do with it.

For my thirtieth birthday, my mother surprised me by giving me a Gucci purse. I was floored. It was the best present anyone had ever given me. I thought, finally, maybe things between my mom and me will change. I used the purse daily for a few months and then it started to fade in colour and fall apart. I told my mother that we should take it back to the store where she'd bought it to get either a refund or a replacement.

"Well," she said, "I guess we could do that IF the purse wasn't a knock-off!" She started laughing like a hyena. "Do you think I would buy you a real Gucci purse? I bought it from some guy in a tavern that I was drinking in. And YOU never knew that, did you, STUPID!"

Yeah, it was time to take stock. Time to start climbing that ladder.

THE ANIMAL HOSPITAL JOB was about the lowest rung on the ladder, I figured. I euthanized mice caught on sticky pieces of paper that people preferred over standard snap traps. I thought this was more humane. So the technicians would bring the traps to me and I would kill them. I also inspected stool samples for the vet. It doesn't sound like much. But I liked the work. I really did. I liked working with animals and it really didn't matter which part of the animal. I started to feel like I was needed. I also felt I was good at what I was doing. Like I had a natural talent for it. I knew I had to take another few steps up the ladder: I decided to work towards a veterinary degree.

Now, it turned out that Guelph had one of the largest veterinary colleges in the country. I knew I wouldn't be admitted there immediately, but perhaps I could score some credits at the University of Guelph, which had a mature student program and provided married student quarters for anyone enrolled in its programs.

The animal hospital agreed to change my work shifts to evenings and weekends. Plus Shane, who preferred construction to modelling, could easily find work in the Guelph area while staying with Michael and me in the married student residences. It was a crazy plan in so many ways. From party girl with no education to wealthy suburban socialite to divorced cocktail waitress with a teenaged son to university student, all in four years.

Because I was enrolling as a mature student, the admissions standards were different than for a regular student. My biggest hurdle would be writing an admissions test. Just in case, I decided to introduce myself to as many people at the university as I could. I have always been much better with people than with tests. I passed the test.

I can't tell you how proud and excited I was when I was assigned a student number. I felt like I had passed into an elite fraternity. I was no longer "stupid" Cathy. I was a university student. The dream was to show the world that I was not stupid, that I was smarter than I had had a chance to demonstrate up until then. Only smart people went to university, and they did it to become even smarter and succeed at whatever they chose to do. I loved it there. I wanted to stay forever.

I studied as hard as I could. But it was exhausting. Plus I had my part-time job at the Holiday Inn and my volunteer work at the veterinary college, not to mention trying to be a mother to Michael and a girlfriend to Shane. But I just wanted so badly to do something with my life. The "something" was still ill-defined and badly focused but it was there. Of all the things I have done in my life, admirable and regrettable, none has marked me as lazy, and my years at the university represent in some ways the height of my ambition.

One day while volunteering at the veterinary college, I blew up at a woman who brought her sick dog in for an examination. The poor animal was in agony, but the woman didn't seem to give a damn. I screamed at her that she shouldn't be allowed to have a pet if she was dumb enough to think that maggots infesting the vulva of her female beagle was something she could ignore. I really lost it. "The sickest bitch here isn't the one with four legs," I screamed at her. "It's you!"

Administrators at the college suggested if I couldn't keep my emotions under control, maybe I'd be better off dealing just with animals and not with their owners, and I saw their point. I resigned from my volunteer services, and I missed the work and the people. But I never regretted blowing my top at the dog owner.

It's funny, but sometimes—maybe too often—I seem more sensitive to the suffering of animals than I do to that of the people around me. I suppose it's because animals can't help being what they are, so treating them badly seems so unnecessarily cruel. People usually have choices.

Considering the long and bumpy path I had taken to arrive at university, I refused to feel as though I didn't belong there, despite the fact that some students were ten years younger than me with real high-school diplomas and loving parents fussing over them. I arrived at classes with the attitude that I had as much right to be there as anyone.

I discovered that I had an aptitude for some subjects, including complex ones like microbiology, and the philosophy of medicine. We worked with lab partners in microbiology class, and one day we were asked to do mouth swabs of each other, transfer them to a Petri plate and do a visual analysis under the microscope. We were looking for bacteria and other organisms, which I found in my partner's samples, but I also found spermatozoa! Naturally I asked if she'd had a date with her boyfriend the night before or if they'd been fooling around before class that morning, and presented her with the evidence.

I liked the other kids. I liked them all. I made friends with foreign exchange students, with jocks and athletes, with everybody. The professors as well. They didn't intimidate me. If I received a low mark on a paper, I made a point of tracking down the professor and asking for an explanation, or asking if I could have an opportunity to explain my side. I refused to let a bad mark just lie there as evidence that I was unable to do the work. Time and again, my concern or my explanation of things earned me a better mark. And in case you're wondering, my chances of success were just as high regardless of whether the professor was male or female. You succeed on the basis of your relationships in life, and I treated women the same as men.

I did a lot of partying while at Guelph, usually with my son and his friends. One snowy winter's night while Shane was away visiting him mother in Edmonton for a few days, Michael and I and a couple of his friends decided to visit a bar. A line of people extended from the bar's entrance out onto the sidewalk, so I dropped the guys off in front of the bar and told them to get in line while I parked the car. When I joined them in the lineup, a guy standing behind us thought I was cutting in and told me to go to the back of the line.

"Hey, I don't even do lines normally," I said. He was bugging me. I was cold and uncomfortable and wondering if going to this bar was really worth the hassle. "They were saving my place, all right?"

Then Michael, his friends and I started talking and laughing about nothing very important. The guy behind us, however, just couldn't leave things alone.

"So what's up?" he sneered. "You go around picking up young guys for fun? One of these guys is your boyfriend, is that it?"

The comments were really getting under Michael's skin but, like a good mother, I advised him to ignore the comments. And we both did, until the guy said, "So what're you going to do? Pick one of these guys, take him back to your place and give him a blow job?"

That did it. I turned around and punched him so hard he flew back into the people behind him, who had to catch him to prevent him from landing on the sidewalk. Michael and his friends, of course, thought the whole scene was hilarious and they laughed about it for weeks, even years.

At university, I discovered that I had an excellent memory for things I was interested in. I just couldn't regurgitate them back on paper for exams the way they were in my head. I had a natural aptitude for English and scored great marks in that subject. I did well in anatomy and microbiology because those subjects depended on memorizing pictures and involved concepts that I could somehow grasp quite easily.

It was in classes like statistics and chemistry where I really screwed up. I didn't have the fundamentals of mathematics needed to handle those subjects, and my learning disability (which I didn't know I had until years later) made things even tougher. But I stuck at it. I needed something. More than that, I needed to *prove* something.

For five years, the University of Guelph was my town. Just walking among the old stone buildings seemed to make me smarter, or at least more confident. Knowledge seemed to seep into me, and if I could have I might have stayed there forever. I felt protected from all the wrongs of the world. Nothing nasty and threatening, I believed, could happen on the university campus, because it was a place where knowledge and education were valued above everything else. Beatings, abuse, starvation, they all existed somewhere else. Not among Gothic stone buildings and young people laughing and learning together.

I was serious about learning, serious about obtaining a university degree. I hired a tutor for mathematics and chemistry studies, a woman whose help I wanted so badly that I often slept at her house after a long evening of studying, of trying to grasp what I needed to know, so I'd be ready to get started again first thing in the morning.

Michael and were getting along pretty well. At least, I thought so. The truth was, maybe I was too busy to notice what was going on.

One day the police showed up at our door. Some expensive exercise equipment had been stolen from an apartment complex and they suspected Michael. But he denied it and I believed him.

I began getting restless. I had been a student for three years and I felt like I was no closer to my goal.

One morning on campus I saw an interesting notice in the want ads. A local hospital was looking for a morgue assistant to work with its resident pathologist. Whoever got the job would help perform autopsies and "generally assist in the administration of the facility and its inventory." *Inventory?* Was this a morgue or a supermarket? I assumed the phrase meant tracking corpses coming and going or at least making sure they were on the right shelf. The pay was good and the prospect of being employed in the medical field, even the dead part, was too much to resist. I would be working with corpses but that wasn't a turnoff to me. Somewhere there had to be living and breathing doctors and nurses and that was good enough for me. The way I saw it, I hadn't had a lot of success with live people anyway. Maybe I'd do better with dead ones.

The more I thought about it the more excited I became, and early the next day I was back at the veterinary college asking for an application form.

When she heard I was interested, the girl who handled student jobs at the college looked me up and down as if I was a soiled piece of laundry. "Are you a vet student?" she asked.

I told her no, I wasn't, I just volunteered.

"So are you in pre-med studies then? What program are you in?"

I was in general studies and I think she was trying to get me to back off, but instead I had a few of my own questions for her. I asked what the qualifications for the job were, besides being a student at the veterinary school or being pre-med. She wasn't anxious to tell me. She mumbled something about understanding medical terminology and having innate skills, that kind of stuff. In fact, it was pretty obvious that she simply wanted me to go away. So I did. Why go to the dirty, greasy rag when you can go to the train conductor?

Whenever I can't get answers from somebody, I start moving up the chain of authority. In this case, it meant going directly to the pathologist instead of screwing around with someone who wouldn't even hand me an application form. Besides, to me, no really means maybe.

I made calls to the hospital and learned the name of the pathologist: Dr. E. T. Ling. Hanging around the hospital cafeteria a couple of days later, I watched him arrive for lunch, and my first impression was, Do I really want to work with this guy? His face seemed fixed in a permanent frown behind heavy glasses. About forty-five years old, he looked as though he hadn't smiled since he was a kid, and probably not very much then. But I heard he was brilliant and admired by all the medical professionals who worked with him even if, I learned later, he intimidated them.

The next day I phoned Dr. Ling, introduced myself, said I was interested in the job and asked about the necessary qualifications.

"I am looking for someone enrolled in either pre-med or pre-vet programs at the university," he said in his gruff speaking style, "or who is in veterinary studies at the college. They need that kind of background."

"But wouldn't it count," I asked, "if someone lacked those specific qualifications, maybe had a few of them I mean, but had a really keen desire to do the job? Wouldn't that be at least as important?"

No, he said. He had told me the qualifications, and those were the kind of people he wanted to choose from.

I could have thanked him and gone back to another waitressing job to earn money, but I didn't. I wanted that job, damn it. More than anything else I wanted to work alongside somebody as highly regarded as Dr. Ling. There was no way I could fake being pre-vet or pre-med to get hired. I'd have to sell myself on my determination, which doesn't sound like much compared with memorizing *Gray's Anatomy*, but it was all I had. If Dr. Ling didn't think a ton of ambition made up for not having some courses under my belt, I'd have to convince him that it did.

The next day I plopped myself in a chair outside the morgue office and waited for him to finish an autopsy. When he came out of the lab, his white coat as fresh and clean as when he put it on that morning (a hint at how meticulous he was in his work), I stood up and introduced myself.

"Hi Dr. Ling," I said. "I'm Cathrine Ann. I called about the job posting yesterday."

He remembered me. "We have our list of applicants in now," he said, "and we'll be making our selection sometime in the next few days." He wasn't being very friendly. Maybe he was just busy?

I wasn't on that list, I knew. And I wouldn't be on it unless I could persuade him right there on the spot.

"You really have to give me a chance," I said. "I realize you might be very busy, doctor ... " He started to walk away down the corridor. I chased after him. Okay, so I was getting a little desperate. "There must be so many things you're looking for that have nothing to do with the classroom the person sits in every day, and I have them. I know I have them. I love this stuff and I never missed an episode of *Quincy* either!"

I don't know whether it was my words or the tone of my voice, or the joke I somehow managed to throw in as I was babbling away, but something made him stop and look back at me. And before he spoke, before he said a word to me, I knew I had him.

Keeping my voice under control, trying to walk that fine line between enthusiasm and desperation, I told him about my studies at university, my understanding of anatomy, my good marks in microbiology, my work at the animal hospital doing diagnoses, and that most of all, I just needed a break. Would he give me a chance? Please?

When I finished, he actually appeared to smile, or maybe I just imagined it when he said, "Come in tomorrow at three o'clock and I'll test you on your anatomy."

Yay, Dr. Ling! Yay, Quincy! I swear I danced all the way out of that hospital.

I STAYED UP most of the night reading *Gray's* and every other medical book I could borrow from the library. I was going to impress Dr. Ling and his department. Who the hell was smarter than a doctor, especially a specialist like a surgeon or a pathologist? Did doctors and surgeons have stupid people working alongside them? Not a chance. You had to be smart to work in medicine, and that's what I was going to prove—that I was smart enough to work with doctors or anybody else. That's why I went back to school in the first place. I didn't just want to carry books under my arms like I did when I was a kid, now I wanted to read them, to absorb them, so that I would really be seen as smart and not be the phony my mother always told me I was. I was going to achieve things that nobody ever expected me to achieve, things I always knew I could do if I had the chance.

I was at Dr. Ling's office at two-thirty the next day, expecting some kind of quiz in which he'd ask me the names of principal veins and arteries.

But he didn't. He came out of his office looking as grim as the first day I saw him. "Let's get started," he said, and I trotted behind him down the corridor to the morgue. Why are morgues in hospitals always in the bowels of the building? It was a bit of a scary walk down, down, down almost to where I thought the frickin' boiler room should be instead. I'd been terrified of dead bodies ever since my grandfather's funeral, so it was pretty ironic that I was going for this job. But thinking first is never something I was good at doing. I even missed my grandmother's funeral because I was too scared to see her dead. And although I did go to my Aunt Olga's funeral, I had to stand at the back of the room where she was laid out, unable to go up close for a personal one-on-one goodbye. I passed on all the other family members' funerals too. But if I got the job, I wouldn't be working on my own, would I? No, Dr. Ling would always be with me, I figured. Anyway, I felt like a real medical student so it didn't matter if we were heading to the boiler itself. He instructed me on everything in the room, the ventilation, where the lockers and staff areas were, the scale, all the instruments and how to dress for work in the morgue. I took all of that in and then followed him right up to a cadaver on a stainless steel autopsy table, noticing that he was watching me to see what my reaction would be. As long as he was there, I was fine. Without saying a word he yanked the sheet off the naked body and went to work.

The woman had been about fifty, maybe fifty-five years old when she died. There she was, lying on this cold steel table, and Dr. Ling told me to put a block under her back so that it would arch and thrust her chest upward. She had lovely blond hair, and when Dr. Ling turned aside to get an instrument, I went to put the block under her back and in doing so I ended up touching her hair—and it slid off her head. I was already nervous, but I wasn't expecting that. I almost jumped back, which made Dr. Ling smile.

"I assume she was a cancer patient," he said, lifting the wig from the table and tossing it aside. "Notice no hair anywhere on her body, likely the result of chemotherapy."

Other than that, I knew nothing about her but as I've mentioned, I'm curious by nature. Although I was removed from her as an individual, I wondered what type of life she had had and if she had kids and so on. I wasn't nauseous or repelled by the idea of watching this woman's body be cut open. But it did occur to me that she might get up and start walking around like a scene out of *Night of the Living Dead*. I was trying to think only of the questions Dr. Ling would ask me, and how I would respond so I could get the job.

I didn't flinch at all when he made two deep cuts into the body, starting at each shoulder and meeting in a V shape at the bottom of the sternum, before starting a vertical cut down to the pubic bone (I remember the neat way he curved around the left side of the navel). Then he took what looked like a kitchen hand blender, but was actually an electric tool called a Stryker saw. Using this saw, he cut through the rib bones before lifting the rib cage up and out of the way, and there were all the organs, the intestines, the blood vessels, everything that had kept this woman alive all those years, for us to see. I think Dr. Ling worked more on behalf of the living than did other specialists in medicine. I mean, without pathologists, other doctors would never learn how to extend the lives of their patients.

I watched every move he made, amazed at how efficient he was at a job that most people could not imagine doing. Because he worked so quickly, it was difficult to keep up with him as he cut through the inferior vena cava, the pulmonary veins, the aorta and pulmonary artery, and the superior vena cava, leaving the aortic arch intact (I was following all this thanks to my studies the night before), He took blood samples from various locations and placed them in small labelled vials.

He made quick cuts to separate the lungs and removed them before lifting the liver, kidneys and intestines out of the body cavity. After weighing each organ, he wrote its weight in grams on his clipboard, then cut thin slices from every major organ and placed each slice in separate labelled jars. Every step was accompanied by a short comment into a microphone hanging over the table. "The heart is free of scars, although with notable evidence of arteriosclerosis ... looks like she'd been a smoker in her youth ... healthy liver ... ," and so on.

Now and then he looked across to see if I was turning pale or about to faint or throw up. But I was fine. Each time he looked at me I smiled and moved a little closer. I didn't want to miss a thing.

Nothing having to do with the job disturbed me, not even when he opened the stomach, took a sample of its contents and poured it into a glass vial. That's when I realized he wasn't going to test me on my anatomy. Instead, he had tested my ability to work with him without throwing up or passing out, and now he was teaching me, in an off-handed way, about the job itself. I watched as he used a scalpel to cut through the scalp in a line starting behind the left ear and going over the crown of the head to the same location behind the right ear. Then he yanked the scalp away from the skull in two directions, as though peeling a tangerine, pulling the front half down over the face and the rear portion back over the neck. In less than a minute with the electric saw he had cut a line all around the skull and lifted off the cap, exposing the brain. After snipping the spinal cord and cranial nerves he lifted the entire brain from the skull.

I was fascinated by how neatly and efficiently he performed all these steps, as smooth and professional as a Las Vegas magician doing tricks on a stage, except there were no dramatics, no "Hey, look what I did!" theatrics. Dr. Ling was the coolest professional I had ever encountered. I watched everything he did, not just carefully but up close. When he opened the chest cavity and when he lifted the skull to expose the brain, I stood as near as I could without getting in his way. Maybe it was my ability to watch the autopsy without fainting or being revolted, or maybe it was simply my enthusiasm for the job, but after Dr. Ling placed all the organs in a bag within the body, sewed the body up and was finished with the autopsy, he nodded at me and said, "Go and tell Human Resources that you're hired."

I had a job. I was taking university classes that would lead to graduation and what I was sure was a fantastic future. I had Michael with me all the time and Shane most of the time. I had plans and an income and, most of all, a life.

Nothing could go wrong.

BEFORE TOO LONG I was doing well enough to perform an autopsy on my own. I did the mechanical work, the cutting open of the body and the removal of organs, while Dr. Ling did the weighing and sample selection, recorded the findings and generally supervised. We made a good team. When all the organs had been examined and weighed and tissue samples obtained, he'd ask me to sew up the body and prepare it for the mortician.

Anything less than perfection was unacceptable to him. I know perfectionists can be a pain in the ass, but he believed there was only one right way to do something, and any other way was wrong. For example, he would start a complete autopsy wearing a freshly washed lab coat. When he finished, the coat would be as white as when he started, not a speck of blood on it. "There is no reason to have blood on your coat," he would say. "It is absolutely unnecessary. If there is blood on you, you have done something wrong." The first time I completed an autopsy without getting blood on me I showed my lab coat to Dr. Ling.

"Look. Not a bit of blood. No jackal around a carcass over here," I said, laughing. He didn't. "Come on, Dr. Ling, that was funny, no?"

He smiled and nodded. That's all the approval I received. It was all I needed.

Over almost a year, we performed more than thirty autopsies together, and I realized he was taking almost as much pride in my work as I was. Whenever he saw me arrive in the morning, his face would light up. He began teaching me things beyond what I needed to know in order to perform autopsies, things I might learn in medical school. He even took me on a tour of the hospital and introduced me to lab technicians, surgeons, radiologists and all the people who diagnosed patients and took care of them, healed them, made them better. I was his protégé, and I was honoured.

In his own way, Dr. Ling inspired me to make a totally audacious dream come true.

I was good at what I was doing in the autopsy lab, but I began to want more. I believed I could become a full-fledged medical doctor.

There was something else as well. I honestly wanted to make Dr. Ling proud of me. Unlike so many other people in my life, he trusted me, and he had encouraged me to go beyond what I believed I could do myself. Earning a medical degree would make him proud of me. That was something I wanted. I told Dr. Ling that I planned to apply to a medical school and become a doctor. He thought it was a wonderful idea.

Of course, I'd have to even the odds first. Oh, what a web we weave …

There were several medical schools within an hour of Guelph, but I rejected them right away. They were too close, making it easy for them to perhaps check my school records. Somebody at McMaster Medical School, fifty kilometres away, might know somebody at the University of Guelph and start asking embarrassing questions. Nearby medical schools were also the most popular, receiving three or four times as many applicants each year as they accepted. To get better odds of acceptance I would have to go elsewhere.

After researching various medical schools, I decided to apply to the University of Saskatchewan. How many people want to be in the prairies? I figured I'd have a better chance being accepted there than at, say, the University of Toronto. I made calls to Saskatchewan to find out what the requirements would be and deal with the paperwork. Basically, that was working from the inside out. I figured with my background that would not be nearly enough. I had to have a plan for working my way in from the outside.

Of course, I had a formidable hurdle in my path to Cathrine Ann, MD. No college degree and what grades I had collected over the last few years were not that impressive. It would take me years to take the courses I needed to fulfil even the basic requirements for entrance into medical school. I figured I had only one option: I'd forge the records. I would cheat my way in.

CHAPTER TWENTY-FIVE

Dad and med school

MY MOTHER DIDN'T TELL ME about dad's death until two days after he passed away in March 1990, when I was thirty-four years old and still attending university. He died from upper respiratory disease, not cirrhosis of the liver, as everyone had expected. At the time of his death at sixty-seven he was still living in the apartment near High Park, which was as run down as every other placed he'd lived throughout his life. In one of the two bedrooms he stored cans of paint and paint thinners and all kinds of other combustible material, and who knows why. Anyway, one night while he fell asleep smoking, as he often did, all the stuff stored in the second bedroom caught fire, and in one huge explosion his apartment was pretty much obliterated. Amazingly, he was okay. He reminded me of a dog or some other animal that just "was." He was someone who accepted whatever happened to him without overreacting or even reacting.

So it wasn't the explosion that killed him.

One night he went out to the bar while his apartment was being repaired and he was staying with a neighbour. He and the neighbour went to the local watering hole and as usual, they got plastered. A couple of young guys picked a fight with him and beat the crap out of him. I went to visit him at St. Joseph's Hospital a few weeks later. He was all busted up from the fight with a broken leg and was using crutches. A few days later he slipped on the front step to his apartment—yes, he was drunk—and he broke his pelvis.

Things just got worse and he ended up in the ICU. But that experience didn't kill him either.

Sometimes I could only marvel at the man's tenacious staying power. A few weeks before he died I visited him at his "newly remodelled" apartment. It was just as dark and dingy as it had been before the explosion. Plus, it reeked of smoke. He had an old queen-sized mattress on the floor in the bedroom, boxes for a dresser and a beat-up old kitchen table with two vinyl chairs. At least he's consistent, I thought.

He asked me if I needed a few bucks and I did, but I said I didn't want to take money from him. He insisted. Then he saw me looking at a four-inch-square blue metal box on the table with a picture of dogs and cats on it. I picked it up and took the lid off, but it was empty.

"What's this?" I asked.

"Oh, someone came around to my apartment from somewhere and I bought it from them. You can have it if you like it." I didn't want to take that from him either. He had so little as it was; he always had so little. He insisted.

He'd had a soft spot for dogs all his life. The only picture he ever carried around with him was a photo of his dog Butchy and me at around three years old, with me playing on a wooden duck that he claimed he had made himself. Often when he was drunk and alone he would stare at that picture and kind of rub his thumb on it like it was a magic lantern and moan, "Oh, my Butchy. I loved that dog so much. Do you know he used to stay outside the bars and wait for me? Oh, that dog. My Butchy ..."

I guess he lost the picture of Butchy in the fire. Anyway, I took the tin box and the few bucks he insisted I have, gave him a hug and left. I would never see him alive again.

WHEN MY MOTHER CALLED ME to tell me he had died, she claimed she knew I was studying for examinations at the time and didn't want to distract me, so she waited a few days before breaking the bad news. I didn't believe her. I think she didn't believe that anyone, including me, really cared that he had died.

When I came home for the funeral with Michael and Shane, I learned that Dad's family was upset because my mother had insisted on a closed casket service. Dad's family wanted to say their goodbyes to him, but all they got to see was a coffin. There wasn't even a picture of him on the coffin, the way there is at most memorials. She had refused to pay to have Dad embalmed. Instead he was slathered with some salve to keep the smell down and wrapped in clear plastic, and then the casket was sealed.

"Dad left money to pay for his funeral," I said to Mom. "Why didn't you have him embalmed?"

"He left shit. The veterans pay for his funeral," she said. Which confused me even more because she always insisted he was never in the army. Then she added, "What difference does it make when he's ten feet under?"

"Six," I corrected her.

"Ah, let him rot, however many feet down he is."

We gathered at the grave. My mother talked to he funeral director a bit and shook hands with him and then we walked over to the gravesite. She stared at the coffin, took a deep breath and quietly said, "I'd never be buried with that rotten goddamn son of a bitch! Cremate me and keep my ashes."

"And what am I supposed to do with your ashes?" I asked her.

"Who cares?" she said, shrugging her shoulders. "I'll be dead. Do whatever you like."

When they lowered the casket into the ground, I looked around the cemetery. This would be the most beautiful place he had ever lived, I thought.

Toward the end of the funeral, with all the family and friends still gathered, my mother shocked me. She turned to me and hugged me. She started crying. Everyone stared and nodded in sympathy. So I began to cry too. Maybe my mother was right. I was a phony. But I had learned from the best. I didn't believe her crocodile tears for a second.

CHEATING MY WAY into medical school would require a serious plan—and it helped to have an accomplice.

Like me, Chloe was struggling. She wanted to become a veterinarian as desperately as I wanted to become an MD. Over lunch one day we talked about the prospect of our being accepted as medical and veterinary students. We honestly believed we could handle the work. There was just that stupid barrier called admissions.

First, we would need copies of our university records and transcripts that we could reproduce and alter to our advantage. We needed to match everything about the university's official reports, right down to the exact typeface and size and the paper the reports were printed on. This would take more than access to a Xerox machine; we needed a professional print shop. Not just any print shop, either. We needed an outfit hungry enough to take our bribes without asking embarrassing questions about the purpose of our forgeries, and run by somebody who would print just about anything except maybe counterfeit money.

We found one by checking the Yellow Pages. I insisted on choosing among the printers who couldn't afford big display ads but instead advertised themselves in plain small type, because they would be the most hungry; smaller advertising budgets might mean less incoming revenue. No printer would help us if they didn't need the money, I figured. It was easy enough whiting out old marks and inserting new ones to raise our averages. We did the same things with all the classes we needed as prerequisites plus we threw some extra classes in just to raise the profile.

Night after night, we hovered over documents with our white out and markers and cut and pasted and checked and double-checked everything to make sure we had added up everything correctly before turning them over to the printer, an old guy who meant well and needed the money but who made more than his share of mistakes. Once, the typeface wasn't perfect; another time the watermark wasn't the exact shade of pink used by the university. Then, after we finally had perfect forgeries, I discovered that the medical school would not accept records supplied directly from applicants.

All that work and all that time and planning—for nothing. Where the hell was help from Rochdale when I needed it?

Earlier, I had contacted a woman in the admissions department at the University of Saskatchewan and had remained in touch—just to keep a contact. I called and arranged to meet her and tour the campus. I flew off to Saskatoon, checked into a small hotel across the street from the campus and stayed up all night. Not studying—worrying. Could I really pull this off? Why not? I had come this far. Every person I met, from the front-desk clerk to the waitress in the coffee shop where I tried to get through breakfast, learned about my ambition because I told them, even being without asked. "I'm here to be interviewed for medical school," I volunteered to them all. "Going to school. Medical school. I'm going to be a doctor!"

In my meeting with her, I mentioned matter-of-factly that I happened to have my academic records with me—I had bundled them in an official University of Guelph envelope—and didn't it make a lot of sense for me to leave them with her instead of trucking them all the way back to Ontario and bugging the university to package them from there?

She agreed, and I handed her the records. It was our little secret.

Several weeks later I received a letter inviting me for a personal interview, which I passed, and then I was advised that I was admitted to medical studies at the University of Saskatchewan. To become a medical doctor. Holy crappola!

When I told Dr. Ling, showing him the letter of acceptance and telling him I would be leaving within a week, he smiled the widest smile I had seen on him or any other man, and he almost ran for the telephone to call his wife. "Cathrine is going to be a doctor," he told her. He sounded more excited than me. "She has been accepted at the University of Saskatchewan! Isn't that wonderful?" I realized he must have been speaking to his wife about me in glowing terms over the past year, and I could tell by his words and expression that he was almost as proud of my being accepted at medical school as as if I was his own child.

When he hung up he took me to the cafeteria, where we celebrated with a slice of lemon meringue pie, my favourite.

"You know, Cathrine," he said, "my whole family and I will fly out to Saskatoon to see you graduate. You've been the best assistant I've ever had, and I know you'll be a first-rate doctor. I'm so proud of you."

I have never felt so horrible in my life.

OF COURSE THINGS with Shane didn't last. His lack of ambition was driving me nuts. We had a series of breakups and reunions. Then it was over.

I now had to plan the move across the country. Years later, I would meet up with him and find that he was as unmotivated as ever. He also confessed that he'd been unfaithful when we lived together in Guelph. Even though we hadn't been together for years, my heart hit the floor. Why did that shit always happen to me? And what was wrong with me that I couldn't stay with one person? I just didn't get it.

In July 1991, Michael and I set off in my Plymouth K-car for Saskatoon, this time accompanied by a friend of Michael's named Dan. Michael claimed Dan was an orphan, with no foster parents to care for him and no home. Could he live with us in Saskatoon? Sure he could. For some reason, having Dan around made me feel less of a fraud. I guess it allowed me to pretend I was being the responsible adult.

The three of us squeezed into my car—my horse Harry riding along behind in his trailer—and aimed it west.

In Saskatoon we found a small two-bedroom apartment with a large pantry. We had food and furniture and heat, and with a tiny bit of support still coming in from Henry, I figured I would be fine working the summers until I became a bona fide doctor. Dan needed a place to sleep, so we covered the pantry floor with a mattress and that's where he spent the nights.

I WAS IN MEDICAL SCHOOL. I couldn't believe it. It still bothered me that I had cheated my way in but I believed so intensely that I had what it would take to succeed that I convinced myself I deserved this opportunity. I had done what I needed to do. I would become a healer. I would be a credit to my community.

My introduction to the world of medicine was less triumphant than I had imagined.

A lot of the students were from privileged families whose parents were physicians and surgeons. This didn't bother me, but their attitude did. Many of them acted like snobs except when they were acting like children, especially some of the male students. When ob/gyn class was announced they giggled among themselves and said, "Great, we get to see some pussy today!"

I insisted on being me, refusing to change just because I was among some privileged kids who were ten years younger and a lot wealthier. I didn't tone my language down much either. As a result some people loved me and others despised me. What else is new? And yes, I admit that some of it probably had to do with my own feelings of insecurity.

The classwork was difficult and time consuming. I struggled to keep up. It didn't help that I enjoyed partying as much as ever and rarely turned down a chance to get out and dance, drink, socialize, whatever just like the other students. In spite of that I managed to score great marks on some subjects. Not all of them. Just some. Once I scored an honest 95 percent on an anatomy test—thank you, Dr. Ling—and a female colleague accused me of cheating. It was art class all over again.

Other things took the shine off my opinion of the medical profession and higher education generally. I found out that another female student lied about not being available to take a test because of some kind of family emergency. When arrangements were made to let her take the test, her boyfriend—also a med student— gave her the answers. The truth is, I could not believe how much cheating was going on.

So, sure: how could I of all people be complaining about people cheating? The thing is, I cheated to get into school because I so badly wanted to be a doctor. Once in I worked my ass off in school. They were cheating just because they were lazy or they felt entitled.

I'm not saying I was right, but it is what I believed. When someone says I can't do something my first reaction is to prove that I can; it doesn't matter how I do it.

I loved the clinical studies part of my studies when we had a chance to interact with actual patients. I loved the chance to help people through pain and suffering, even as a student with forged admission documents. In fact, the biggest complaint made about my clinical studies was my tendency to form deep relationships with the patients, making them laugh and making them trust me. I should be more emotionally detached, I was told.

I also did volunteer work at a local women's shelter and the local prison, which was an eye-opener and a confidence builder at the same time. I found that women spoke openly to me—without any coaxing. It was like we had an immediate bond of understanding. Plus, I finally realized that I never wanted to end up there ever again.

I FINALLY FIGURED OUT why I had had so much trouble with tests in the past. I have ADD (attention deficit disorder). As treatment for my ADD, the clinician prescribed Prozac. I've never liked taking medications of any kind. My reluctance to take Prozac was reinforced when I asked the opinion of a couple of senior students at the medical college. They were not surprised that I had ADD, but they were totally opposed to taking Prozac. Word was spreading throughout the profession about the high incidence of suicide by Prozac patients.

At least that is one decision I have no regrets about.

THE CHRISTMAS AFTER my first year I returned home.

It had turned out that Dan was not an orphan after all. He had just wanted to hang out with Michael. With Dan not around Michael had become restless too. He decided he didn't like life on the prairies and moved in with my mother in a high-rise apartment in Toronto. Was I sorry to see him go? Truth is, I may have resented more the fact that he preferred living with my mother than with me. I figured that since I was so busy with school and volunteer work and everything that maybe it was better for him.

All the way there on the airplane I wasn't feeling well, and I began to recognize the symptoms during the flight. At my mother's apartment I knew I had pneumonia, and I crawled into her bed to sweat it out. The following day I felt so bad I actually broke my own rule about drugs and asked Mom to go to the drug store for some medication. She couldn't. Or wouldn't. The weather was bad, she wasn't feeling well herself, I wasn't that sick, whatever. Later that day, Michael asked where a couple of his shirts were. "At the cleaners," Mom said, already shrugging into her coat. "Wait here, I'll go and get them for you." And she was out the door before I could ask if, as long as she was out, maybe she could get those medications after all. Some things never change.

I felt well enough to celebrate New Year's Eve with Michael and his cousin Anthony. They bought up the bar that night. I should have wondered how he could afford it. Turns out he lifted a credit card. I should have been angry. I wasn't. I was only angry because I didn't feel well enough to imbibe all that champagne.

EVENTUALLY, HOWEVER, the workload—the partying—began to wear me down. I was falling behind. The teacher assistants who coached me were encouraging. "We don't care who you are or where you came from," one TA said to me, "we think you'll make a terrific doctor, and we'll help you get through this."

But I think they were developing some doubts.

I was told I would have to repeat my first year. The administration was puzzled. They could not reconcile how it was I had scored so high at Guelph but had scored so poorly in Saskatoon. I panicked. I couldn't blow this. I would have to try harder.

Midway through repeating my year at medical school, I could tell the show was about to end. I still wasn't able to drag those marks up. One day I received a registered letter from the university.

I knew what it said before I opened it. Things were not, in the opinion of the university, what they appeared to be and I would have to explain things to the university board.

I consulted a lawyer. He read the letter, made a few telephone calls, and told me I could remain enrolled at the university while we contested the board.

I decided not to fight it. All at once, I realized what I had tried to do and I asked myself if I was crazy thinking that I wouldn't get caught. I collapsed on my bed and cried. My mother's voice played over and over in my head: "You're a liar. You're an actress. You're a goddamned phony."

As I had done with everyone and everything in my life I couldn't handle, I fled, running to someplace new where I could reinvent myself again.

CHAPTER TWENTY-SIX

The mob

THE K-CAR AND I barely made it to Calgary, driving all night through the bald-ass prairie darkness.

I bought a tea and a newspaper, scanning the Help Wanted columns. Someone outside the city wanted a barn hand to clean the stables and do other chores. The wages weren't much, but the job included a small apartment and offered an opportunity to board Harry. It was too good to pass up, and I nursed the old car out of Calgary to the thoroughbred stable, which was part riding arena and part ranch. I told Daizy and Tara, my dogs, that everything would be all right.

They had expected a guy, or maybe a younger woman, and I literally had to beg for the job. "I'll work just for a place to sleep," I offered, "a chance to work around horses and whatever you agree to pay me. That's all."

The owners went along with it. It was clear that they had no other serious applicants. I would work with the horses, which I enjoyed, and get to board Harry for free. In return I had a couple of rooms above the stables and a little money left over. I arranged to have Harry transported from Saskatoon and got him settled on the ranch, my dreams of becoming a doctor or veterinarian or anything else associated with medicine long gone.

The stable manager was a creepy older guy who occupied an apartment next to mine. "You gotta keep your apartment door open all the time," he warned me. I let him know that if he decided to come in while I was there, he'd be wearing a horseshoe for a hat. He never tried coming in. I think he just liked the idea of being able to boss around a younger woman.

I've worked hard at a lot of things, but never as hard as I worked at that stable. To this day I don't know if the manager was upset with me because I would refuse to leave my door open, or if he thought I would beg him to give me less work and offer him something else in return. I did neither, and my entire day was filled with carrying heavy feed bags, mucking out stalls, sweeping the barn, exercising and grooming the horses and doing every damn thing the manager ordered me to do. My workday began at six in the morning and ended at seven or later each night when I could barely make it up the stairs to my apartment and fall into bed. I loved the horses, I loved the outdoors and sometimes, when I could actually stop long enough to enjoy it, I loved the peace and quiet.

But after a few months I could no longer handle the work. I made arrangements for Harry and headed to the city to find something better.

I WAS SLEEPING in the back of my car at night, freshening myself up in public washrooms each morning, and treading sidewalks office corridors the rest of the day, in search of work.

I took the only job that I could find available, which was working in a customs brokerage company at the airport. The pay wasn't bad but the hours were ridiculous. I started work at three in the morning and finished at eight.

I found a two-bedroom apartment downtown, and after I had settled in a bit I convinced Michael to move back from Ontario to be with me. I was proud that Michael had completed high school, but he really didn't have his sights on a real job or profession. I suppose one of the reasons that he agreed to come out west was simply because he had nothing better to do. He got a job at a convenience store—where quite often I shopped for free. Michael and I went out clubbing some nights, just like we did in Guelph.

I WAS WALKING through Calgary one day, when I passed an office and saw a strikingly attractive woman with a large cast on her leg.

I went inside and asked what had happened to her leg. She explained the accident that had caused the break, I told her how much I loved her hair and soon we were talking a mile a minute.

We had lunch together later that day, and then a couple of other times after that and before I knew we were best friends. It turned out that Tanya had soured on her job after finding some files of soft porn pictures her boss had taken of his "clients."

Tanya and I told each other about everything: backgrounds, the men we loved and hated, the things we wanted to do, the places we wanted to go, all of that. My mother came out to visit just like she did in Saskatoon and she and and Michael and I went to Banff and had a great time. Seemed like old times. I even found a new boyfriend, a decent-looking guy who was fun to be around until, after I left for work one night, he hit on Tanya, who told him she wasn't interested.

"It's okay," he said to Tanya. "Cathrine won't mind."

"No, she won't mind," she told him. "She'll just fucking kill you!"

When she told me what happened I was so upset I dumped both him and the job. Then, my landlord confiscated Michael's prized mountain bike in exchange for the rent that I hadn't paid. I hadn't paid my half of Harry's board either and I had to think of something to do to earn money and do it fast. Michael decided he wanted to move back to Ontario again and I thought that under the circumstances, he probably should. He would get a better job there, plus he started missing all his old friends. Michael never gave me shit about the bike, and I promised I would make it up to him.

He was much more understanding with me than I was with him at times. Well, most of the time.

So there we were, two good-looking girls without a boyfriend or a job between us, monthly rentals due on our apartments, boarding costs for Harry and, oh yeah, we still had to eat. What were our choices? The subject of working for an escort agency came up.

Uncle Johnny's words to me at sixteen when I so desperately needed money still echoed in my head. Lots of things had changed since
then, but when you're totally down and out, when nothing else
seems to work and you're a woman without ties or obligations, the
option remains.

I had promised myself I wouldn't starve again and I wouldn't
be homeless again. Tanya thought the idea sounded intriguing, but
I wasn't sure she was cut out for that life. She had great parents and
a fabulous upbringing and had shared no horror stories with me
about her past. Anyway, I began calling escort agencies in town.
That's how I found Carole.

Carole had been running an escort agency out of a dingy
apartment over a street-level office. Her rules were simple: The
agency took the calls from clients from ads in the Yellow Pages and
local newspapers. The girls charged $150 for a half hour and $300
for a full hour, and paid the agency $20 per call. The agency called
you out fifteen minutes before your time was up, so even less time
was officially involved than what the guys thought they were paying for. (Yes, some women called the agency but only for other
women, not men.) Whatever call you took, you knew what you
were expected to do. You just didn't know who you were expected
to do it with. That's the easiest way to explain the business.

I signed up right away. Tanya would end up signing a few
months later. To tell you the truth, I still am not sure why she opted
in. Not only did I not encourage her, I actually warned her off.
Well, her life ... her choice.

At the time, Calgary had an interesting law about escort
agencies. They were legal as long as they were owned and managed
by a woman. I suppose this represented the city's concern about
women being exploited. Henry once told me, "Men talk dirty to a
woman and it's sexual harassment. Women talk dirty to a man and
it's three hundred dollars an hour."

Most of my clients were businessmen from out of town, horny
husbands, shy kids looking for an experience and lonely men who,
it often seemed, wanted conversation or a dinner date as much as
they wanted sex. I used to say being an escort was like eating from

a bowl of Cracker Jack—you never knew what you were going to come up with next; every handful was different. When the men were married, I sometimes tried to guilt-trip them and often it worked. "Wow, you're married?" I would say, picking up a picture of the supposed happy couple and slowly shaking my head while the victim watched. "Just take the money and go!" was what I sometimes got. See ya!

The personalities of the other women in the business were very different. At one end of the spectrum were sweet, gentle souls who wanted to help the other girls. At the other end were out-and-out bitches, tough broads who carried weapons in their purse and were prepared to use them. More often than not, their mouths were their best weapons. They verbally attacked and sometimes even slapped or pushed you if you got scheduled to take a call they thought they should have gotten, stressing the point that they, not you, had seniority at the agency. Then you'd have to take the calls they didn't want. Like the really late-night calls when they were home relaxing and couldn't be bothered getting all dolled up for an hour.

You had to be careful. People are often curious about what occurred when I knocked on a strange hotel room door not knowing what or who was behind it. In reality, it was all predictable and on my part strictly business. This doesn't mean I was nasty. In some ways I had the same attitude as the woman who checks you out at Wal-Mart except with me, I got paid before rather than at the end of the sales transaction. I would say a few friendly words, scan the merchandise, add up the total, do the job, thank you very much and where's the next customer?

That was my attitude, my way of dealing with what I was doing. Not all the girls followed the same routine. For example, I never bargained, never gave discounts and for sure never gave it away. You want half an hour? That's $150. You want a full hour? That's $300. You want something special? Forget about it.

Some girls liked their clients so much, or felt sorry enough for them, that they would lower their price or even perform for nothing. They would return to the agency and admit that they'd done it for half price "because the guy was so cute!" I never understood that. For one thing, my involvement was purely professional, and professionals always stay with the posted rate. Would you really expect to negotiate a price, for example, with a dentist to fill a tooth? In addition, I didn't want to have any personal involvement with the men. The idea of feeling anything beyond whatever was necessary to perform the service wouldn't make the work any easier. It would make it far more difficult.

Girls who slept with some guys for nothing amazed me with their stupidity. "Maybe he'll call me sometime," they would explain. "He promised to call me!" They were hopeless romantics who refused to believe this was all a business and that most likely the guy just wanted to get their services for free.

It's true that some clients claimed they wanted to rescue the girls from the life and would make all kinds of promises, acting as naïve as some of the girls. I met my share myself. My reaction was to play the game, laugh it off and reply, "After you've called me ten times we can talk about it." Then when we got to ten, I would add on another ten visits and so on. A few believed me when I said they had to fulfil a quota of visits with me before they could call me without going through the agency. Some clients acted out their own romantic fantasies, taking me shopping for clothes or jewellery, surprising me with perfume. Sometimes I encountered gay men who wanted to experience sex with a woman. Some said they would switch to playing for the other team because of their encounter and others said no way, I'm gay! Some were cross-dressers whose interest was shopping, not sex, buying clothes for me and for themselves, but with the cover of a having a woman along. Others just wanted to massage my body for an hour straight or kiss my feet.

Some days I hated what I was doing and other times I loved it. I never felt that the men were losers because they had to pay a woman for sex or their company. Some girls hated their clients, treating them badly and complaining about them over and over. Some were lesbians, and I wondered how they could spend such intimate time with men they despised, no matter how much money they were making. I liked the freedom I had and I believed that

I simply didn't fit in with normal society. And when it got down to it, I believed that I made people happy regardless of how badly I might at times have felt about myself.

After paying the agency fees, I could earn around five grand or more a month for working part-time. If I'd worked full-time, that would have been about the same amount of money I might have made after graduating from medical school, completing my internship and setting up a medical practice—a procedure that might have taken me five years or more, if I were fortunate. I was sending money to Michael and paying all my bills on time. Tanya and I ate good food and drank fabulous drinks. Our wardrobes grew and so did our friendship. We rode in her hot convertible sports car singing at the top of our voices along with the radio. Yup. Life was okay as a ho. I fit right in.

Okay, I wasn't saving lives. But I wasn't ruining them either. I was scratching for a living, employed in what I considered a different kind of profession. We all find ways to deal with the good and the bad in life, especially the bad. That's how I dealt with this part of my life, and eventually the experiences merged into one long, uninteresting series of work shifts, with a couple of exceptions.

That year a TV series based on a popular western novel was filmed in and around Calgary, and many of the actors and production crew became clients, giving us a little brush with Hollywood and a look at how weird some people in show business can be. One of the producers, or maybe he was a writer, would hire a girl or two or five, get himself naked and have the girl(s) order a pizza while he hid in the closet. If a girl could seduce the pizza delivery guy, the guy paid her a $1,000 bonus. The girls had to get creative among themselves, if you know what I mean, to get the pizza delivery guys as hot as the pies they were delivering. And sometimes a rock star or two travelling through town would book four or five girls at once just to be able to crawl into bed with them all.

There were lots of drugs around. One time I walked into a biker headquarters and the five-foot-long coffee table had a mountain of cocaine on it. I never touched it. I wasn't interested. I had my experimental phase when I was younger and only drank alcohol if

I was socializing. Some girls would work in exchange for drugs. I used to say, "Why don't you get paid and then buy your own drugs and party with people you choose to party with?" I couldn't figure it out. Maybe some girls were lonely. You know, not every man is willing to share his girlfriend with a whole city ... and the tourist population too.

Now and then a pervert appeared, wanting us to urinate on him or perform some other disgusting act. Whatever fetish you can name, someone, somewhere, is willing to do it for enough money. I rarely encountered freaks, so it wasn't a big deal to me. The most upsetting kind of guys I dealt with were married men, and if I couldn't get them to pay up and send me on my way, leaving them broke and feeling guilty, I would think they were pretty low.

It was even worse when the men wanted a call to their home. I would show up at a private home with the wives and kids absent to spend an hour in bed with the husband, the same bed he and his wife made love in. Scattered around the rooms would be pictures of the guy's wife and children, smiling back at me. I hated that. I hated it so much that I often took something small belonging to the wife, maybe perfume or a hairbrush or a piece of cheap jewellery, something she would miss for certain when she returned home and that the husband couldn't explain. I didn't need or want the perfume or jewellery, and I never took anything of real value. I just wanted to create some uncomfortable minutes for the husband when he realized what had happened to the items.

The most frightening call I ever made was to a motel room where two men waited. There was only supposed to be one, and the sight of the second guy worried me immediately, especially when I realized they were both junkies and the second guy was passed out on the floor in the motel bathroom, the needle still in his arm, blood pouring out onto the floor. I wanted to leave, but I didn't. But I did tell the man who was functional that if the other guy roused himself and came near me, I was bolting. And oh yeah, it would cost him double.

WHY WOULD A WOMAN work as an escort? Their reasons fell into every category you can imagine. Some, like Tanya and me, were single, unattached women in need of employment, biding our time until something better came along. Some were dabbling simply to absorb the experience, others to support their kids and husbands and more than a few were supporting a drug habit. Others were in it for keeps. But I thought that, regardless of why they held the job, we all were above the girls who worked on the Track, the four-block downtown area where street hookers worked, the ones who gave every penny to their pimps. They were just plain stupid as far as I was concerned.

I was amazed at the number of girls whose husband or steady boyfriend had no idea what their woman was doing in her spare time. One of the prettiest young girls, whom I'll call Mary, had a live-in boyfriend who didn't know she was in the business. She was out on a call one night when a telephone request came from a private home and somebody recognized the address—it was Mary's place, and the guy calling in was obviously her boyfriend. To protect her we changed the address in the logbook, but a girl who knew Mary took the call. Mary never learned about her boyfriend's own after-hours activities. Not from us anyway. I just hope Mary didn't end up paying for it with her money. The loser didn't work.

After some time things began to slide, as they always do. Tanya began doing drugs—cocaine, grass, whatever she wanted and could get her hands on—and it occurred to me that maybe she wasn't as happy in the business as she pretended to be. She started hanging out with girls that I had no interest in socializing with, and that bothered me a lot. We still saw each other, but infrequently, and I missed all the time we used to spend together. Then she blamed me for contacting her parents and telling them what she did for a living. That was not me. Maybe she was looking for a way to not be friends, I don't know.

One evening, entering a popular downtown bar, Sole Luna, with Tanya, I saw a man for whom the word gorgeous was barely adequate. Somewhere in his mid twenties, he had perfect features, café-au-lait skin and an obviously great body inside his designer jeans and crisp shirt. His long brown hair was perfectly coifed, and one single braid with a handful of coloured beads hung from one side of his hair. Not a look that I normally favour, but the whole package was too good to resist. So I didn't. This was a hunk. As he slowly made his way through the thick crowd, I passed behind him, leaned forward and kissed him on the back of his neck.

He was cool. So cool that he didn't speak or follow me around the bar. He just looked around at me and smiled, showing me perfect white teeth, and for the rest of the evening when our eyes met he would smile a little and nod his head. Very cool.

Finally he walked to where Tanya and I were seated and introduced himself. I was struck first by his mild accent and then by the fact that he had a mild stutter. The stutter was actually endearing, as though it represented his only definable flaw.

His name was Jamie. He said he was half Lebanese and half Hungarian. He was in business with a group of other Lebanese-connected men, all of whom referred to each other as cousins. It was impossible to identify the exact connection between them, either through family or business. Everybody was a cousin.

For the rest of that evening we—Jamie, his friend, Tanya and I—had some laughs before saying goodbye. Before I left, Jamie asked for my address and I scratched it, along with my telephone number, on a piece of paper. Then I headed home to my apartment. Maybe, I thought, he'll call me some time. Or maybe not. No, he'll call. I crawled into bed and quickly fell asleep.

About an hour later I was awakened by the sound of someone entering my room through the bedroom window. As I was trying to decide whether to scream or hit the intruder with a lamp, the man said, "Shhh!" and laughed softly, and I realized it was Jamie.

And that's how it began. A relationship with an outrageously charismatic man who carried an aura of danger about him that he could never erase and I don't think many women would want him to anyway. As a woman, you either grasp this appeal immediately or you don't. I can say only that we began an intense relationship, one that evolved into the most frightening and dangerous of my life.

I avoided telling Jamie what I did for a living. I don't recall that he ever asked or even cared. He liked parties and bars, and enjoyed having me on his arm when we got together with his cousins, all of them emanating the same aura of danger but none of them with Jamie's magnetism.

I continued working for the escort service and juggling my evenings when necessary to be with Jamie. Concealing my line of work was easier than it first appeared because Jamie worked hours similar to my own. To prevent my pager ringing at inopportune moments with Jamie I would book the entire evening off, which meant I made no money. He wanted to see me more and I was feeling even greater pressure. For several weeks I managed to conceal my work, until one evening Tanya and I walked into a bar and there was Jamie across the room. He smiled and waved, and I returned the wave. He nudged the man next to him and gestured toward me, obviously announcing that I was his girlfriend. The man turned to look at me and I almost fell to the floor. He was one of my clients, a guy I had been with maybe three times. When our eyes locked, he couldn't hide his surprise. Then he spoke to Jamie, nodding his head and pointing in my direction, clearly telling him who and what I was. Jamie's expression changed. His smile vanished and he glared at me before turning his back to me.

"I'm busted," I said to Tanya. "He knows what I do. That's it. We're through."

Not quite. Jamie worked his way across the room to where we were standing, leaned toward me and said, "You'd better go home now."

By this time I had regained my composure. Nobody was going to tell me what to do, not even gorgeous Jamie. "Why?" I asked him.

Jamie leaned even closer and his voice took on a menacing tone. "If I were you," he said, "I would do it. I would go home. Right now."

And I did.

An hour later he showed up at my apartment, very angry. At first I believed he was angry because it had been a friend who revealed what I did for a living. That was part of it, but as he went on venting his anger I realized there was more to it. He was hurt as well. "I really liked you," he confessed. "I've told all my cousins how crazy I was about you, how much fun we have together, how happy you make me feel and now I discover *you work as a fucking escort girl!*"

When he calmed down, I reminded him that I had no idea what he did for a living and he had never asked what I did. Now he knew. And now he gave me some idea about the way he made his money. I wasn't sure I wanted to hear it.

Jamie's business amounted to doing whatever the cousins chose to do to make money. Essentially, they were a branch of the Lebanese Mafia, running bookies, loan sharks and other rackets while at the same time owning businesses and doing honest work. Jamie's quiet manner, generosity and sense of humour were all at odds with his responsibility within the group. He was the enforcer. If somebody refused to pay up or generally did anything at all to upset the bosses, Jamie was dispatched to do whatever it took to bring the person back into line, which included threats and beatings and sometimes involved brass knuckles and a baseball bat and who knew what else.

Eventually Jamie got over his rage without becoming violent toward me, which was a relief. He told the rest of his cousins what I did for a living and they weren't shocked at all. I'll bet they didn't tease him about it either, because the next time we got together he could hardly wait to talk to me about a business proposition.

Jamie and his cousins wanted into the escort business, and they needed me to be their front. The escort services were big business and the Lebanese guys wanted a piece of it. They couldn't get their hands on the money without a woman running things for them, and I was it. Jamie's crowd would find space to rent for the office, get the telephone lines installed and protect the operation. I would pose as the owner, pay for the licences in my name and run the show on the inside. We would divide the profits.

I had been working with the escort service for about a year and was getting a little weary of it. Still not sure where my life was headed, I didn't want it to be an endless chain of night calls to hotel rooms and the homes of married men who had managed to get their wives out of the house for a couple of nights. Sitting behind a desk sounded more attractive and more profitable. I could still do calls on my own, just to boost my own income. So I agreed. Jamie's friends weren't the kind that you said no to.

It was a smart move on their part, in the beginning at least. I had a good mind for business—I'd proven it in the past—and I had absorbed a good deal of knowledge about marketing and managing a business that involved sending attractive women across town to meet strange men with sometimes strange needs.

I knew, for example, that a man's fantasies went to work as soon as he began thinking about hiring a girl, and they continued to work while he flipped through the telephone book to choose the service. Successful enterprises offered what appeared to be several distinct escort services, which covered most of the choices the guys might have, plus a little bit of built-in flash. In reality, the telephone numbers all led to the same office and the same person answering the telephone, which was me, and I would send off whichever available girl came closest to the request.

Along with business skills and experience, I had another quality to apply: I didn't use drugs. Not only that, I didn't want girls whose primary motive for getting into the business was to keep themselves in cocaine or heroin or whatever they needed to get them through the day. I wanted girls who were in it for the money to buy stuff that ordinary people appreciated: nice clothes, some jewellery, a good car and a vacation now and then. Girls who were in it strictly to get and stay high were bad news. The clients became pretty good at recognizing who they were and paid them off in dope. Too many girls would choose $75 or $100 in cocaine, placed right in their hand, over the $300 per hour they were supposed to be earning.

When dope was all the girls cared about they were nearing the end of the line and were bad news. I could tell the druggies when they showed up looking for work and sent them on their way.

BEFORE RECEIVING A LICENCE I needed to pass an interview with the police, who were interested primarily in how and where I would recruit the girls, and in reminding me that the law prohibited the girls going out on calls after one in the morning.

Once the ads began to appear, I knew the girls would find me faster than I would find them. I already had some girls in mind I planned to hire immediately. Tanya had decided to stay with Carole—who, of course, was none too pleased with my decision to start my own agency. She called me one night and was really pissed off. "You ungrateful bitch! You're stupid, you know that? I give you six months tops." She hung up.

I didn't care what Carole thought. Besides, I had found out that she had won a brand-new custom-built mansion in a lottery. Shit, some people have all the luck.

JAMIE FOUND OFFICE SPACE on the second floor of a building where one of his cousins manufactured shoes, just a place to take calls and crash and for the girls to gather. I worked out expenses and figured we would have to earn $5,000 a month just to break even. At least I had my dogs Daizy and Tara to keep me company and give me a sense of security.

I began with three girls, and Jamie managed to sleep with all of them within a few weeks. I soon had a roster of about ten, which was sufficient to meet the incoming-call demands, but not enough to pay the bills. They were the usual cross-section of bored housewives, out-of-work secretaries, lesbian man-haters and party girls loving the excitement and the money. Not once did I attempt to talk them out of the business. It wasn't my job. These girls had come to me, and as long as they were of legal age, sober and not heavily into drugs, I gave them work. Looks and age were never an issue.

If they had a problem on the job, some guy who acted like a jerk in one way or another, I would protect them where possible. Usually this consisted of phoning the guy and telling him not to call the agency any more because we had cut him off. The men either treated my girls nicely or they did without. A couple of times, Jamie was in the office when I made those calls and before I knew it, he stormed out of there with the guy's name and address to provide a personal and up-close warning. I hated it when he did that and would try and argue with him to not do it. But he never listened to me. I would hear him speed off in his car, cousins in tow, and knew pretty much what was going to happen. "That shit could ruin our business," I told Jamie. "So could assholes who are a problem," he'd say.

The girls knew what to do, I knew how to run a business, although my paperwork was always sloppy, and Jamie and his cousins were pleased each week when they showed up to see that everyone was working, even though they weren't able to claim their portion of the profits yet. We had a growing demand, an efficient means of satisfying it and, as they say in other lines of business, a good product. But no business grows hugely over night. I didn't know how long it would take, but I started having my doubts.

The police would visit now and then to make sure we were sticking to the rules and that the girls were treated well. There was never a concern on their part. In fact, they told me on several occasions that they were pleased to see somebody was doing a good job of running an escort agency in town, keeping the girls off the streets and generally making their job easier. They knew the score. They said that every big city had a sex trade and no one was ever going to stamp it out, so they might as well see that things ran smoothly, with no complaints. Which is ironic, because the only really memorable problem arose one night when I received a telephone call from a cop.

He asked if I had a girl named Tiffany working, and I said yes, we had. He described her to me—really cute, tall, slim, young, lots of fun, always laughing and enjoying herself. "That's her," I said. "Do you want to see her?"

He started to cry. "That's my baby," he said. "That's my daughter."

When he composed himself, he got down to business with me. None of his pleading and begging would make her get out of the business. Now the pressure was on me. Either I drop his daughter from my list of girls or he would make my life hell. So I agreed, and I guess I succeeded because later I heard his daughter was working as a waitress in Canmore, a small town nearby, out of the city and out of the sex trade. I hope her father was happy. Too bad for me though, because she made the agency a lot of money.

The scariest event involved the time we needed new girls and Jamie decided to recruit some from the Track. Many girls on the Track were gorgeous, parading up and down the sidewalk in lingerie or bustiers, their thighs bare all the way up to their asses even in winter, and you had to wonder if the guys who stopped and picked them up really wanted them for sex or if they just felt sorry for them in their high heels amid the mounds of snow.

I had attempted to talk some of the girls into giving up the street and joining us as escorts, which was both safer and warmer when the cold weather arrived, but without much success. Jamie figured he could do the job better than me, and one night we began interviewing the girls, telling them not only could they avoid freezing their asses off on the street, but they would get to keep everything they earned less our $20 fee. Sure, the pimps bought them cheap little fur jackets and sexy boots, but if the girls were with us they could buy whatever they wanted with their own money.

The girls listened without saying much, but at least one of them must have told her pimp what was going on, because when we showed up a few nights later to talk to the girls again and see who would come work with us, I heard what I thought was a car backfiring and then saw a big black dude across the street shooting a gun at us. Jamie and I ran to the car hearing "ping," "ping," around our feet but we made it to the car unscathed. Jamie squealed the tires to get the hell out of there and I sat in the car in shock, unable to speak. Later, he pointed to a bullet hole in the passenger side of his car. The side I was sitting on! The next time, I suspected, the pimp wouldn't be aiming at the car. He would be aiming at us, and that was our last attempt to find new girls from that source.

As time passed, the novelty of the cousins' investment began to fade for them. In the beginning I guess they liked the idea of investing in an escort service, like a bunch of kids buying a candy store. The novelty was replaced by greed and suspicion. I just wasn't making enough money to satisfy them. They wanted a bigger return on their investment, and one way to get it was to ignore the law that restricted us from sending girls out on calls after 1:00 a.m. They told me to send girls out any damn time of the night if a call came in, and to hell with the 1:00 a.m. curfew. Even though this attracted attention from the police, which I didn't need, they insisted I keep doing it. Worse, they began to suspect that I was skimming the profits.

I moved out of the office and into a dismal attic that Kathy, an escort who worked for us, let me live in, But she had six kids, all from different fathers, and two kids slept in her bed. So she sometimes needed her attic back for a few days every week or two for the kids to sleep in when their daddy du jour slept with her in her bed and the kids had to beat it. In Kathy's attic I had a mattress on the floor and nothing else. Even Daizy and Tara hated it there, pacing in circles non-stop and panting like crazy. On the days she needed her attic back, I found abandoned houses or apartment complexes in the midst of being built to sleep in. Kathy let me take a pillow and blanket and it was my younger years all over again, except I wasn't running away from drunk and fighting parents, I was running away from people far more dangerous: the mob.

The cousins were starting to put the heat on me. I'd get unexpected visits during which I was asked, "Why can't you pay the rent?" and "Where's all the money going?" And they would pore over the master logbook of calls for hours, adding and re-adding numbers over and over again. My math wasn't so good, but I didn't need a calculator to tell me something wasn't adding up.

I might borrow a hundred or two out of the cash drawer from time to time, but the real drain on the company was Jamie. Soon he was coming by almost every night, stuffing cash in his pockets and telling me not to say anything to his cousins because he would square things up later, everything was cool. Some months he walked out with a couple of grand, making it difficult for me to cover the bills and still leave something to give the cousins for their investment, which was really nothing at all when I started to think about it. I was the only one who had really invested anything. I was working my ass off and they were just sitting back expecting to get their palms greased from my can of oil.

I liked Jamie, so I covered for him when I could. It wasn't easy and I knew it was going to blow sky high pretty soon. Because I couldn't afford to buy anything new, I was too poor to even swap price tags. I was barely eating; my dogs were the only ones eating every day. Our business was going well enough, but the money that Jamie took was adding up. Finally I was one month late in paying the rent and then two. I was borrowing money from the business for the bare necessities like food every second day or so and gas to get to the few calls I took myself. If I didn't keep the girls working, they'd leave and go work somewhere else. I was earning zilch running the Lebanese escort service and I regretted quitting work for Carole. Her six months prediction was about right. Tanya had been smart to stay with Carole. Everything was a hot mess again. Things were so bad I had to abandon my car when it broke down because I couldn't afford to have it repaired. Meanwhile, Jamie used the escort service like his personal ATM and didn't have a care in the world.

I didn't tell the cousins about Jamie's skimming the profits because I was afraid if it came down to a "he says, she says" debate, I wouldn't win. If Jamie called me a liar in front of the cousins, I would be a liar because I wasn't blood and I was a woman. I began to feel the walls closing in on me.

Jamie's cousins kept dropping by unannounced, thumping their way up the front steps and ordering me to bring all my paperwork into the boardroom, where they would study the books in even more detail than before and question the amount of money we were making. I never learned the cousins' real names, only their nicknames. They referred to themselves in slang, or spoke in their own language, which meant nothing to me. When they spoke English, their names sounded as if they had watched too many gangster movies—Bones and Faddie, names like that.

One of the cousins, obviously the leader, was scary. He and a couple of other cousins dropped in one night with Jamie and an escort from another agency, of all people. He called me into the boardroom, then put his face into mine and told me he didn't like the way things were going in the business. Neither did I, I said. I thought he'd have a little sympathy for me, but he wasn't interested.

"We're not making enough money," he said. "Somebody is taking cash out of the business and it's gotta be you."

I told him it wasn't me.

"Then who is it?" he demanded. "Where's all the money?"

Trying to soften my words I looked at Jamie and explained that he took money from the company now and then. "Don't you, Jamie?" I said. "Tell them."

Jamie did what I expected him to do. He covered his ass. First he said I was crazy, and then he admitted he took some cash from time to time but he always put it back and besides he put some of it against the rent every month.

They bought Jamie's version, which terrified me. I had heard enough stories from him and the cousins about beating up people who crossed them. I also knew what they did to their very own customers who gave the business a bit of grief from time to time, and it wasn't pretty. Jamie and the cousins left without slapping me around, but I could tell by their attitude and by Jamie's look as he left that I was still in trouble.

The following day, I gathered all my belongings and asked Kathy if I could borrow her car. She had no insurance on the car, it didn't have a muffler, the motor for the windows didn't work, it guzzled gas like a baby drank milk and the tires were bald and it was now winter. I was up in the office, getting things organized, when I heard the front door open and several sets of heavy boots start climbing the stairs. I knew immediately who it was, and I was not going to stick around to see what they wanted. Every fibre in my being told me to run. I grabbed the money that was in the cash box and flew down the back stairs with the dogs. I hustled them into the car, jumped behind the wheel and took off. My heart was pounding a mile a minute and I started crying uncontrollably.

I WASN'T SAFE in Calgary and I had nothing to go back to in Saskatoon, Guelph, Toronto or anywhere east. The car moved and it kept moving all night long, driving west through the Rockies toward Vancouver. We were running away again, me and the dogs and a borrowed jalopy. Somehow I'd managed to get out of Cowtown alive.

CHAPTER TWENTY-SEVEN

A second chance

I UNDERSTAND THE DRIVE from Calgary to Vancouver—passing through the heart of the Rocky Mountains—is beautiful. I couldn't tell. It was dark and I wasn't interested in looking anyway. I just wanted to put as much distance between Jamie's cousins and me as I could. I stopped only for gas, Diet Pepsi for me, water for the dogs and washroom breaks for all of us. I arrived in Vancouver with the morning sun.

After Shane and I'd split up for the last time he'd returned west, choosing Vancouver over Edmonton. He told me this in a letter. I had kept the letter with his address, folded in my wallet. I called him from a pay telephone, telling him I was in town and needed money. An hour later he appeared at the restaurant, looking as good as ever. I wish I could say so did I. I had gained a lot of weight since he had seen me last. Blame it on the lifestyle. Long days and late hours and lots of junk food. Shane said I looked great. The liar.

We talked about old times. I was feeling bad about the way I'd treated him and how hard I'd pushed him. I should have let him be who he was and not someone I wanted him to be. I asked if he thought we might have made it. He thought for a minute and shrugged his shoulders. No, it was for the best. Actually, I felt hurt. How come? I wondered.

Turns out he hadn't actually been faithful to me in Guelph.

I WASN'T GOING TO RUN anymore. I would get back on my feet and finally make something of myself. Being in the Vancouver area was a good start. It was mid-winter and Calgary had been bitterly cold and covered with snow. I settled in a town called Burnaby. No matter what happened now, I wasn't going any farther. I had run out of land. The next stop going west was Japan so I knew I had to make BC work. Barely a block from the restaurant I spotted a sign promoting an escort agency.

The agency was one in a string of operations managed by a guy who lived two hundred kilometres away in Whistler. When it came to running a business he had more in common with franchising than Jamie and his cousins would ever understand. He operated escort agencies in Prince George, Prince Rupert, Victoria, Kelowna, Vancouver and Whistler. Being a good businessman who knew how to protect and enhance the company's assets, he was fair with the girls he employed. As a matter of fact, he had married one of them. Just as I had in other places, I watched and listened, absorbing information and learning how and why he did things. I might have learned more if I had attended business school, but I doubt that sitting in a classroom and reading textbooks would have been as interesting.

His business strategy suited me perfectly. He favoured girls who didn't mind moving from location to location within his chain of agencies, spending two weeks in each town before moving on. This was fine with me because he paid for our accommodation in hotels and motels in each city, and I didn't have anywhere to live anyway. Everyone knew what was going on but it was all legal and, more importantly, they were paid on time every month. All the calls coming into the escort agency were answered at the head office in Burnaby, twenty-four hours a day, and then the girls would be dispatched to the respective hotels via the fax machine that was in every rented hotel room. They had the system down pat.

It also helped that regular clients knew the setup, especially the ones who liked a different girl each time. I suppose with new girls arriving every two weeks they could avoid being bored. Anyway, it worked. Business was good, I was making money, and with the agency covering my hotel bills I figured I didn't need a permanent place to stay. I even had enough cash to cover the cost of transporting poor Harry through the Rockies to a small boarding ranch outside Vancouver. I had neither the time nor the inclination to ride and groom him myself every day, as I had back in Ontario or in Saskatoon, but I visited him when I could, taking apples and carrots. As time passed and my income dropped, because the escort business fluctuates like any other, I had to move Harry to cheaper stables where the care wasn't as good, but he was with me and he knew me when I came to visit. I kept in touch with Michael by phone regularly; he was working selling cellular phones and doing well for himself. He said that he wanted to move to Vancouver and do the same type of work, so we talked about when he would come out. I was looking forward to seeing him again because his moves back to Ontario had me missing him a lot. I realized that he was more of a friend to me than anyone else had ever been. Although I didn't have a real place to live, I invited him to move in with me until he got settled on his own. I told him that he would love BC. I got him all excited about moving out, and I liked that we would be together again.

For this to happen I knew I'd have to put down roots, so I found a cheap basement apartment. Now I could work for the escort agency near home more frequently rather than at the satellite hotel rooms. I got settled into the apartment; Michael would be with me in a month.

I sent a cheque to the girl in Calgary whose car I had borrowed. I paid her more than it was worth but she had threatened to call the police and I just didn't want the hassle. I bought myself a cheap used car.

Often a bunch of girls would get together at the agency in Burnaby and socialize while waiting to get sent out on calls. I would take my two dogs to the agency with me when I visited, and when I went on calls, they stayed in the car. We all heard and traded stories about customers. One girl returned from a day-long call to say she had spent hours in a decrepit house with an old guy who paid her top dollar to talk with him. He didn't take her to bed or even touch her. He paid her, hour after hour, to sit with him in his house and keep him company. When the other girls heard about it, they almost climbed over each other for a chance at a call from him.

My favourite story had to do with a guy who hired me for an hour, or so I thought. When the hour was up and I started getting ready leave, he said, "How about staying for a couple of more hours?"

"Two more hours?" I said. "Sure, but that will cost you another six hundred bucks." I was thinking that he was going to barter and I knew I wouldn't be staying if that happened.

He said that would be no big deal and picked up a hammer, which gave me something of a fright—until he took the hammer not to me but to the wall of his house. It was a rundown farmhouse, but it was still better than most places I grew up in. He punched a big hole in the wall amd pulled out a bag of money. He didn't believe in banks, I guess.

I WAS GOING OUT with many men, and they were all great guys, physically at least. Here I was juggling dates with a fireman, a lifeguard, a ski instructor, a body-building trainer and an actor who worked as a stand-in for an actor playing an action hero in a TV series—all of them younger than me.

Michael had been living with me for a few months in my basement apartment and he slept in the living room. He got a job selling cellular phones, but I didn't ask him to contribute anything at all to the rent, bills or groceries. I even convinced my mother to move out with us too—I don't know what the hell I was thinking. Actually, I do know what I was thinking. I was trying to have the family life that I'd wanted all along. My dad was dead, my mom was living alone because her sisters had all died too, and she was lonely. Plus, she really missed Michael and he missed her. I have to say, though, that putting the three of us together was pretty crazy. We were all stuck in some mode from way back when I was still trying to win my mother's love and approval and still wasn't going to get it, and Michael was acting like the parent instead of the kid. The three of us used to argue for hours on end, each of us trying to be right. We all needed therapy, or separation, and it was still a few years away—for me anyway. Michael chose separation.

I was proud enough of my life that I was invited to appear on an episode of *The Maury Povich Show* featuring older women who insisted on dating only younger men. The deal included flying me and Michael along with one of my boyfriends to New York City for the appearance, where we would spend a couple of nights at a great downtown Manhattan hotel (courtesy the show) with access to a vehicle and be paid a stipend. I invited my mother to come along, but she declined. She said she didn't want the whole world knowing that her daughter was stupid enough to date guys young enough to be her son. I didn't quite see it like that. I simply wanted to have fun and I didn't want to date older guys who were usually divorced and had less money than me, with wives who were probably sitting pretty with alimony and the marital domain while the exes lived in a cave like I did. Also, I kind of figured that if I associated with people my age or older, I might feel old too. I had invited the ski instructor to come along with me but he backed out almost at the last minute, so I flew there with Michael only and we had a great time together.

When I wanted to be alone I could be alone without being lonely. I had my dogs and my son and my mom, and although we spent more time arguing than anything else, I still kept trying to have that family unit that I'd never had. Sometimes I would go to the movies alone, and before the lights dimmed I would look around at the couples sitting together and talking, being close to each other like men and women are supposed to be. I recalled when my mother saw a couple walking on the street hand in hand and she would say to me, "Yeah sure, wait until he gets you home and he kicks the shit out of you!" I wondered if there really was a guy out there who would be faithful to me and love me unconditionally forever. I had seen too much as an escort. I had seen too much in my family and growing up. Life threw a lot of lemons at me and I tried to make as many margaritas as I could. But I still didn't know where I was going or where I would end up. I just knew that something had to give.

When watching other couples, I never felt sorry for myself. I would imagine their lives like a movie. How would it play out?

I thought about my own life as a movie. Would there be happy ending? Who the hell knew?

IN JUNE 1998, I went to a local bar with my friend Charlotte. Charlotte was a bit older than me and was a widow. One night she went to sleep beside her husband, the love of her life, and the next morning he was dead beside her. Charlotte was now making up for lost time. She had two daughters younger than me and she partied harder than the both of them together.

That night the dance floor was mostly croweded with couples—except for a man who was dancing by himself. He was gorgeous. When he finished dancing, he settled himself alone at a table near the dance floor with a pitcher of beer. I walked across the room and introduced myself. His name was Marc; he had just turned twenty-three and he worked as a cook at Earl's, a popular chain of restaurants in the Vancouver area. Twenty-three? I needed a drink. He kept talking but he was shy and quiet, so I had to ask all the questions.

He said he wanted to become a teacher, then confessed that becoming a teacher had been his father's idea. Marc was living with his father. He was a drug addict but had kicked his addiction on his own. I thought that was really admirable. I had seen too many people who just gave in to their addiction and had never met anyone who'd managed to kick it on his own. This guy was special. We danced, the two of us on the floor together. At the end of the night, I didn't want the bar to close. I offered to drive him home but he declined; he lived only a few blocks away. I was amazed. Even if he lived next door, wouldn't he want a woman who paid him as much attention as I did to drive him home? But he didn't. I was thinking, In all likelihood some guy is going to call me through the escort agency tonight and pay me to be with him, and here you are turning me down when my company would be free? Don't you know we were meant to be?

I was hooked.

We saw a lot of each other. I was trying to work only during the days and then booking off nights, which put my job in jeopardy. One morning I couldn't bear the idea of missing him all day and asked how much he was being paid. "Eight-fifty an hour," he said. I said I would pay him ten-fifty an hour to stay home with me. I only had to get to my calls to make the money. At first I told Marc I was a doctor. How else was I supposed to explain why I wore a pager that went off all night long resulting in my leaving him for hours at a time?

Eventually I had to tell Marc what I did for a living. He was shocked. I told him about my life. I talked and talked. He listened. I figured with all the shit I had told him he would be disgusted and that would be that. I saw it coming.

"Cat," he said finally. "We all have trouble in our lives. But we love each other and I know that we can both do better. I believe in you! And by the way, that's one hell of a life story."

Okay, I admit: I did not see that coming.

LITTLE BY LITTLE I gave up the escort service work.

It was a crazy time. I was happy about that. But that meant we didn't have much money coming in. We had to start economizing. I gave up my car. Then Marc lost his construction job and couldn't find work. I stopped the escort work completely and we didn't have enough money to pay the rent, so we gave up the apartment. Actually, we had planned to move to a trailer park, into a trailer owned by one of the girls I knew from the escort service. The trailer was fully furnished so we held a garage sale, disposed of all the furniture I had acquired, loaded the dogs into Marc's truck and headed for the trailer park, where the owner announced that no dogs were allowed and he was making no exceptions. And by this time, we had three dogs! That's when we started living in Marc's truck. We were homeless. And out of work.

Marc and I searched the newspapers for work and we went to a few interviews. But we never got hired. It's pretty difficult going for interviews when you're homeless, but we managed. I would just have to think of something else.

Marc's father had a cabin in Washington state, about an hour's drive past the border. We started staying there, without his family's permission. We were hungry and still trying to figure out what we were going to do. One day we found a deer on the side of the road that had been struck by a car, and Marc and I wrestled the carcass into the pickup to carry it to our cabin. I had never tasted wild game, but the idea of venison cooked in the small oven in our cabin sounded good to me. Plus, the dogs would be in heaven. We thought the animal had been a recent road kill and the meat would still be fresh, but the animal was infested with worms, and when Marc began butchering the deer, the worms emerged by the thousands, wriggling out of the animal's nose and mouth—a more sickening sight than anything I had witnessed while working in the morgue with Dr. Ling. We used almost the last gallon of gas in the car to carry the deer carcass back to where we'd found it. I told Marc I thought we would laugh about that one some day.

I collected unemployment insurance but Marc was ineligible. We had three dogs to care for, so our options were limited. We began camping wherever and whenever we could or sleeping in the pickup. I refused to go back to the escort service and Marc couldn't find work anywhere. We scrounged food wherever we could. Including garbage cans. I had seen bleak times before, and this was bad. Back in Guelph I had met a guy who had served time for robbing a bank. I thought about it. What did I have to lose? All my life I'd expected to wind up in jail again. I had been there before. It wasn't that bad. Maybe that was the ending of my movie.

WHAT IN THE HELL were we going to do?

Opportunities are often difficult to recognize because they don't call out to you, with a trumpet fanfare, "Hey, over here, Cathrine! Just do such and such and your life is going to change beyond your wildest dreams!" Maybe I wasn't really ready for big change and success until I met Marc. Who knows? And opportunity often comes disguised as hard work, which may explain why I missed most that came my way. I tried to go with the grain as much as possible, not against it, because I wanted things easy in my life.

One day when Marc and I were driving around in our new home—his truck—I asked him to stop by where I used to live to pick up my mail, which I had asked the new tenants to collect for me. I was expecting my very last Employment Insurance cheque and was getting worried about how we would make money. Trying to get real jobs posed a problem because we didn't live anywhere. Plus we wanted to be together 24/7.

As Marc drove, two plans began to brew in my mind. One was an easy plan A: we could rob a bank—I had some old connections that I could contact. Plan B was more difficult: starting a legitimate business.

Marc wasn't too keen on plan A and I began to think about who would take care of our dogs if we ended up in jail, and did I really want to drag the poor guy down with me? We tossed around some ideas about businesses we could start without capital and there weren't a lot of choices.

When we got to my ex-apartment, I jumped out of the car and collected my mail. Back in the truck, I ripped up the few bills and flyers and opened the cheque. I was just about to toss the insert that accompanied it, but something made me pause and read it. I figured it was going to say something to the effect of, "Yup, this is your last cheque, loser. Now what are you going to do?" But instead it announced the start of a non-profit/government project called SEEDS (Self-Employment and Entrepreneur Development Society). If I had a great business idea, I could qualify to receive a condensed business-training course and a nominal stipend over a number of months to help me get started.

Well, hadn't Marc and I just been talking about this very subject not five minutes ago? It was a sign. It had to be. Well, maybe I would do what I had to do just to get the stipend. I could always think about a business idea later. But Marc convinced me that I could make this work and said he was behind me, whatever business idea I came up with.

As we continued to drive, I started to think. A jet ski business?

No. A consulting business? No. A pet sitting business? No. I called my son to see what he thought. Michael told me about a relatively new type of business called Mystery Shopping and Customer Relations Monitoring. It was huge in the U.S. but not popular in Canada yet. I was so excited by the business concept he described that I had Marc pull the truck over so I could take neat notes on the pieces of bills that I had just torn up. Michael knew that poor customer service was a pet peeve of mine. Somehow I just knew that this was going to work. Starting a business was this derelict's last stop.

So I made an appointment and in I went to pitch my idea. The SEEDS admittance panel loved the idea and I was accepted into the program, even though on the first day I was still homeless. Regardless, I never missed a class. And this was the first thing in my life that I completed.

When I graduated from SEEDS I tried to get a business loan. The loans officer said, "Wow, Cathrine, that is an amazing business plan—one of the best I've ever seen."

"You mean I've got the line of credit?" I yelled.

"No, but it's one hell of a plan!"

It took me ten years to become an overnight success. In our first Consumer Connection office, I didn't see a run-down dump of a house with urine-soaked carpets from the previous tenant's eight dogs that were never let outside. I didn't see a mattress that we got from a second-hand store. I didn't see the three chairs and table that we got from the garbage and used for making endless sales calls. Instead, I saw what could become the headquarters of Consumer Connection. I saw professional offices with a real live receptionist. I saw staff who were happy to come to work. I saw beautiful furniture including my huge desk where I would sit running my own little empire. At McDonald's, where we ate most days, if at all, I didn't see a statue of Ronald. Instead, I saw a maitre d' ready to seat my husband and me at the finest restaurant in town.

That's when my mantra was born: Dream it. Believe it. Be it. Starting my company and making it a success was the most difficult thing I have ever done. When I was exhausted from working twenty-hour days seven days a week and I needed a helping hand,

I looked down to the bottom of my sleeve and there it was. When other people had weekends and evenings and holidays, Marc, Michael, and I (we were all partners) only saw a lengthy to-do list. Not only did we have a business, we had a family business and that threw even more wrenches into the mix—to my eternal regret, Michael and I had what would eventually become a permanent falling out.

I worked so hard for so many years that at times I didn't know where my strength came from. Especially when you consider that I was in a rut for most of my life. In some ways I still was. Being in a rut is like being in a grave, just with different dimensions. My company often made me feel that I was being buried alive.

Because Michael and I parted ways, I was often afraid that that would be Marc's and my eventual fate too. But that didn't happen. Instead, we became closer than ever. We built a company that would be seen as a leader in the industry, and I went on to win numerous business awards and accolades that would make any business graduate proud—except I'm no business graduate. Yes, I had SEEDS, but everything I learned about business took years to learn, not months.

But even today, successful and happy in my life and work, I am still often afraid. I never feel content and relaxed. Maybe that's because I realize that I could lose it all. I love what I do, but I know to remain a success I will have to work as hard as ever, albeit differently now than when we started off and then for years thereafter. Though the hours are still long, now we have staff and years of experience under our belts. I've learned a lot of lessons about running a successful business and I imagine very few of them you learn in school. School wasn't where I learned how to balance a chequebook or get along with others when I really didn't want to, or how to work as part of a team or figure out the gazillion other things necessary to become a success in life or work. If you want something in life, you will find a way to get it. But you have to want it badly enough.

Ironically, my street smarts have helped me tremendously in my business. On the streets, I learned about people—their behaviour, their likes and dislikes, and how to read them with just a glance. This knowledge continues to work very well for me as we're on our way to being in business for two decades.

I am living proof that dreams really can come true.

CHAPTER TWENTY-EIGHT

Struggles, heartbreak and the whole damn thing

I'M CONVINCED THAT EVERYBODY needs help in sorting out their lives amid all the baggage they've picked up over the years. We all carry that kind of baggage around. Some of us just have more of it than others, and some of the baggage is heavier than for others, and none of us can really handle it on our own. Not totally. I knew I couldn't; I had enough baggage to sink a ship.

I'd known it for most of my life, of course. I'd looked for help and appreciated it, right up to the time I wanted to tear the head off the shrink at the Clarke Institute who treated me more like a file than as a totally screwed-up young woman trying to make sense out of her life. The sessions I had with him helped me, but even with Marc's love and support and the success of Consumer Connection I was still struggling with all that baggage around my neck. Well, inside my head actually, but it felt like it was choking me. And just because we started a business didn't mean the challenges ended. I wish that were the case, but in a way, things got even more stressful and crazy. It was just a new dimension or layer of crazy. And I didn't just stop being bad overnight either. Like when we got business cards done up with the title President under my name. I felt that I needed a bit more uumph! So I added B.Sc. (Hons.) after my name until a potential client asked me, "Cathrine, what did you major in at university?" It was a dumb idea anyway, so I had new cards done up shortly after, dropping the lie. I thought that I had to come from a place that was better than I did to fit in and to make something of myself. I still thought I had to even the odds.

Not all the weight I carried was emotional either. The skinny little scarecrow girl from the slums of Toronto had ballooned into a 260-pound woman who refused to walk past mirrors or, if she couldn't avoid them, avoided looking at her reflection. Marc said he had never seen anyone deal with food the way I did, so it was no wonder that I got so fat. When we went grocery shopping I started eating in the grocery store, but now I paid for what I ate. So, by the time I got to the cash register, I had maybe an empty barbecue chicken container and an empty cheese package and an empty cupcake container ... The cashier would hold up the empty containers and look and me and I'd just shrug my shoulders and smile.

"Cat, wipe your face," Marc would say. More often than not, he would just wipe it for me like I was a two-year-old. When we got into the car, I would have a small picnic on my lap while Marc drove. And then when we got home, I would continue eating while Marc put the groceries away. Marc would find a time to talk to me about this strange behaviour. "Cat, I've never seen anyone gorge food the way you do. Are you okay?"

I would reply, "Marc, I don't know if that food is going to be there tomorrow. I feel like I need to eat it all at once. But I hear you ... and by the way, I'm starving again. Can we go eat?" It was crazy. So, my solution to binging would be barfing. And I didn't need anymore damage to my teeth than had already been done. I refused to smile as it was. From all the stress I had endured, I had apparently been grinding down all my teeth while I slept. The dentist told me that he had never seen such a devastating case of grinding. For someone that loved to smile and laugh, that really affected me.

I remember the first time that I realized I was fat. It was in Saskatchewan, when I attended the medical college's welcome party for all new students, of which I was one. I wanted to look spectacular and the only thing I ended up looking like was, well, fatactular. I was wearing size 16/18 on a good day and there were very few good days, if you know what I mean. Size 16/18 was snug. I guess it wasn't the first time I realized that the pounds were piling up, because I went to a doctor at about 220 pounds, and he said I was obese. That really stung. He also gave me a prescription for pep pills, but it seemed they only made me eat faster.

So there I was at a fabulous event, trying to make friends at my new school, hoping I looked good enough wearing a huge, bright, flower pattern stretchy jacket, a black stretchy-wasted skirt and a black stretchy top. Most everything you wear when you're fat has to be stretchy, because you can't be assured that you won't keep getting bigger day to day. Plus, when the waist expands like it does with stretchy fabric, you can stuff your face even more without feeling full.

I was a mess. I ended up standing next to the food table, watching everyone else mingle and have a good time. At the after party, at a hot senior medical student's place, I got plastered and passed out. To this day I feel horrible about barfing all over my stretchy new outfit and his new couch.

For the next couple of years, I put being fat out of my mind. I figured by the time it took me to get thin anyway, fat would probably be in fashion.

What the hell happened? Couldn't I be happy without being gigantic and without doing something negative to myself? And how could I be really successful if I couldn't control my own weight?

I was pushing 300 pounds until just before I met Marc. I stayed fat longer than I would have liked, even though I tried every stupid diet going: grapefruit diet, soup diet, blood-type diet, and herbal diet—and then things got serious when I started the binge and barf diet. I was pretty desperate.

You'd think someone who thought people would like them more if they looked better would be more inclined to lose weight. I had to convince myself that I just wasn't "that fat" and it just wasn't "that big of a problem." You know, I had a lot of excuses. It got easier not walking past mirrors, and I took to buying shoes and accessories instead of clothes. I had a handful of stretchy outfits and a gazillion pairs of shoes, of which most were stilettos—why, I don't know, because fat people don't do well in stilettos. Barefoot was what I preferred. When I did have to wear shoes it always ended up being flats. Mostly I used to just look at the stilettos, dreaming of the day when I would wear them.

After all of my half-assed attempts to lose weight failed—or

I failed, rather—I went to another doctor and got Fen-Phen diet pills. They were amazing! Instant will power to diet. I started to lose weight and got inspired: I started working out and ate only one small meal a day, usually a Lean Cuisine or something like that.

When I met Marc, I looked pretty sickly. Even though I was exercising, I was burning through my muscle along with the fat. But I was down to a size 10, and having thrown out all the moo-moos I vowed I would never be fat again.

Sure. After I met Marc, I put the weight right back on again. It didn't even creep up on me. I mean one day I was lean and the next I was fat again. It was like I was in some messed up version of Cinderella and at the stroke of midnight, I was transformed into the pumpkin. So there I was, back in size 18/20. (Yes, I had graduated from 16/18.) They say that if you lose weight too quickly, you will gain it all back ... and more. And that's just what happened to me. It was all Marc's fault, I decided. I was sure if he had told me how fat I had gotten, I would have lost weight. We laugh about that today, but initially I really did think he could have at least let me know when I started to get a bit fluffy. Marc said he loved me whatever way I was. I would love to call him a liar, but you know, the fact is, he did. He was with me regardless. However I looked was good enough for him. But it wasn't good enough for me. I vowed to make another serious attempt to get healthier and look better, but this time do it the right way and keep the pounds off. I was achy all over and my knees were becoming a problem and I felt like I was getting old before my time.

Marc and I started going to the gym together and in a few months I had dropped to where I thought I could bear mounting a scale. I was 260 pounds. Who knows how big I had gotten before I weighed myself? I started reading everything I could on body-building and weight loss and even saved my pennies to hire a personal trainer every so often. I hovered around 230 pounds. It seemed impossible to get any lower than that. Of course, I still believed that I could lose weight my way—that is, simply by eating less than I did at 260, which did nothing to help me lose very much weight. I learned that weight loss couldn't be achieved by diet pills or starvation—at least not for me. I wanted to do it fast—I want to do everything fast, because that's my style—but this time I decided I wouldn't torture my body or mind. I would change the way I thought about food. I needed to eat to live, not live to eat.

A couple of years had gone by and although I was now in a size 16, that wasn't good enough. By the time I discovered a doctor who would really help me once and for all, I was scheduled for knee-replacement surgery. To get ready for surgery I signed up to start a very restrictive but healthy diet based on eliminating all starchy carbs and sugar and even some fruits and vegetables and the weight started flying off. I became a gym rat and Marc and I made health a priority. I committed to the diet and exercise program so fiercely that I went down to a size 10 in a few months and felt great. People actually started telling me that I was too skinny! Now that was a first.

I gave away all of my old clothes, had a space organizer company come in and redo my closet and then filled it up with new fabulous clothes and shoes—because I even lost half a size on my feet so all those stilettos didn't fit!

I'm proud to say that I have pretty much maintained my new weight of 175 pounds for a couple of years now. There is "no weigh" that I'm going to replace my whole closet again, that's for sure. Oh, and as for the surgery, I went back to the surgeon and after my exam, he looked at me and said, "Knee replacement surgery? What knee replacement surgery?" and we both laughed.

THE ONLY THING that I could not make happen was to generate honest love between my son Michael and me, and make him understand that despite all the crap he underwent as a child, the constant moving from one home and relationship to another home and relationship, the endless series of men, the days and nights he spent alone while I did whatever I felt I needed to do, he was the first person I truly loved and always did and always will. My therapist told me something poignant when I discussed this with her during one session. "Cathrine, do you think that someone that becomes a mother so young as you were, who had the life that you had, could really raise a child that would be inclined to have a healthy, normal relationship with his mother when he grew up?" Wow ... that hit me like a ton of bricks. Of course Michael was going to have problems. I had problems. It made sense. But the guilt of causing him grief in his life from the way he was raised tears me up inside. I feel like I did a crappy job and although at the time of writing of this book he no longer chooses to have me in his or his family's life, my heart is open and I hope that he reads this book and understands a bit of what I went through and why I am the way I am. I would love to meet my grandchildren too.

At each stop along the way in my life, Michael had been with me most of the time. From the earliest years in Toronto through my marriage to Henry, my years in Guelph, Saskatoon and Calgary, Michael was there. Sometimes he was a better parent to me than I was to him. When we were apart, my mother looked after Michael with a degree of care she never exhibited for me. Even to suggest that Michael and I had a normal mother-son relationship, whatever that is, would be a joke. When he was still a teenager with me in Guelph we went to movies and bars together. He knew how I supported myself in Calgary and Vancouver. I can only guess what it means to a young man when he understands that his mother works in the sex trade. He has been hurt, he has been lonely, and he may feel he has been neglected from time to time. But I always loved him in the only way I knew how. I hope someday he can forgive me.

The times we spent together were precious to me, and most of them, I know, were precious to Michael as well. I'll admit that, by the time he reached his teenage years, he and I were more friends than mother and son. But friends can have great times together. Friends can love each other and support each other. Friends can have adventures that shape them and their relationship, and Michael and I had plenty of those. Someone once told me that a parent should never be a friend to his or her child.

By the time I launched Consumer Connection, and I credit Michael completely for the idea, Michael was in his late twenties, had his own career, his own relationships and his own identity. I had asked him to join my company. It probably should not come as a surprise that the experience was awkward at best and did not work out. I suppose I was trying to make up the best I could for lost time. For things I should have done but failed to do.

It may sound heartless, but at a certain point we all need to stop making apologies about the past and start living in the present. What's done is done; what hasn't been done can be done a lot better. Truth? It's easier said than done. As I would discover.

It was amazing. After all the disasters and heartbreak of my life, all the years of being told I was a failure, I was proving everybody wrong, including myself. Consumer Connection might not have been the world's biggest corporate breakthrough but we were successful and growing, becoming the best in our field, which is what I wanted all along.

But my corporate success was not enough to salvage my relationship with Michael. We had a major falling out. It was ugly and heart-breaking and in the midst of all the pain I was feeling, I wondered if I deserved it. This, I told myself, was payment for all the bad things I had done in my life, the thefts, the lies, the abortion, the selfishness. The universe was settling the score. I believed that I deserved Michael's rejection and all the pain I was feeling. I welcomed the pain, I searched for it, looking for each and every hurt I might have inflicted on others and turning it upon myself, day after day, until I honestly didn't want to live anymore. After everything, I gave up.

I was sliding, sliding out of reality and away from the disaster that had become my life into the same kind of self-flagellation that some extreme religions demand. I was also, in a sense, running away again.

In the past, with Henry and Shane, in Guelph and Saskatoon and Calgary, when disaster hit I had run away physically, just getting the hell out of town. With Michael's actions and comments I escaped not physically this time but mentally. I finally succumbed to a full-blown nervous breakdown and I couldn't work—couldn't do a damn thing for over a year.

Marc ran the company, and ran it well. I spent up to twenty hours a day in bed, running through everything in my life that had led to this point, realizing that my strength in creating, shaping and managing a successful business had hidden my weakness in handling not only my current life but aspects of the life I had led in the past, all the ways I had sought happiness and a sense of belonging at any price because I believed I deserved it. And I did. I just paid too high a price, I suppose. And asked others to share the cost as well.

It has since become clear to me that my relationship with Michael had been emotionally incestuous. Besides being mother and son, for many years we were good friends, hanging out together, watching other people, trading stories, each telling the other our troubles. I loved having my son as my best friend, but it was a mistake, a terrible mistake. Michael knew everything about me, which, under the circumstances, meant that he knew too much about me, and I knew too much about him. Each of our lives was an open book to the other, and that's a lousy arrangement between a mother and a son.

Through all of our years, especially the times when Michael felt abandoned by me, a reservoir of anger had been building within him. I understand this. I've been angry much of my life as well. The difference between Michael and me has been my ability to forgive. I'm not boasting. It's just something I have learned about myself. It's why I still maintain a relationship with my mother, and feel protective toward her. It's why I have contacted various members of my family and visit and talk with them about us and about life; I feel a need to maintain that relationship and forget the past.

I can forget the past. I remain hopeful that others around me can forget it as well.

I HAVE SIGNS all around my home and office that read "Believe" and I look at these messages every day. Because that's where it all started. I also have a vision board where I write down all my dreams and aspirations. Some are easier to achieve than others.

My mother is living close to both Michael and me in a suburb of Vancouver. She is eighty-four years old and I think she is fitter and healthier—physically, that is—than she ever was, even though she still drinks and smokes like a chimney. She likes to go for long walks. She says that someone is taking money out of her bank account and she thinks it's the woman that takes care of her building. She says that it's a good thing that she is so strong because what she went though in her life, someone else would surely be crazy by now. She started out with nothing and she still has most of it left. I now feel sorry for her like I used to for my dad. I was sort of hoping that as she got older, maybe she would be the mother that I always wanted. But with all these types of things going on, I need to accept that will never happen.

Nevertheless, Marc and I take her on shopping sprees and out to dinner and we take her on trips to Las Vegas every birthday and Mother's Day. In Vegas, my mother loves to smoke and have some drinks and sit at the slot machines for hours on end. I have never missed sending my mother a birthday, Christmas or Mother's Day card. Ever.

Do I love my mother? I don't know. She is very, very difficult to deal with and even Marc, who is the kindest and most compassionate person that I have ever met, told me that my mother just doesn't like me very much. No surprise there. But it was comforting to know that someone else saw how I was being treated by her and it wasn't all in my head. She still has those looks that she gives me that take me back to when I was a kid and make me feel like shit. And she still tells me to shut up, that my opinion doesn't matter.

I don't have anger toward my mother for how I was raised. Yes, I often feel sad about things. I can feel bitter about being deprived of so much.

But then my mother will say, "Ah quit complaining. You're still here, aren't you?"

Yes. I am.

CHAPTER TWENTY-NINE

Looking back without regrets.
Well, maybe a few...

WE NEVER LOOK BACK on things in our lives until we have something to look back to. And when we're fully-formed adults, we look back with a different perspective than when we're in our twenties and thirties recalling our first day in school or our first crush or our first kiss. Writing this book was like reviewing my life after I died, but I was still alive.

When I look back on the child I was, on the teenager I was, on the wild twenty-something woman I was, and on the wannabe doctor or vet I was, I feel sorry for all of them. I'm sorry for them because they were pretty lost and confused and although there were fun times, it wasn't a life that I would wish for anyone else.

I don't feel sorry for myself. I feel sorry sometimes for the person I used to be. The difference is important. I do feel sorry that I missed out on receiving love and affection from my parents. I do feel sorry that I didn't stay in school and wasn't taught the difference between right and wrong.

Please know that my story isn't about only achieving huge financial success as a way of achieving happiness, although I do now live a very comfortable life far away from where I came from. My story is about the ability to change ones life for the positive either in a small way or in a big way. It's about possibilities. It's about self-belief and inner strength and saying to yourself, I can do whatever I want to do and I won't stop until I get there. It's about getting to your "there" wherever that might be for you in your particular life. It's about surviving and keeping on keeping on. I am not bringing you stories from other people's experiences and saying, see, you should be able to do that too and hope that you get motivated for a few days or weeks. Besides, in my humble opinion, no one can motivate you anyway. We all look for inspiration from others, but we are each responsible for motivating ourselves; motivation comes from within.

I am saying that you can do most anything you want to do for your entire life, because I am living proof that it can be done.

I have shared my life and my very soul with you to be an example of you being able to do whatever you really want to do in your life. Know that your dream, whatever you always wanted in life, is just waiting for you to make it a reality. And the only place that dreams are impossible is in your own mind.

I read somewhere that everyone should reach for the stars. I thought, why just the stars when there's a whole universe out there to explore? That's my attitude and that's how I live my life. My mantra is: Dream it. Believe it. Be it. You are more than welcome to use it as your own.

Oh, and I still love buttons.

CPSIA information can be obtained at www.ICGtesting.com
Printed in the USA
LVOW011551141111

254921LV00014B/46/P

9 781926 645629